WEST BUCKLAND

THE DIARY OF AN EDWARDIAN SCHOOL

The Devon County School – founded in 1858. This building had its foundation stone laid in October, 1860. The building was opened in October, 1861.

WEST BUCKLAND
THE DIARY OF AN
EDWARDIAN SCHOOL

BERWICK COATES

ryelands

First published in Great Britain in 2008

British Library Cataloguing-in-Publication Data
A CIP record for this title is available from the British Library

ISBN 978 1 90655 105 6

RYELANDS
Halsgrove House
Ryelands Industrial Estate
Bagley Road, Wellington, Somerset TA21 9PZ
Tel: 01823 653777   Fax: 01823 216796
email: sales@halsgrove.com
website: www.halsgrove.com

Printed and bound in Great Britain by
CPI Anthony Rowe, Chippenham, Wiltshire

Contents

Acknowledgments

This is the third book I have written about West Buckland School. The first was a miscellany of history, humour, and anecdote. The second was a collection of essays designed to create a mosaic of the life of the School. This one takes the reader right up close – to look at the day-to-day events of the life of the School during one year only – 1907. In each case I have been indebted to the Headmaster for giving me total and free access to any documents on the premises which relate to the School's history.

Once again, no agency connected with the School has made any attempt to exercise any kind of editorial influence. Opinions and comments therefore are mine alone, and can in no way be construed as the official current philosophy of the School, except insofar as the quotations from 1907 School documents represent what the School thought *at the time* – 1907.

As before, I am grateful to Yvonne Reed for her painstaking care in reading and checking a complicated and detailed typescript, to Lorraine Millar for collating, and scanning over 130 hundred-year-old photographs (the more so as she was nursing a broken arm), and to Stephen Prior, who did what you might call emergency editorial scanning at a very late stage at the end of a busy term.

And finally, I suppose, I owe a debt to those boys, teachers, servants, and governors from a bygone age, who, by their efforts and aspirations, recorded (I hope) fairly in these pages, have let us into their lives for a whole year.

Berwick Coates, 2008

Introduction

In 1998 I was told by my Headmaster that I, as a semi-retired, part-time history teacher, would be unlikely to have any more history teaching coming my way. He went on to ask me if I would be willing to set up and run a School Archive. I said, not surprisingly, yes, of course, what a good idea, great, absolutely terrific. Wouldn't you?

In the course of the next two years, I did so. One of the by-products of that work was to have to produce various written pieces for the local media. This in turn led, by various roundabout ways that need not concern us here, to publication of a book based on my work, entitled simply *West Buckland School.* It was, I like to think, kindly received. In 2005, I published a second volume, entitled *The Natural History of a Country School.*

As I sifted through the quite extensive written records of the School's history – 140-odd years of it – I became aware that there was an above-average amount of material relating to the first two decades of the twentieth century, and especially relating to the year 1907. At roughly the same time, a local stationer gave me an out-of-date, unsold diary with a whole A-4 page for each day. It occurred to me that it might be an interesting experiment to put together a school diary for that year. I had plenty to work on: nearly 200 pages of contemporary school magazines, minutes of Governors' meetings, the published accounts, a contemporary school prospectus, minutes of the school's debating society, confirmation records, prize day awards, and so on.

There were photographs too – of the staff, of the whole school, of cricket and football teams, the choir, old boys' gatherings, even the school's servants. Many of them were in remarkably good condition – the photos, not the school servants (though one of them did serve the school for 58 years).

As some of the events recorded in the magazines had both their dates and days of the week included, it became relatively straightforward to concoct a full calendar for 1907. I also thought it would be interesting to retain as much of the original magazine entries as possible – their phraseology, their punctuation (rather fussy, perhaps, by today's standards; or displaying standards of precision which put today's writing to shame, depending on your point of view), their type-size, even their misprints.

The cumulative effect of these verbatim records is, I hope, to present a picture of a whole school's life, its hopes and fears, its unspoken ideals, its self-absorption, its blind spots. The portrait includes, and is intended to include, warts and all. It shows a vigorous, composite, human organism in full flow. Humble maybe, parochial, unsophisticated, inward-looking, a bit rough round the edges, even quaint – all these things. But alive, and proud of school and country.

The School in 1907 reflected Edwardian England at its height – King, Empire, white man's burden, votes for women, drink and temperance, and so on; look at some of the motions in the school debates. It was also the school where, as in many others, the entire first eleven enlisted in 1914 without a second thought, where a music master joined up *at the age of 44* – he couldn't bear to be left behind. When the average school roll was about 130-odd, 56 old members (boys, teachers, servants) died for their country.

It was also oddly forward-looking; the debating society discussed, among other things, a Channel Tunnel and the abolition of the House of Lords – I repeat, in 1907.

There was drama too. A Headmaster resigned. Bankruptcy loomed, and another headmaster had to be recruited from a neighbouring school in Somerset. The whole status and government of the School began to undergo a radical change.

A generation ago, the people who remembered the years just before 1914 were unanimous in their verdict that those years were special, that the world had something – charm, light, grace, sun, innocence, richness, what you will – which shone out despite the poverty and the long hours and the fog and the gas lamps, and which was lost in 1914, never to return. I hope one can catch whiffs of it in this diary of an obscure, small, remote country boarding school in the depths of the Exmoor countryside.

Every piece of information in this book comes from documents on the School premises. I could, for instance, have searched Armed Forces records, local government archives, electoral rolls, War Graves Commission lists, and more. I could have used the Internet to delve into family histories. I could have written to surviving relatives. I have chosen not to.

This is a *School* affair. This is what the *School* did, what it thought, what it knew (and didn't know), what its view of the world, and itself, was. I have tried to restrict editorial comment. I wanted the School's voice to come through loud and clear. Whether that makes you *like* the School is another matter. But I hope it makes you feel its presence. Here was something.

Editorial Note

In order to enhance the flavour of 1907, I have kept the spelling and the punctuation of the contemporary documents I have used – for example, double inverted commas for quotations instead of single ones common today, 'connexion' instead of 'connection', full stops in 'D.S.O.'. Where there is an definite error by today's standards, I have usually retained it, though I sometimes show off my superior knowledge by inserting a scholarly square bracket in order to point out that I am aware of it.

The one exception to this is where a title or quotation appears at the end of a sentence. For instance, if the writer is telling of a book being presented, he might say, and often did, something like:- "W. Smith was awarded a copy of 'Bleak House.'" In fact, the final full stop should come outside the single inverted comma. After a few instances of this, I gave up drawing constant attention to it in pedantic square brackets, and let the writer get on with it.

As this book/diary is devoted to the year 1907, I have not repeatedly quoted it. So where a date (day/month) appears by itself, the reader can assume that it is 1907 that is being discussed. If a date appears outside that year, the year as well as the day/month is supplied. Dates in brackets after a name refer to the time a pupil spent at the School.

Normal type (Bembo 10.5pt) indicates the record speaking for itself – usually straight quotations taken from the School magazine or the Governors' Minutes or whatever. A series of three dots shows where I have edited out certain passages or single words and phrases in the interests of simplicity, brevity, or sheer flow. Material in square brackets comes where I feel that some editorial comment is necessary for making something clearer, or for adding, I hope, to interest and enjoyment. Here I use 8.5pt, to help the reader the more easily to identify it.

In cases like cricket scorecards, I have tried to follow the size, sequence, and spacing of the print. Every little helps. In some titles and sub-titles, I have tried, as accurately as possible, to imitate the font used by the printers of the magazine. Full stops abound, like buttons on an Edwardian lady's boot.

It's a bit like dressing the actor in the costume of the period.

List of Illustrations

The Prospectus

DEVON COUNTY SCHOOL

WEST BUCKLAND

FOUNDED 1858

THE FIRST PUBLIC SCHOOL FOR THE

MIDDLE CLASSES, GIVING A HIGH-CLASS

EDUCATION AT A LOW COST

𝕮𝖍𝖆𝖎𝖗𝖒𝖆𝖓 𝖔𝖋 𝕲𝖔𝖛𝖊𝖗𝖓𝖔𝖗𝖘:

THE RIGHT HON. EARL FORTESCUE
Lord Lieutenant of Devon

𝕳𝖊𝖆𝖉 𝕸𝖆𝖘𝖙𝖊𝖗:
THE REV. E.C. HARRIES, M.A.

𝕾𝖊𝖈𝖔𝖓𝖉 𝕸𝖆𝖘𝖙𝖊𝖗:
G.C. FRY, M.Sc., F.I.C.

𝕾𝖊𝖈𝖗𝖊𝖙𝖆𝖗𝖞:
A. TAYLOR.

Postal Address: Devon County School, West Buckland, South Molton.
Telegrams: Harries, Filleigh.
Railway Station: Filleigh, G.W.R.

=============

[Earl Fortescue was the grandson of one of the co-founders of the School – Hugh, second Earl Fortescue (also a Lord Lieutenant of the County). The other was the Revd. J.L. Brereton, a very busy educational reformer of the middle and later years of the nineteenth century.

Ernest Harries was appointed when the School was at a very low ebb, in fact close to total demise. He pulled the School round, and went on to become the School's greatest head. He became known far and wide as 'Ernie'.

The name of the School reflected the designs of the founders – to set up a school which would cater for the educational needs of sons of the 'middle classes' in the County. It was later changed to 'West Buckland School'. The process of total reorganisation began this year – 1907 – when the original company went into voluntary liquidation, and was completed in 1912.

The telegraphic address has a nice mixture of succinctness and celebrity – as if the Headmaster's name was so well known that these words were all that was necessary. Rather like those millions of letters which are addressed: 'Santa Claus, North Pole'.

As for the railway station, the Prospectus helpfully included a railway map of the South-West, from which prospective parents drew the reassurance that Filleigh (and therefore the School) was connected – by rail – to places like Lynton, Torrington, Bideford, Ilfracombe, Bude, Holsworthy, Launceston, Moreton Hampstead, Princetown, Ashburton, Budleigh Salterton, Sidmouth, Seton, Tiverton, Chard, Hemyock, Minehead, Wells, and Glastonbury. For all that the School appears to be lost in the back of beyond, a glance at the map of mid-century Devon, Cornwall and Somerset would show that on the contrary it had an enviable network of reliable communications to put it within the reach of a wide catchment area of potential parents.

George Cecil Fry was one of the first teachers to come to the School specifically to teach Science, and, as has become normal in schools like WB, soon found himself involved in countless other activities.

Mr. Adelbert Taylor, the 'Secretary', besides being Secretary to the School, was also Secretary to the Governors, a senior master at the School (teaching a huge variety of subjects), a games coach, a keen games *player*, a choirmaster, an organist, and about a hundred and seventy-three other things besides. More of him later.

Back to the Prospectus....]

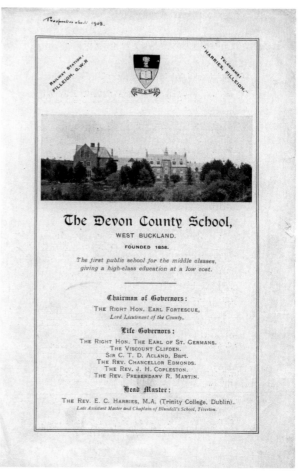

The front page of a prospectus leaflet. The Prospectus proper ran to 25 pages.

Object and Aims.

The School was founded in 1858 by Hugh, second Earl Fortescue, K.G., LL.D., F.R.S., Lord Lieutenant of Devon, with the object of providing for the middle classes, on terms adapted to the means of the less wealthy, a school based on the same principles, and offering as far as may be the same kind of education, as our great public schools. It was one of the original centres for both the Cambridge and the Oxford Local Examinations [the ancestor of 'O' Levels and, more recently, GCSE], which have always formed an integral part of the curriculum. More successes have been obtained on several occasions than by any other school in England, and the first place in the whole examination has been secured six times by boys of the Devon County School. The present course of instruction is in accordance with the regulations of the Board of Education, and is adapted to prepare boys for either a professional or a commercial career. Special attention is given to the teaching of Science and Mathematics. Although Day Boys are admitted, the School consists almost entirely of Boarders, thereby ensuring a high moral tone and a strong *esprit de corps*.

Situation and Buildings.

The School is situated on the western borders of Exmoor, at an elevation of 650 feet above the sea level, overlooking the valley of the Taw and the Dartmoor Hills. The surroundings are entirely rural, there being no town or large village within six miles. The site is one of the healthiest in the country.

[Bracing, certainly. When, in 1909, the 'Officers' Training Corps' was set up, and detachments of West Buckland boys attended cadet camps, they became well known for their toughness. If you could stand conditions at West Buckland, or rather the Devon County School, you could stand anything. A survivor of the late 1920's told me that he went through four years without ever having to go to sick bay. He also outlasted six years of the Second World War and played rugby till he was fifty-eight.]

The buildings are modern and specially designed. They include a fine dining hall (75 ft. by 32 ft.), good class-rooms, well-equipped chemical and physical laboratories (rebuilt 1903-4), carpenter's shop, and forge.

The dormitories are large, airy, and well lighted.

The boys have access to a lending library, a reference library, and two reading-rooms.

All the class-rooms, the dining hall, the library, the reading-room, and the changing-rooms are heated by hot water.

[We are able to date this prospectus pretty accurately. We have in the Archive the original letter from the War Office authorising the setting up of the Officers' Training Corps – in March, 1909. There is no mention here of the actual existence of an OTC, though there is a clear reference to it below – see 'Drill and Shooting'. A near-identical prospectus of just a little later still does not mention an existing OTC, but fees had gone up just a trifle; a single piece of paper had been pasted over the page which gave the figures. The second prospectus raised the charges for day pupils from two guineas

to three pounds – that is, by 90p. – for a term! The reference above to the new laboratories clearly puts this after 1904, the year they were built – which is explicitly stated below. Better still, we know too that Harries' appointment became substantive in May, 1907, and Harries' name appears here as the Headmaster. It would have been perfectly reasonable for a new prospectus to have been issued to indicate that a new headmaster, a new broom, was sweeping clean. So it seems fairly safe to place it in mid- to late 1907 – the second perhaps in 1908.]

Boarding Arrangements.

The School has accommodation for 120 boarders.

The Head Master's house is in the centre of the buildings, and is in direct communication with the dormitories and class-rooms.

The boys are divided into dormitories, each under a Master. All meet in a common dining hall, where the dormitories have separate tables. The Prefects are immediately responsible for the order and moral tone of their dormitories.

The boys' clothes are kept in special rooms, under the charge of the Matron, assisted by a wardrobe-keeper. The boot-room, lavatories, and changing rooms (for games) are on the ground floor.

Every boy has a hot bath in the evening once a week; and boys may have a cold bath every morning, by permission.

[With facilities for 120 boarders, and a School roll of barely 70, the School in 1907 was clearly not being fully exploited. Harries, as the new Head, was facing a challenge – which in the succeeding years, he rose splendidly to meet.

Why was it considered necessary to inform parents that the boot-room was on the ground floor? How many boys clamoured to have extra, cold, baths? What did a wardrobe-keeper do? The title could have come straight out of the household of John of Gaunt.]

Subjects of Instruction.

A boy can enter the School at eight years of age, and parents are strongly urged to send boys at any rate before the age of twelve, so as to enable them to take full advantage of the systematic teaching of the Upper School, and to avoid the loss of time and energy often involved, at a critical period of a boy's life, by a change of schools.

The course of teaching is under the direct supervision of the Head Master, who takes some part of the work of each Form.

Scripture is taught in all the Forms. Boys whose parents desire it can be prepared for Confirmation by the Head Master.

Singing is also taught throughout the School, and in the winter months a Glee Club is formed for the practice of sacred and secular music. Instrumental music is an optional subject.

There is a Reading and Debating Society, which holds meetings during the winter terms.

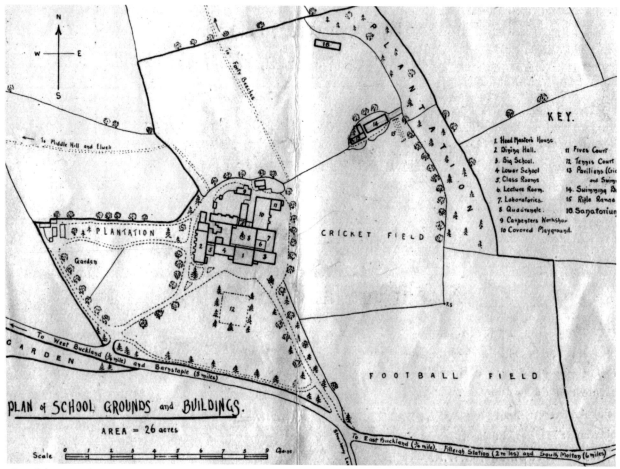

KEY.

1. Head Masters House
2. Dining Hall.
3. Big School.
4. Lower School.
5. Class Rooms.
6. Lecture Room.
7. Laboratories.
8. Quadrangle.
9. Carpenters Workshop
10. Covered Playground.
11 Fives Court
12 Tennis Court
13 Pavilions (Cricket and Swimming)
14 Swimming Bath
15 Rifle Range
16 Sanatorium

PLAN of SCHOOL GROUNDS and BUILDINGS.

AREA = 26 acres

Plan of the Grounds and Buildings.

During the two winter terms, Lectures and Recitals are given at intervals by lecturers and reciters selected by the Head Master. School Concerts are also held.

A. – THE JUNIOR SCHOOL
(Forms I & II.)

The hours of teaching are somewhat shorter in the Junior School than in the Upper School.

The subjects are arranged so as to prepare boys as completely as possible for the teaching which they will receive in the Upper School. They are thoroughly grounded in English, the knowledge and intelligent use of which are so essential as the foundation of all other studies; and also in French, History, Geography, Arithmetic, Writing, and Drawing. No boy learns Latin in the Junior School.

The Science Course (Chemistry and Physics) begins at the age of twelve; but there are simple lessons for junior boys in preliminary Science, including practical measurement.

B. – THE MIDDLE SCHOOL
(Forms III, IV, & V.)

The curriculum is designed to give boys a thorough general education. Nothing in the shape of specialization is attempted. It cannot be too strongly emphasized that there is a large substratum, common to all higher education, which is intended to train the faculties of accuracy, observation, reflection, clear expression, and retentive

memory, in such a way as to fit a boy for any career. This is the work done in the Middle Forms of the School.

The subjects of the Junior School are continued and carried to a higher stage; and, in addition, considerable time is devoted to Mathematics (including Algebra, Geometry, and Trigonometry), and to a systematic Science Course in Physics and Chemistry.

Latin is begun by all boys in the Third Form. This subject (apart from the fact that it is necessary in nearly all professional preliminary examinations) is of high educational value in the training of the memory and as an aid to Composition and a sound knowledge of English.

C. – THE UPPER SCHOOL
(Form VI.)

When a boy has passed through the Middle School, which he should have done by the time he is sixteen, and has given proof of possessing a sound foundation of knowledge, he is allowed a large measure of specialization. Boys are prepared for Scholarships at the Universities in Mathematics, History, or Science; for the London Matriculation; and for the Medical and other Preliminary Examinations. An intelligent boy should be able to pass any recognised Preliminary Examination at the age of seventeen. For University Scholarships a longer course of study is necessary.

It is thus possible to retain boys to the age of eighteen, and to secure for them the immense advantage which belongs to the last years of school life, while they are

A dormitory. Generations of Old Boys, until well after the Second World War, talked volubly about breaking the ice in the wash-basins.

devoting their time to those subjects for which they are especially fitted, and which are of definite practical use to them for their future career. It is very important for parents to bear in mind that a boy who leaves school at sixteen has only the foundation, without the super-structure, of a real education, and loses just those years of moral training and growing responsibility which are the most valuable parts of a public school education.

Advanced Latin, Mathematics, and Science will be thoroughly taught when desired. The laboratories are well equipped for advanced instruction in Science. French is taught on modern principles by an English master thoroughly conversant with the spoken language.

Examinations.

The Sixth and Fifth Forms take the Local Examinations of the Cambridge Syndicate. These examinations, under certain conditions, give exemption from the Preliminary Examinations of various professional bodies, and from the University Previous Examination, or 'Little Go'. The certificates are also of value to boys entering business life, as evidence of a good general education.

Examinations are also conducted by the Masters for the whole School at Midsummer, and for the Junior and Middle School at Christmas.

Prizes are given at Midsummer for all branches of work, but at Christmas Form prizes alone are given. There are several prizes for special subjects, viz:-

ONE PRIZE FOR DIVINITY, presented by the REV. CHANCELLOR EDMONDS, B.D.

ONE PRIZE FOR ENGLISH, presented by MICHAEL B. SNELL, Esq., J.P.
ONE PRIZE FOR MATHEMATICS, presented by SIR C.T.D. ACLAND, Bart.
ONE PRIZE FOR SCIENCE, presented by SIR C.T.D. ACLAND, Bart.
ONE PRIZE FOR FRENCH, presented by the HEAD MASTER.
ONE PRIZE FOR GENERAL KNOWLEDGE, presented by R. Pearse. CHOPE, Esq., B.A.

[The Aclands were a powerful local family. Gentry. Carried a lot of clout. It is often tempting for us mere mortals to cast them as unfeeling semi-aristocrats who married only for breeding purposes, whose idea of emotion was to puff at a difficult jump while out after the stag, and who came nearest to aesthetics when they felt a lump in the throat at singing *God Save the Queen* when they were abroad. However, some years ago, I came across a structure on Exmoor which gave the lie to that. It was the Acland Memorial Hut, and a notice told the traveller who took the trouble to stop and ponder that the spot had been chosen by the youngest surviving son of Sir Thomas Dyke Acland (1787-1871). A plaque bore this delightful and endearing inscription:-

'In Remembrance
of the father who, during more than fifty years, took Sunday walks up this combe with his children and grandchildren, training them in the love of nature and of Christian poetry, this Wind and Weather Hut was built. 1878.'

It is possible that the 'Sir C.T.D. Acland' of the Maths and Science prizes was that loving son. He was certainly one of the surviving sons. I find that thought a pleasing one.

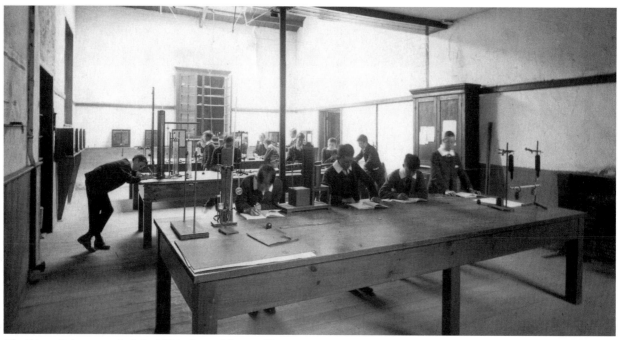

The Science Laboratory – built in 1904. It served for over fifty years.

Michael Snell and R. Pearse Chope were Old Boys who had 'done well'. 'The Rev. Chancellor Edmonds' was Chancellor of Exeter Cathedral, and a Director of the Devon County School Company.]

Scholarships.

The Shephard Law Scholarship, of the yearly value of £25, tenable while the holder remains at the School, is awarded on the recommendation of the Head Master to such boy in the School as has passed highest at the Senior Cambridge Local Examination.

Foundation Scholarships are awarded on the result of an examination to boys living within a radius of fifteen miles from the School. These scholarships exempt the holders from tuition fees, and also entitle them to a reduction in boarding fees.

Entrance Scholarships for boarders, given by the Governors and Old Boys, are from time to time offered for open competition. These Scholarships vary in value from £10 to £15 per annum, and are tenable for three years.

The Laboratories.

The new Laboratories were opened in 1904. In the centre is a Lecture room provided with an optical lantern and demonstration table. It will seat 28 boys. On the eastern side is a large Chemical Laboratory, with benches for 24 boys. The Physics Laboratory is on the northern side, and has accommodation for the same number. There is also a Store Room, which can be darkened for photographic and optical work.

The Science Course is so designed as to train boys in the knowledge of natural laws and in the habits of scientific observation. At least as much time is spent in practical as in theoretical work, and the eye and hand are constantly trained in scientific processes and methods of accurate measurement.

The Workshop. No overalls, but Eton collars for woodwork.

Carpentry.

The Middle School receives instruction in Carpentry and the use of tools once a week. A highly-skilled Instructor visits the School for this purpose.

Boys are also allowed to work in the carpenter's shop in their playtime, and have the assistance of a working carpenter to superintend their work. Simple forge work is also taught.

Games and Sports.

The School playing fields consist of about twenty acres, all quite close to the building. One ground is used for cricket only; no games are allowed upon it during the winter terms, and it has thus been possible to secure some of the best wickets in the county.

Association football is played during the winter terms. The Athletic Sports are held in May. The School possesses an excellent covered Fives Court.

Cross-country running, for which the neighbourhood offers special facilities, is also encouraged. The runs, which are of moderate length, are carefully supervised and invariably accompanied by a Master. The School possesses several Challenge Cups and other athletic trophies presented by Old Boys.

The games form an important part of the school life; all boys are expected to take part unless forbidden by a doctor.

[There were indeed several runs 'of moderate length', but the longest run – the *Exmoor* – first mapped out by the elder Dyke Acland baronet mentioned above, in 1859, covers at least nine miles. Well, it does now. Cancelled only twice in nearly 150 years, it is the School's oldest and most cherished tradition.]

Swimming Bath.

A large open-air concrete Swimming Bath, 60ft. by 30 ft., and varying in depth from 2 ft. 6 in. to 6. ft. 6 in., adjoins the Cricket Pavilion, which has recently been re-built and enlarged. [Completed about 1905-6 – another means of dating this prospectus.] Bathing is always under the supervision of a Master.

Drill and Shooting.

All boys are expected to drill under the instruction of a duly qualified Sergeant Instructor. Steps are being taken to form a Cadet Corps. [It appeared in 1909.] A miniature Rifle Range is in the grounds, and all who wish can receive instruction. A small subscription is charged to cover the cost of the ammunition.

Medical Arrangements.

All cases of infectious illness can be isolated in a wing of the building especially built. It may be mentioned that, owing to the position of the School, epidemics are of very rare occurrence.

The Medical Officer visits the School regularly.

At the beginning of the term a certificate must be signed by the parent or guardian of every boy, stating that he has not been exposed to infection, and in any doubtful case the Medical Officer and the Head Master are responsible for determining the date of the boy's return.

Every boy is required to bring this certificate back with him. Boys who fail to do so are isolated until the certificate arrives.

Arrangements are made by which boys can have their teeth examined. A statement can be forwarded to each parent containing the estimate of cost of the work required to be done. No boys, except in urgent cases, are treated without their parents' consent, but it is of great importance to the boys' health that their teeth should have periodical examination and treatment.

The sanitary arrangements are thoroughly up-to-date, and are inspected periodically by the Medical Officer.

General Administration.

Time Table. – The fixed hours on week-days, at present, are as follows:-

7.15 – 8, Preparation (Summer Term only).
8, Breakfast.
8.45 – 12.15, Prayers, School. (with 15 mins. break.)
1, Dinner.
2 – 4, School.
6.30, Tea.
7 - 8.30, Preparation.
8.30, Prayers, Supper.
9.15, Bedtime for Junior Boys
10.15, Bedtime for Senior Boys.

In Winter there is no early Preparation. Tea is then at 6, and Preparation lasts from 6.30 to 8.30. During the months of November and December, Afternoon School

The Dining Hall – always known as 'the Karslake' after its donor, a clergyman of the 1870s. It is still so used, and still so known.

is from 3.45 to 5.45. [A long lunch-hour to allow time for recreation in daylight? Not a bad idea.]

Wednesdays and Saturdays are half-holidays.

Meals. - The greatest care is taken to provide boys with a liberal and wholesome diet. Porridge is provided for breakfast. Owing to the School possessing a very large garden, a good supply of vegetables is always available. The School being in the country, it is possible to exercise an effective supervision over the milk supply.

Pocket Money. - Pocket money will be advanced to boys by the Head Master on the written request of parents. Not more than sixpence per week is considered necessary.

Clothes. - A list of clothes required is sent before a boy's admission. One dark suit should be included for use on Sundays. School blazers – black, bound with scarlet – are worn when the boys are in change for games, and the ordinary coats are thus saved. Distinctive caps are worn by members of the Elevens. Every boy is expected during the Summer Term to have a straw hat with the School ribbon. All clothes for athletics are sold by the Matron at the School, thereby combining uniformity of costume with a minimum of expense.

Reports. – Reports on boys' work are sent to parents at the end of each term. Should occasion arise, the Head Master will communicate with parents during the term concerning their boys' progress and conduct. It is the Head Master's special wish to be in full communication with parents about their boys, and it is his hope that they will freely inform him of any matter which may cause them anxiety, and rely upon his discretion in dealing with it.

The Headmaster's House. Headmasters actually lived with its booming stone stairs and flagstones until 1997, when a modern house was built.

Visitors. - The Head Master is glad to see parents or those who wish to see the School, by appointment. The Station – Filleigh, G.W.R. – is two miles from the School, and carriages should be ordered in advance from Mr. J. Dallyn, West Buckland, South Molton (Telegrams: "Dallyn, Filleigh"). The charge for a conveyance from the Station to the School is 2/- [10p].

Holidays.

The School Holidays consist of about fourteen weeks, viz., three in April, seven in August and September, and four at Christmas.

All boys must return punctually on the appointed day, unless leave of absence has been previously obtained from the Head Master.

Arrangements can be made by which boys from India or the Colonies, or others, may stay at the School during the holidays. Particulars can be obtained from the Head Master or Secretary.

Fees.   Per Term.

	£.	s.	d.
Tuition and Boarding Fees (boys over 13) ...	11	11	0
" " " " (boys under 13) ...	10	10	0
(A slight reduction is made for brothers.)			
Tuition Fees only...	2	2	0
Stationery, Games, Library, School Magazine, etc.	0	10	0
Athletic Sports (Summer Term only)...	0	2	6
Text-books (see below)	(variable)		

OPTIONAL EXPENSES.

	£	s	d
Instrumental Music	1	11	6
Rifle Club	0	3	6

Text-books are supplied to boys at net cost, but second-hand copies can often be purchased from the School. The School, if so desired, will re-purchase from boys who are leaving those books which are in good condition and likely to be sold again.

The Boarding Fees include medical attendance, but in the case of illness requiring a special nurse, the charge is borne partly by the parent and partly by the School.

In the case of boys prevented *by illness* from returning at the beginning of a term, a proportional reduction in the Boarding Fees for that term is made.

[Decimal coinage, which was introduced in 1971, replaced 240 pence in the pound with 100. There were twenty shillings ('s.') in the pound, and twelve pence ('d.') in the shilling. There was also an even older currency called a 'guinea', which was a pound and a shilling. So 11 pounds and 11 shillings was 11 guineas. Why '£', 's' and 'd'? It was Latin – referring to three old Roman coins – '*libri*' (hence '£'), '*sestertii*' (hence 's.'), and '*denarii*' (hence 'd.').]

Notice of Leaving.

Notice of a boy's leaving must be given in writing to the Head Master *at the beginning of the term*. In default of this a term's fee must be paid.

Railway Communications.

Filleigh Station can be reached from London (Paddington), via Taunton, in 4¼ hours; from Exeter in about

Diagram of Devon's railway network. Probably far better even than the present range of services of buses, never mind the trains.

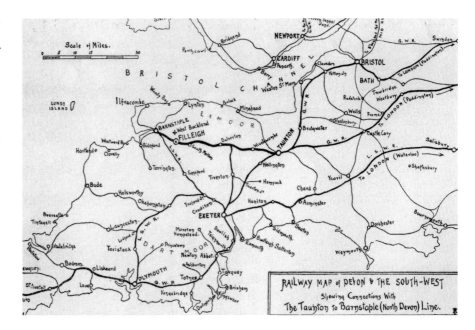

2½ hours, either via Dulverton (G.W.R.) or via Barnstaple (L.S.W.R. and G.W.R.); from Bristol in 2½ hours, via Taunton.

[Printed by]
HICKS, WILKINSON & SEARS,
4, DORSET BUILDINGS,
SALISBURY SQUARE,
LONDON, E.C.
Telephone: HOLBORN 1777
Telegrams: "BAMBUSA,
LONDON."

[In a near-contemporary document, the School published 'a few opinions' of the Devon County School.]

Four Archbishops of Canterbury –

Archbp. Longley, formerly Head Master of Harrow. It stands on the same level, in all important respects, with the great public schools of this country.

Archbp. Tait, formerly Head Master of Rugby. A great deal of the idea of the institution was borrowed from the great public school with which I was connected.

Archbp. Benson, formerly Head Master of Wellington. The success attained in the University Examinations is such as the boys may well be proud of, and it is a success that must become a tradition of the School.

Archbp. Temple, formerly Head Master of Rugby [and Bishop of Exeter]. I regard the School as one of the glories of Devonshire. It brings within the reach of the great body of the middle-class an education of the very highest character. It gives them an education precisely such as will fit them most admirably for their after lives. There is, also, a real religious education given without in the slightest degree infringing on the rights of conscience.

Rev. Dr. Rigg, President of the Wesleyan Training College, Westminster. It gives an education which is at once liberal, practical, and suitable to the different requirements of the professional man, the farmer, and the tradesman. The education is given on principles that are Christian, on principles that are generously catholic. The School is managed on the principles of the Church of England, and it ought to be managed on the principles of some particular church. But, at the same time, there is no attempt at proselytization – you respect the scruples of those who are not attached to the Church of England. [Sort that one out.]

The Right Hon. the Earl of Devon. The education given is calculated to encourage a high sense of responsibility on the part of the boys – not merely by developing their intellectual powers, but by the moral tone which is communicated, by the high sense of honour which is fostered, and by the sense of mutual relation and regard for each other's interests which spring up naturally in a public school education. [The Earl's family name was – is – Courtenay. He was connected with the School from the outset. One of the first two houses in the School was named after him.]

Sir C.T.D. Acland, Bart. In the Cambridge Local Examinations it has, again and again, scored a greater number of successes than any other school in England. [Acland was one of the four pioneers who set up the 'Locals' in 1858. The other three – Temple, Brereton, and Fortescue – were all closely connected with the School.]

Rev. Preb. Brereton [a founder]. It is connected with no party, identified with no sect, dedicated to no saint, and signalized by no symbol except the motto "Read and Reap". [As succinct and eloquent a testimonial as you are likely to get.]

"The Globe" Newspaper. In so far as healthy and comfortable living, careful religious training, and sound, useful education are concerned, it may well be adopted as a model for the guidance of future efforts.

W. Ayshford Sanford, Esq. [whoever he was].
I regard it as the Eton of middle-class schools.

[The School also helpfully provided a list – with addresses - of ' "Old Boys" to whom reference may be made'. There were 54 of them, spread over London and 21 counties, from a surprisingly wide variety of walks of life: Clergyman, veterinary surgeon, solicitor, barrister, university professor, banker, Royal Navy College instructor, a principal at the Patent Office, a chief clerk at the Thames Police Court, accountant at the India Office, stockbroker, borough engineer, champion golfer, chief constructor at HM Dockyard, auctioneer, Welsh rugby international, and *Punch* cartoonist.]

December, 1906

Register of Directors of the Devon County School

The Right Hon. Earl Fortescue	Castle Hill. Filleigh.	Peer.
The Rt. Hon. The Earl of St. Germans	Port Eliot. Cornwall.	Peer.
The Viscount Clifden	Lanhydrock House. Bodmin.	
Sir Charles Thos. Dyke Acland	Killerton. Exeter.	Bart.
The Rev. Chancellor Edmonds	The Close. Exeter.	Chancellor of Exeter Cathedral.
The Rev. J.H. Copleston	Offwell Rectory. Honiton.	Clerk in H. Orders.
The Rev. Prebendary R. Martin	Exmouth	Prebendary of Exeter Cathedral.
J. Mortimer Esq:	Woodville. South Molton.	J.P.
J. Mothersdale Esq:	N.P. Bank do	Bank Manager.
[National Provincial, once one of the 'big five' – N.P., Westminster, Lloyds, Barclays, Midland.]		
J.F. Wilkin Esq:	Rose Ash do	J.P.
G.C. Smyth Richards.	Filleigh do	Estate Agent.
G.A.W. Thorold. Esq:	Hudscott. Chittlehampton.	J.P.
C. Pearce. Esq:	Pilton House. Barnstaple.	Tanner.
M.B. Snell Esq:	5, Copthall Buildings, . E.C.	Stockbroker.
	Nr. Tokenhouse Yd	
James Sanders Esq:	South Molton	C. C. J.P. Coal Merchant & Wool Stapler.
W.P. Hiern Esq:	Barnstaple	C.C.

['C.C.' – County Councillor]

[This is taken from lists in the Register of Directors, from 1906. There is no entry for 1907, probably because of the School's change of status – see 23rd February, 30th May, 15th June. There is no record in the 1907 Minutes of attendance by the Earl of St. Germans, Viscount Clifden, Sir Charles Dyke Acland, Revd. Chancellor Edmonds, Revd. Prebendary Martin, or J. Mortimer. And curiously, Director Clifden, though a Viscount, does not have 'Peer' printed after his name. J.Mothersdale resigned during the year, and there were four new 'prospective' governors mentioned (not 'directors'; it ceased to be a private company) – Revd. J.H. Thompson (the first Headmaster, 1858-88), D.J.C. Bush (who was to serve 27 years), R.P. Chope (who wrote endlessly for the *Register*), and Revd. J. Newman.]

2th December – The Directors accepted the resignation of Mr. W.A. Knight, M.A., and shortly afterwards offered the Headship to the Revd E.C. Harries, M.A.

January

Accounts.

———

𝔇𝔯.		TUCK SHOP						𝔗𝔯.		

	£.	s.	d.			£.	s.	d.
To Stock, Jan. 1st, 1906	0	19	7	By Receipts-				
" Cadbury Bros.	20	5	6	1st Term		20	11	0
" T. Dunn	13	3	9	2nd "		28	0	0
" Elliott and Fry	5	12	6	3rd "		19	9	3
" Dornat and Co.	3	5	6	" Value of Stock		4	8	10
" Wallaces, Ltd.	0	8	0					
" Thornby and Co., and								
Various, per Matron	12	10	0					
" Balance to "Games"	16	14	3					
	£72	19	1			£72	19	1
To Stock, Jan. 1st, 1907	4	18	10					

[Actually, the second column comes to £72 9s 1d., not £72 19s 1d. Who pinched ten bob?]

𝔇𝔯.		ATHLETIC SPORTS.						𝔗𝔯.		

	£.	s.	d.			£.	s.	d.
To Prizes –				By Subscriptions –				
Sly & Co.	4	5	3	Governors, Friends,				
H.R. Williams	1	17	0	and Masters		13	16	0
A.W. Gamage and Co.	10	8	1	Boys		9	5	0
" Printing, etc.	3	5	6	" Balance from				
				"Games"		1	6	10
" Steel Die for Medals	2	10	0					
" Advertisements	0	13	6					
" Various payments	1	8	6					
	£24	7	10			£24	7	10

[For an explanation of pre-decimal coinage, see page 18.]

Monday, 7th January.

School List. – Lent Term, 1907

Head of the School: S. Bendall, Bristol.
Prefect: J.B. Harris, South Molton.
W.M. Burridge, Bratton Fleming*
Sub-Prefects: W. Saunders, Kingston-on-Thames.
[A purist will tell you that it should be 'Kingston upon Thames'.]

V.A.

W.L. Armstrong, Shipley, Yorks.
H.J. Harris, South Molton *

V.B.

R.T.H. Hooper, Teignmouth
L.K.V. Job, Ledbury, Hereford
H.H. Jones, Exmouth *
C. Lewis, Chittlehampton
L.G.H. Major, Oakhill
A.O. Parker, Winchcomb, Glos.

N.K. Pearce, Kingsbridge
T.H. Richards, Ilfracombe
R.W. Seldon, Lincoln
E.H. Trudgian, Tregony, Cornwall*
J.I. White, South Molton
A.L.J. Youings, Barnstaple

IV.

E.A. Adams, Taunton
A.H. Austin, Verwood, Dorset
A.S. Ayres, South Molton*
F.J. Brooks, East Buckland
J.L. Buckingham, North Molton
C.E. Drake, Tiverton*
W. Elworthy, Swimbridge
A.J.E. Helps, Bridgwater
H.E. Hicks, Berrynarbor
W.F. Kingdon, South Molton

H.F. Lovell, Chulmleigh
H. Matthews, Hayle
R. Maynard, Bude*
A. Pearce, Barnstaple
A.E. Preston, Natal
R.M. Read, Exeter*
H.J. Richards, Chulmleigh
F.E. Sanders, Barnstaple*
D. Squire, Filleigh
H.G. Woolaway, Chittlehampton

III.

G.W. Anstey, Filleigh
W.E. Ayre, North Molton
C.M. Barnecutt, Exeter*
V.J. Battershill, Exeter
H.C. Batting, Silverton
F. Chave, Wellington, Som.
S.D.S. Craddock, Filleigh
E.B. Driver, Montserrat
L.W.E. Grant, Exmouth
C.G. Harris, South Molton
H.G. Hopper, Lee, Kent

W.G. Jewell, Gillingham, Dorset*
F.S. Lee, Thorverton
R.D. Medland, Bude
A.P. Moor, South Molton
F.J. Pike, East Buckland
M.R. Roberts, Ilfracombe
E.H. Southcombe, Cheltenham
P.J. Were, London
S.J. Widgery, South Molton
T. Williams, King's Brompton

II.

F.W. Balman, Chittlehampton*
T. Bendall, Bristol
J.L. Carter, Exmouth
F. Hooper, Bideford

W.W. Owbridge, Teignmouth
E. Pearcey, Silverton***
B. Webber, South Molton

[* left at Easter[

22

The Devon County School – pupils and staff. We can name about a third of them. In February, 1907, the boys totalled 66 – in a school designed to take 150. By the end of the year Harries was beginning to get the numbers up; they averaged just over 130 in the First World War. Today they touch 700.

A distinguished Old Boy – T.R. Potbury, who married on 7th January. He was one of a whole family of Potburys who attended the School. Clever too.

Marriage.- At St. Paul's Church, Plumstead, on January 7th, THOMAS RICHARD POTBURY (1880-84), of 35, Park Parade, Harlesden, N.W., to Minnie, eldest daughter of the late John Drew, of Sidmouth. [Thomas Richard was one of a whole dynasty of Potburys, three of whom attended the Devon County School at the end of the nineteenth century. Two of them – J.A. in 1876, and T.R. himself, in 1883 - became Head Prefect, and both became teachers. See also 4th December and 14th December.]

Tuesday, 8th January.

We much regret to announce that the Head Master has resigned his post, and will leave the School at the end of the Lent term … [Mr. Knight had in fact tendered his resignation on 2nd December, 1906 (*qv.*). By 11th January, at the Old Boys' Dinner, his successor – as 'Head Master Elect' - was already much in evidence.]

When Mr. Knight became Head in 1900 there were only 31 boys in the School. The numbers gradually rose to 80, and have for the last two years been fluctuating about 70. Among the more notable School events which have occurred during Mr. Knight's tenure of office may be mentioned the building of the new Chemical and Physical Laboratories, the construction of the new Swimming Bath and a new Cricket Pavilion, and the formation of a Rifle Club …

The Rev. E.A.S. Young, B.A., Second Master and Chaplain, 1904-6, has become a Master in a private preparatory school at Folkestone, and Mr. E.B. Waite has become Modern Language Master at Grantham School.

Mr. G.H. Grimes, B.A., St. John's College, Cambridge, and Mr. J.P.R. Marichal, B.ès L. (Besançon), B. ès. Sc. (Nancy), have joined the Staff this term.

The Rev. E.G. Beckwith, M.A., who, as Rector of Filleigh and East Buckland, has been indirectly connected with the School for about twelve years, has accepted the living of Highweek, Newton Abbot. He is succeeded at Filleigh by the Rev. A.R. Fuller, M.A., late Curate at Holy Trinity, Chelsea.

W. Saunders (entered Jan., 1904) has been made a Sub-prefect.

We tender very hearty thanks on behalf of the School to Mr. F.W. Matthews, Hayle, Cornwall, who has presented us with a very handsome silver cup, to be known as the Swimming Cup. It is nine inches in height, and stands on a plinth bearing a silver shield, on which the School arms are engraved. Mr. Matthews is the father of one of the present members of the School, an "Old Boys" Scholar. ['H. Matthews, Hayle', in Form IV.]

Our neighbour at Elwell [a nearby hamlet], Mr. W.L. Miles, has taken much interest in the Rifle Club, and last term presented a silver spoon to each of the winners of the monthly Competitions. [See 2nd April.]

We have also to return thanks to Dr. G.W. Hill (1870–4) and to Mr. H.B. Squire (1868), who have each promised to give a cricket bat as a prize during the coming summer. [It may be worth checking up to see if a later entry records the presentation of these bats. See Prize Day, 29th July.]

The "In Memoriam" notices in this number are by the Rev. J.H. Thompson, to whom we have previously been indebted for contributions to the early history of the School, such as he alone can write with intimate knowledge. We hope that he will write for the *"Register"* on many future occasions.

We are informed that an illustrated article on the School will appear in the April number of *Health and Strength*. [It did. See 8th April.]

We are again indebted to Mr. R.P. Chope (1874–81), not only for the two articles he contributes to this number ("Old Boys in the Admiralty Service" [see 8th February] and "Football in the Past" [see 22nd February]), but for much valuable help in other parts of the *Register*, and particularly in connexion with Old Boys' News and the report of the Old Boys' Dinner. [See below, 11th January. More of Mr. Chope later. You will find it difficult to avoid him.]

Wednesday, 9th January.

The School has acquired … a very good optical lantern, thanks to which our programme of entertainments during the Christmas term was much more varied and extensive than usual … the movement for the purchase of a lantern was started in the Debating Society, whch voted £2 for that purpose. The rest of the required sum was obtained chiefly from the Masters, Miss Denny [the Matron], and the present boys, a large majority of whom contributed.

We are informed by the Rev. G.T. Llewellin [sic] that the late Baroness Burdett-Coutts visited the School in 1868, with a large party who were shown round by the late Earl Fortescue.

We acknowledge with thanks the receipt of the following contemporaries:- *The Blundellian* (2), *the Kyrtonian, The Burfordian, The Framlinghamian, The Aluredian.*

[Framlingham had been founded as Suffolk County School, similar to the D.C.S. It was Brereton's hope that similar county schools would one day cover the whole of England. Many were founded; only a handful survived.]

The somewhat staid official character of the *Register* appears to have palled on some of the livelier spirits of the Third Form, who last term started a rival paper (in MS.), called, we believe, the *Junior Herald*. Our circulation has not seriously declined, and we venture to hope that there is room for both journals. [Sadly, no copies of this maverick periodical survive. One of the great losses to English literature, one feels.]

The next *Register* will be published about the last week in May. All contributions should reach the Editor by May 4th.

Extra copies of the *Register* can be obtained from the Editor at 6d. each. [2½p.]

Badges inscribed with the School monogram can be obtained from the Matron, Miss Denny, at the School. The price is one shilling. [5p.]

Friday, 11th January.

Old Boys' Dinner.

'Then Hail to the School that, by good grace of Heaven,
Took root and bore fruit on the Hills of North Devon.'

These words, taken from the "Song of the Devon County School", and written by the Rev. Preb. J.L. Brereton, M.A., echo the sentiments of all Old Boys who were present at the Annual Dinner held at the Holborn Restaurant on January 11th, under the Presidency of the first Head Master, the Rev. J.H. Thompson, M.A., and the Vice-Presidency of Messrs. G. William Hill, M.D., B.Sc., and Francis A. Wells, B.A. A more genial gathering it would be difficult to imagine. Old memories were revived, acquaintances of happy school days renewed, and reminiscences of perhaps the happiest days of one's life recalled. As a proof of the enthusiasm of the Devon County School Old Boys, it may be mentioned that the gathering on Friday night drew together 'Boys' from all over England at great personal inconvenience to themselves. But, after all, who would miss such a gathering?

After the loyal toast had been drunk with musical honours the roll call was read over by the Secretary, who took the opportunity of thanking Mr. W.E. Grills for his generosity in providing the artistic programmes.

Among those present were:- W.S. Abell (Assistant Constructor, Admiralty), Dr. W.N. Alexander, F.W. Askham (Chief Accountant in the Army), J.R. Barber, Hubert Bath (Royal Academy of Music)[composer of the School song, and, many years later, of a stalwart item from post-war British film music, *Cornish Rhapsody*], C. Bendall (Bristol), H.H. Bennett, Dr. J.H. Blight, M.B., B.S. (Chesterfield), F.J. Butcher, W.S. Butcher, C.E. Byles, M.A. (Author of *'The Life of Hawker'*, &c.), H.R. Champion (Bristol), A.H. Chard (Bristol), G.M. Chard (Bristol), R.P. Chope, B.A. (Principal of Abridgments and Printing Branch, Patent Office), Capt. T. Chope, A.R. Congdon, F.J. Couch, A.C. Cramb (Borough Electrical Engineer, Croydon), Emile d'Oisly, G.C. Fry, M.Sc., F.I.C. (Master), W. Gard, R. Garrett, W.E. Grills, Rev. E.C. Harries, B.A., (Head Master-Elect), G.W. Harris, Prof. T.A. Hearson, M.Inst.C.E., M.Inst.N.A., J.A. Hill, C.A., Harold H. Hilton (Golf Champion) [twice Open Champion, no less], Dr. T.E. Honey, R.N. (Devonport), C.W. Johns (Stock Exchange), J.C. Johnson, J.H. Kempton, B.A. (Rhyl), John Lane (Publisher), E.O. Lisle, A.F.C. Martyn, J.E. Messenger, T. Mills (Stock Exchange), R.A. Mountjoy (Seamen's Registry Office), Harry Packer (Welsh International Footballer), Dr. T. Perrin, W. Perrin, H. Pickard, A. Podmore, T.R. Potbury, B.A., A.E. Pride, A.J. Pride, A.T. Saunder [the *Register* prints no 's'], J.W. Shawyer, A.W. Shelley, M. Shephard, A. Small, M.B. Snell, J.P.

The Old Boys' Dinner at the Holborn Restaurant in London. Joseph Thompson, the first Headmaster, is standing at the left. Between the wars dinners were held, among other places, at Simpson's and the Dorchester.

(Stock Exchange), R.J.B. Snow, H.B. Squire, W. Strong, A. Taylor (Master), P.R. Tremewen (Stock Exchange), F.J. S. Veysey, F.R. Wadman (Templecombe), T.R. Warden, H.R. Wells, J.B. Wells, P.E. Wells (Winchester), J.R. Western, W.C. Wheeler, J. Wreford.

Letters or telegrams of regret for inability to attend the Dinner were received from a large number of Old Boys.

The first toast, "Success to the Devon County School," was proposed by Mr. FRANCIS A. WELLS, B.A., who said it had been his privilege to mix with boys from other great public schools, and he had heard many interesting stories of meetings in remote and wild lands between men who as boys had been scholars together, had played together, and, possibly, had been castigated by the same brawny arm – (Laughter) –, and it was always to be observed how deeply ingrained was their love of their old School. He was sure the boys of the Devon County School loved their old School with no less depth, and enthusiasm, and gratitude. There were not many who were able to help directly towards the prosperity of the old School, but, at any rate, most of them might be looked to to add to its prosperity as "producers of the raw material" – (Laughter) – and also to act as walking advertisements or commercial travellers for it. He could not help mentioning Mr. Thompson, as he had done an enormous amount of work for the old School in conjunction with the Old Boys. (Cheers.) He would wish him, and those who with him were doing their best

for the School, "God-speed," and he hoped that they would again see their old School as it was in the days of "Auld Lang Syne". He impressed upon the Old Boys the necessity of restoring the School to its former high position. [The School had twice in the previous decade been driven perilously close to the reefs of closure.] He believed the tide had already turned, and he thoroughly believed that under the control of the new Head Master its future prosperity might confidently be expected. (Loud applause.)

Mr. G.C. FRY, M.Sc., F.I.C., to whom fell the duty of responding [possibly because the Headmaster, Mr. Knight, had absented himself so as not to cramp the style of the new Headmaster, who *was* there], said that his qualification for doing so arose solely from the fact that, as a present Master of the School, and, he hoped, a future one, he knew something about the School from the inside. He assured them that the School was sound in the head, and, what was perhaps more important, sound at the heart. (Cheers.) He had some qualification for comparing things, because he had been a master in four or five schools in different parts of England, and he stated deliberately that he had never met a finer or a better lot of boys than those at West Buckland, and those who had been there in recent years. On behalf of the School he thanked Mr. Hubert Bath for composing, and Mr. Emile D'Oisly for singing, the School Song they had just heard, which, he hoped, would be an essential feature at all future gatherings. He thanked Mr. John Lane for presenting 100 volumes to the School Library. He was also pleased to thank Mr. Chope and Mr. Grills for gifts to the School. The Library was still a small one, and there was plenty of room for more books. They had recently secured an optical lantern, and he invited any of the Old Boys to visit West Buckland and introduce some new slides if they were able, and relate their experiences. They needed more money to carry on the School efficiently, but the greatest need of all was boys – a lot more boys, - and he urged upon the Old Boys the necessity of helping the School in this respect. (Cheers.)

Mr. T.R. POTBURY, B.A., proposed the toast of the Head Master Elect, Rev. E.C. Harries, B.A., who is now a master and Chaplain at Blundell's School, Tiverton. He said that he and everyone else had been very pleased to know that, if the resignation of Mr. Knight had to be accepted, Mr. Harries should be selected to fill the post. Mr. Harries had the heartiest good wishes of the boys and also of the Old Boys' Association. He did not suppose that his task was an easy one, but he would enter on his duties with the assurance that he had the hearty co-operation of everyone connected with the School. The School itself was an ideal one in situation, and parents of boys ought to study this when selecting a School for them. The speaker recalled some humorous incidents in connection with his school days, and remembered some of his contests in the field. There had been titanic contests in the dormitories also, but he assured the Chairman he took no part in them. (Laughter.) He trusted that a new chapter in the School's history would be opened, and that the name of the D.C.S. would be once more one to conjure with in the west country. (Applause.)

Rev. E.C. HARRIES, B.A., in reply, acknowledged with pride and gratitude the honour done him by the appointment to such a responsible position as the head mastership of the first County School in England. He had been appointed by the unanimous choice of the Governors of the School and backed up by the unanimous approval of the influential Old Boys' Association. The success of the School in the past had been great, but he felt confident that its success in the future would be still greater, if it was the will of the Almighty. If anything was wanted to encourage him in the task he was attempting, it had been given to him; as since his election he had been inundated with letters of congratulation. (Applause.) Referring to the present condition of the School, he said that they were doing very excellent work, and he could assure them all that the efficiency of the School showed no sign of depreciation. (Applause.) The situation of the School stamped it out as enjoying one of the most healthy surroundings in the British Isles. Illness was never seen there, and it was impossible not to be healthy after being there. The conduct of the boys had always been exemplary, and he could not remember any serious offences. He also had a word to say with regard to the hospitality and efficiency of Miss Denny (the Matron). He thought the springing up of Day Schools had something to do with the diminution in their numbers, but he urged parents not to send their boys to Day Schools, but to Boarding Schools, where they were well cared for and educated in a manner that would fit them to face the

world single-handed. (Applause.) Another cause was, no doubt, the decrease of the rural population, but, if the Old Boys' Association, which was now scattered throughout all England, would only send their boys to their old School, they would be helping it in the best way possible. The boys should first have a good general education, at the end of which they could specialize for anything. They might not all be good athletes, but they should be good sportsmen. (Applause.) The Jubilee of the School would be celebrated within the next two years, and he thought they ought to do something uncommon to commemorate it. (Cheers.) He thanked them all for the confidence reposed in him, and, given health and strength, he would strive to keep up the best traditions of the D.C.S. (Loud Applause.)

Mr. G.W. HILL, M.D., B.Sc., in proposing the health of the Chairman, said he had some diffidence in doing so, as he had already done this task three times. Still, he was never tired of eulogizing Mr. Thompson, as they all, he was sure, had a very great opinion of him. The speaker gave one or two humorous reminiscences of his old school-days, and stated that he felt sure that no better Head Master than Mr. Thompson ever existed. (Applause.)

The CHAIRMAN, in reply, expressed his pleasure at seeing again so many of the old faces and reviving so many old memories. The School had passed through a time of trial, but this had brought out in a remarkable way the expression of the loyalty of the Old Boys to their old School. It was, indeed, owing to the Old Boys, and especially to Mr. Michael Snell [an Old Boy, now a stockbroker, who was organising a financial rescue package], that they had every reason to hope that the difficulties were being surmounted, and that the School would now enter upon a new course of prosperity. Happily the Old Boys' Association would in future have direct representation on the governing body. Its representatives would not be mere officials who knew very little about the School, and possibly cared less, but they would have a very great interest in it, and a very great knowledge of it, and they would help in future to carry on the School's old traditions and its old individuality. (Cheers.) It was not a new School started under new conditions, but it was old School merely changed. That evening had its own special interest. They had to "Welcome the coming and speed the parting" Head Master. They wished the "parting" Head Master, Mr. Knight, every prosperity and success, and they hoped to see him among them on future occasions, as his head mastership was a feature in the history of the School, to which he had given the best years of his life. (Hear, hear.) Mr. Harries, the "coming" Head Master, was entering upon a difficult task, but he was no stranger to the School, he was personally popular, and there was a general feeling that he was the man for the post.

Mr. HAROLD. H. HILTON, ex-golf champion, proposed the toast of the School Sports Club. He said that, although his connection with the Devon County School was in his very youthful days, he had a vivid recollection of many exciting incidents, particularly of a fight with another small boy, who, he was told, was present that evening. He urged upon those present the necessity of cultivating sports of all kinds, as he was of opinion that all boys should be athletes as far as they were physically fit. (Applause.)

Mr. HARRY PACKER, whose name is familiar as the old Welsh Rugby footballer, supported the toast. He though [sic] there was no question at all that the sports part of a boy's education was very little inferior to the book part, for the good qualities of a boy were moulded far more on the playing-fields than in the class-rooms (Cheers.) The School had always turned out fine athletes, and he trusted they would continue to do so. (Applause.)

Mr. A. TAYLOR, in responding, entirely endorsed the remarks of the two proposers to the toast, and thought great attention should be paid to the sports part of the School. He hoped it would always be so, as he should be sorry to see sports not catered for in the School. (Applause.)

Mr. H.B. SQUIRE proposed the toast of "The Old Boys' Association," and thought Mr. Shawyer deserved the greatest thanks for his work in connection with it. Mr. Wheeler [a later caretaker headmaster, in 1952] ably co-operated with him in his endeavour to get as many Old Boys together as possible. (Cheers.)

Mr. R.P. CHOPE, B.A., President of the Association, responded. He congratulated the Association on the large increase in the number of members, and hoped it would long continue to grow at the same rate. [It did. During his two-year presidency, he trebled the membership.] He [said] that the Association had been able in the past to give considerable assistance to the School … with the co-operation of the present Head Master, and he had no reason to think that its influence would be any the less under his successor.

During the evening an excellent musical programme was carried through. The chief item was 'The Song of the Devon County School,' the music of which was composed specially for this occasion by Mr. Hubert Bath, the well-known composer, a native of Barnstaple, who himself accompanied the singer, Mr. Emile d'Oisly. [See 29th July.]

The following is the programme:-

Song – "Father O'Flynn" … … … Dr. W.N. ALEXANDER
Song of the D.C.S. – "Hail to the School" … Mr. EMILE d'OISLY
Song – "Gypsy John"… … … … … Mr. R. GARRETT
Song - "My Inquisitive Kiddie" … … Mr. A. H. CHARD
Zummerset Yarns … … … Mr. FRANK R. WADMAN
Song – "Beauty's Eyes" … … … … Mr. G.M. CHARD
Song – "Dermot Astore" … … … Dr. W.N. ALEXANDER
Song – "Richard of Taunton Deane" … … Rev. E.C. HARRIES
Song – "Will o' the Wisp" … … … … Mr. R. GARRETT

Encore – "The Lowland Sea."

Song – "Queer Questions"… … … … Mr. A.H. CHARD
Song – "Anchored" … … … … Mr. E. ORCHARD LISLE

Sunday, 13th January.

The Choir.

E.A. Adams, A.H. Austin, C.M. Barnecutt, H.J. Harris, C.G. Harris, A.J.E. Helps, H.G. Hopper, H.H. Jones, L.G.H. Major, R.M. Read, H.J. Richards, F.E. Sanders, R.W. Seldon, J.I. White, A.L.J. Youings. [The Choirmaster was the tireless Mr. Adelbert Taylor.]

Monday, 14th January.
The beginning of the Lent Term.

[This date is not explicitly given in the record, but the magazines for the same time in 1905 and 1906 give 20th January as the operative date. This would put the beginning of the Lent Term for 1907 on a Sunday, which seems unlikely. It seems equally unlikely that the date would have been put further back, to the Monday, 21st January, as this would cut out three quarters of the month. So, as these, and most dates like them, have to be shunted around every seven years, I have taken the liberty of pushing it back to the previous week.

Incidentally, the School Year, originally, consisted of not three terms, but four – Lent, Summer, Michaelmas, and Christmas. Many boys, as a rule, were able to go home only during the long summer holidays, and maybe for Christmas. When the new railways made long-distance travel easier, and boys could get home for each holiday, the School, in order to save costs, changed its year from four terms to three – in 1878.]

Saturday, 19th January.
The Football First XI. for the Easter Term is as follows:
[a paraphrase to fit the diary form]

Goal – C. Lewis.
Backs – A.E. Preston , E. H. Trudgian.
Half-backs – W.M. Burridge*, J.B. Harris, W. Saunders.
Forwards - H.H. Jones, R. Maynard, H.J. Harris*, R.W. Seldon*, S. Bendall* (Capt.)

A. Pearce, F.E. Sanders, and P.J. Were will also be considered. [another paraphrase]
*Old Colours

[Lewis, who kept goal for the School till he left in 1909, was widely considered to be the best goalkeeper the School ever produced. See his biography.]

Thursday, 24th January.

Runs.

A very decided keenness was shewn in the Runs … and fortunately the weather was fine on every occasion. Space will not permit of detailed accounts except for the Exmoor. A. Pearce is specially to be commended for his running; he came in first in each of the events except for the great one, and it is mainly owing to him that Court-enay can show an advantage over Brereton.

[As the School is situated in Exmoor, it follows that there is plenty of scope for cross-country running. In the atmosphere of muscular Christianity that prevailed at West Buckland right from the start, it was not long before a tradition of such running was soon built up. Each run collected its own name, and by 1907, there were several of them – the Railway Run, the Beeches Run, the Tuck Run, the Long Run, and the Short Run (and, in the Autumn Term, the North-West Run and the Bray Run), which were all a sort of composite overture to the big one – the *Exmoor*. More of that at the appropriate date.

It is not possible to pinpoint the exact date of each of the first five, because luck would have it that, though the dates of the runs are given in the reports of 1906 and 1908, they are absent in those of 1907. So I have taken the liberty of spreading them at roughly the same intervals of time as they were in the previous and following years. The spirit and the interest are the same.

An explanation of the two names – Brereton and Courtenay. In the early days, there were two dormitories, named as above – Brereton after the founder, Revd. J.L. Brereton, and Courtenay, after the family of the Earl of Devon, whose forebears went back to Norman times, and who put money into the early shares of the School Company. So when competitions were arranged, it was an obvious tactic to organise the boys by the two dormitories. Later a third one was added – Fortescue – named after the Second Earl Fortescue, joint founder with Brereton. An entry in the records of the *Exmoor* race recorded that 'the Fortescue' ran for the first time as a separate house in 1911. It became a tradition to put the definite article before each of the house names. It was not always adhered to, as a reading of some of the following reports will show. Some time after Harries became Headmaster, he changed the nomenclature 'dormitory' to 'house', to bring the School closer in spirit to the more fashionable public schools, one suspects. In 1918, a fourth house, 'the' Grenville, was added. These four houses survive to this day.

One final point. The races were usually organised by a system of handicaps: that is, the smaller boys were given early starts, to make up for their lesser size and strength. It sometimes resulted in the most unlikely boys winning races, because the handicaps had been inaccurately estimated. This was changed in 1908, the year of the fiftieth Exmoor and the School's golden anniversary. Race starts were still staggered, but final positions were reckoned by times, not by order of finishing.]

THE RAILWAY RUN.

BRERETON		COURTENAY	
S. Bendall	19	A. Pearce	20
N.K. Pearce	16	L.K.V. Job	18
R.W. Seldon	12	R. Maynard	17
M.R. Roberts	11	J.B. Harris	15
T. Williams	10	C.G. Harris	14
W.M. Burridge	9	H.J. Harris	13
	—		—
	77		97

Courtenay won by 20 points

[The first boy home was awarded 20 points, the second 19, and so on.]

Friday, 25th January.

The Reading and Debating Society.

[This was set up in 1903 after a recent Inspectors' Report had pointed out somewhat tartly that the School catered well for the boys' work, and for their sport, but for very little else. Within a few years, Mr. Knight, the Headmaster, had produced a Rifle Club, some Science laboratories, a Swimming Pool, a Reading Room, and this, the 'Reading and Debating Society'. The first Secretary was a G.E.L. Carter, whose grandson, Mr. R.L. Carter, Head of Physics at the School from 1982-2006, took charge of the Society's successor, the Phoenix Society.]

There was an examination held for the election of members from the V form [sic]. The Subjects for essays were:

The Year 1906
Earthquakes & Volcanoes
A Modern Naval Battle
Future Travelling

As a result of the Examination the following boys were elected members of the Society

R.T.H. Hooper
L.K.V. Job
H.H. Jones
C. Lewis
E.H. Trudgian

Monday, 28th January.

[The Auditor, Joseph Kingdon, reported,] 'I have examined the School Accounts, for the year ending 31st December, 1906 … and do hereby certify the correctness of the … Balance Sheet.'

The Reading and Debating Society.

[Average attendance this term was about 11, which represented roughly 17% of the entire pupil body – nearly treble some of the best attendances today. Attendances in the Christmas Term were even higher. This was the 102nd meeting. The Secretary usually indicated the number – see later minutes. Minutes are recorded as closely as possible to what the Secretary actually wrote.]

Before the opening of the meeting, G.C. Fry Esq. [Science teacher – in charge of the Society. He was usually 'in the chair', according to the Minutes.] made a short speech in which he welcomed the new members and hoped that all the members would settle their subjects for essays and debates as soon as possible.

The minutes of the previous meeting having been read and confirmed, S. Bendall proposed "that this House is in favour of a Channel Tunnel".

The Hon. Member said that it would greatly facilitate & increase commerce. It would also shorten the time for mails & passengers & would be a bond of natural good-will between England & France.

He thought that if it is possible for us to guard our coastline, if would surely be possible to guard the mouth of a Tunnel. A guard could be placed at the mouth, which could cope with the greatest force that could be sent against them by means of the Tunnel.

The cost would be partly paid by the French, & in the event of this being the only objection, it would be put aside. Besides advantages it would be a great engineering feat.

W. Saunders, opposing, thought that there were enough taxes imposed on the British public already, without having an additional tax, to raise several millions for a Tunnel, which would probably not pay.

The Tunnel would be a great convenience to fussy old people who get sea-sick, but if they considered the danger they would risk in going through the Tunnel, they would rather travel by sea.

The Hon. Mem. went on to say that the Severn tunnel was very damp & pumps have to be working continually. The Channel Tunnel would probably be 3 times as long & if the pumps broke down, anybody in the Tunnel would be drowned.

Then again, a great difficulty would be experienced in ventilating the tunnel.

G.C. Fry Esq. said that if an invasion were made from France, the French would first land some troops on the English coast & then proceed to capture our end of the Tunnel. Troops could then be poured into England by means of the Tunnel. He thought that it would not pay, & that a great difficulty would arise in the settlement of gauges. On the whole he thought the Tunnel would not be a success as air-ships would take the place of trains.

H.J. Harris thought the Tunnel would increase murders, as several murders have occurred in tunnels.

W.L. Armstrong described an arrangement by which trains could run on two different gauges.

L.K.V. Job, who made his maiden speech, said that as we were all British subjects, we ought to like the sea, & not to encourage a Channel Tunnel.

J.B. Harris was of the opinion that the Germans would probably in the end make use of the Channel Tunnel. He asked why the last Channel Tunnel bill fell through.

W. Saunders summing up said that nearly all the boats that cross the Channel belong to English companies, & if the Tunnel were constructed they would perhaps be ruined.

The Tunnel might be blown up at any moment by a fanatic. He quite agreed with Mr. Fry that the Tunnel would be useless on account of the progress of air-ships.

S. Bendall, in conclusion, thought that Mr. H.J. Harris was wrong in his statement that murders occurred frequently in tunnels. Murders are not committed any more in tunnels than they are anywhere else.

He thought that the risks taken by going through such a tunnel would be no greater than those taken by ships & air-ships.

He also contradicted Mr. J.B. Harris' statement about the Germans.

The House then divided & the motion was lost by 8-2.

The House adjourned at 8.30.

End of January entries

February

Friday, 1st February.

Old Boys' News.

An Old Boys' "Social" was held in the Baronial Hall at the City of New York Restaurant, 47A Bedford Row, Holborn. The chair was taken by Harold H. Hilton, Esq., the famous golfer. [This was one of a series of social gatherings started in the autumn of 1906 'on the suggestion of Mr. G.M. Chard', and which had 'been continued… without any diminution of initial success'.]

Among recent literary announcements are a book by the Rev. J.F. Chanter, M.A. (1863-7), Rector of Parracombe, entitled "A History of the Parishes of Lynton and Countisbury"; and a book on "Great Golfers in the Making," by thirty-four of the most celebrated living players, including H.H. Hilton (1877).

F. Parkin (1882-5) has recently been elected an Alderman of the City of Exeter.

J.F. Sanders (1890-2) has been gazetted Second-Lieutenant of the 4th V.B.D.R. ['Volunteer Battalion of the Devonshire Regiment.' It became 6th Battalion, the Devonshire Regiment in 1908, when the Territorial Army was set up. It was recruited from North Devon.]

S. Algar (1903-4) has passed the recent examination of the Surveyors' Institution, qualifying as a student.

We have just been informed that A.G. Grist (1886) was appointed, last August, Chief Veterinary Surgeon for the Orange River Colony [in South Africa]. We are unable, at the moment of going to press, to obtain any further particulars.

T.H. Watts (1897-1903) played centre half for Oxfordshire v. Berks and Bucks in the Southern Counties Championship. He scored two goals, as did also G.R.W. Dickinson (Master, 1904), who was playing centre forward. Watts is playing for Notts County in their First League and Cup matches whenever his duties allow him to get away. [See also 20th May. Talbot Henry Watts was killed in the First World War.]

J.R. Barber (1898-1904) is Captain of Crouch End Vampires; W.S. Goff (1891-3) of Exeter City Rugby 1st XV.; and J. Pearce (1900-5) of Barnstaple A.F.C. F.J. Couch (1884-7) has been selected to play for Middlesex.

Saturday, 2nd February.

Football – FIRST XI. (WITH MASTERS)
v. BARNSTAPLE Y.M.C.A.
Lost 4-1

Played at Barnstaple … on a most wretched ground, and resulted in a defeat for the School by 4-1. Considering the bad conditions (the grounds at Barnstaple always seem to be some inches deep in mud), the game was well contested, and, as is usual with the Y.M.C.A., was played in a sporting manner throughout.

Sunday, 3rd February.

In Memoriam.

WILLIAM MILLER

… When the first Head Master arrived upon the scene [in 1858], the School had no pupils, it had no local habitation, hardly indeed a name. Then three boys applied for admission. What was to be done with them? Where was the School to he held? Where could it be held, at all events, temporarily, till a more permanent arrangement could be made? At this time of doubt and difficulty Mr. William Miller came forward with the hearty good feeling which characterised him. He put the chief rooms of his house at the service of the new School, and there, in his house, the Devon County School was started. His parlour was its first schoolroom, one of his bedrooms was its first dormitory, the room you enter when you open the front door was its first dining hall, the good and kindly Mrs. Miller was temporarily its first matron …

Those familiar with the early days know well how ready Mr. and Mrs. Miller were, in every possible way and in every emergency, to exert themselves to the utmost for the good of the School … [Mrs. Miller had died in about 1896. Mr. Miller lived on till he was 84.]

As years went on, the School won for itself many friends, but among them Mr. and Mrs. Miller occupied a unique position: when they saw, rising and increasing, the beautiful buildings of the afterwards far-famed County School, and other County Schools formed after its model in different parts of England, they could look back – and not without natural pride – on the days when the first County School in England was carried on in their house…

Mr. Miller … was not unknown in other ways. In days when wrestling was a favourite pastime his fame as a "wrastler" was spread far and wide through the west country. The story of his deeds in the wrestling world … might form the subject of a not uninteresting article. It cannot be told now. We can now only lay as it were a wreath on the grave of one who, when help was needed, did hearty yeoman service for the School.

Monday, 4th February.

The Reading and Debating Society.

The 103rd meeting was held. There were 11 members present. After the usual reading of the minutes, W.L. Armstrong suggested that if in debates the Hon. Mover & Opposer opened with two or three points, other members would have more to say. G.C. Fry Esq. quite agreed with the Hon. member.

J.B. Harris then read a paper on "Charles Gordon". The Hon. Member commenced his paper by saying that

Gordon was born at Woolwich Jan 28th 1833. He went to school at Taunton & at the age of 16 entered the Military Academy at Woolwich.

In 1854 he volunteered to go to the Crimea, & he then gave an account of his work in the Crimean War.

After the war he joined the commission for settling the boundaries between Russia, Turkey & Rumania. He enjoyed this life for a time but soon got tired of it, & set sail to join the English troops in China.

When he reached China, the Allied British & French troops had taken Pekin, & the Chinese were negotiating for peace. A commission met but there was a quarrel & 26 British subjects were seized & imprisoned. For this act the Chinese were severely punished.

In 1862 Gordon had his attention called to the Tai-ping rebellion. He took the command of the Ever-Victorious Army & defeated the rebels at several places, but on the disbanding of the Ever-Victorious Army, he resigned.

He now returned to England & was appointed to the command of the Royal Engineers at Gravesend. During the years 1872-73 he travelled through Bulgaria & gained intimate knowledge of the ways & means of the Turkish Government.

At Constantinople he met Mubar Pasha, & entered the service of the Khedive, but after completing a line of forts on the Albert Nyanza he returned to London with the firm intention of finally quitting the Khedive's service. However he was prevailed upon to return, & took up his residence at Khartoum.

In July, 1882, an insurrection broke out under the Mahdi, & Gordon, who was on his holiday, was immediately sent for, & and sent to Khartoum.

The Arabs suffered a reverse at Tamai, for which they determined to wreak their vengeance on Khartoum.

Soon Arab tribes surrounded the place, & in Dec.1884, Gordon's position became helpless. Omdurman had fallen, but Gordon never wavered, refusing all idea of surrender & doing his best for his country.

At last on Jan. 26th – 1888 [1885, actually, before anyone writes in – there is no way of knowing whether the mistake was Harris' or the secretary's], the Arabs made a final assault & entered the town. Gordon at the head of about 20 men drew near the church. A band of Arabs emerged from a side street, & then there was a volley, & the bravest man of the day was no more.

G.C. Fry Esq., after congratulating the Hon. Member on his paper, said that the death of Gordon was one of the his earliest memories, & he could still remember the feeling of helpless rage, which passed over England, when it became known that the Relief Expedition had arrived too late.

Since Gordon's time, the Hon. Member went on to say, black prisoners have often been enlisted and drilled, & have fought with success. At the Battle of the Atbara we captured several thousands of blacks, & when the final battle was fought at Omdurman hundreds of these prisoners fought for us.

He thought that the Mahdi's insurrection was similar to the rising of Mohomet [sic], 1300 years before. The Mahdi like Mohomet was a religious maniac whose Gospel was one of fire & sword.

S. Bendall, also congratulating the Hon. Member, said that Gordon refused all presents etc. for his services in China, & returned from that country no richer than he had left England. This was a contrast to Clive, whose great weakness lay in receiving bribes etc from the natives of India.

The House adjourned at 8.20 p.m.

Tuesday, 5th February.

The Old Boys' Football Match will not be held this term.

Wednesday, 6th February.

Football - FIRST XI. (WITH MASTERS)
v. BARNSTAPLE.
Draw 1-1.

In this match at the School … Mr. Knight made his last appearance, and right well did he play. In no slight measure was the draw of one all (slightly in favour of the School), due to his tackling and general defence at full-back, and his assistance will surely be missed next football season.

The game was very even from the start to the finish, the whole of the home team playing very well, particularly S. Bendall and H.H. Jones, the two wing forwards.

Thursday, 7th February.

THE BEECHES RUN.

BRERETON		COURTENAY	
S.Bendall … … …	19	A. Pearce … … …	20
R.W. Seldon … …	17	W. Saunders … …	18
A.E. Preston … …	16	H.J. Harris … … …	14
H.H. Jones … …	15	L.K.V. Job … … …	13
W.L. Armstrong … …	12	A.S. Ayres … … …	11
W.M. Burridge … …	9	J.B. Harris … … …	10
	—		—
	88		86

Brereton won by 2 points.

Friday, 8th February.

Old Boys in the Admiralty Service.

[The author of this piece was Richard Pearce Chope, from Hartland, an Old Boy (1874-81). He combined awesome ability and fierce energy with firebrand interest in the School and the Old Boys' Association (see 11th January). One of the results was a series of ponderous articles about various aspects of School history, which the hapless editors of the *Register* often found difficult to digest. As it happened, though, this particular one does give a good flavour of the sort of boys the School produced, and the sort of work they went into, and, it would appear, did very well at. It is possible in the space

R. PEARSE CHOPE, B.A.
(Hon. Treasurer of the Old Boys' Association, and
Representative Governor of the School).
From a Drawing by Vernon Hill.

Mr. Chope's bookplate. It betrays a little of the ego which appeared to drive him to his relentless campaign of forcing favours on the School.

to reproduce barely half of what he wrote. Indeed the editors themselves sometimes admitted to having to cut his original scripts. Very brave of them.]

'PEREGRINE WILLIAM PEPPERELL HUTTON … entered the *Britannia* as a Naval Cadet in August, 1864 … served in the Ashantee War, 1873-4, and was awarded a medal. … He died in the British Hospital at Monte Video on 14th April, 1887.'

'CLAUD ARTHUR WILLIAM HAMILTON . . . Sub-Lieutenant on 21st October, 1880 … Captain on 30th June, 1903 … received the Egyptian Medal and Khedive's Bronze Star … during the Burma Annexation War … he obtained the India Medal with clasp for Burma.'

'HENRY MANATON OMMANNEY entered the *Britannia* as a Naval Cadet, but died in the Naval Cadets' Hospital at Dartmouth on 19th December, 1885, before he had completed his course of study.'

'THOMAS ALFRED HEARSON entered the Admiralty service in 1863 as the first of the then newly formed class of Engineer Students … he graduated with the highest distinction of Fellow, 1st Class … In 1873 he was appointed Instructor in Applied Mechanics and Engineering at the foundation of the Royal Naval College at Greenwich … until 1884, when he was permitted … to accept an appointment under the Indian Government as Professor of Engineering at Cooper's Hill College … Among Mr. Hearson's inventions are the strophometer (a speed indicator) … and the anti-stylograph, the first practical nibbed fountain pen … In 1899 and 1900 he was one of the examiners in the Mechanical Sciences Tripos at Cambridge, and for many years he was an examiner in Machine Construction and Drawing for the Science and Art Department, South Kensington … etc.'

'GEORGE HENRY HEARSON [a brother, it seems] became an Engineer Student in 1866 … in 1884 he

received the sanction of the Admiralty to … accept an appointment in the service of the Chinese Emperor as Professor of Mathematics and Engineering at the then newly instituted Naval College at Tientsin … In 1887 … he received permission from the Queen to accept and wear the order of the Double Dragon of the Chinese Empire. He died on 6th November, 1900.'

'HUGH REGINALD HEARSON [yet another brother] became an Engineer Student in 1877 … and resigned his commission . . . on taking up an appointment in the service of the Chinese Emperor as Professor of Mathematics and Engineering at the then newly instituted Naval College at Nanking … established a private practice as a Consulting Engineer at Shanghai.' [See 16th August.]

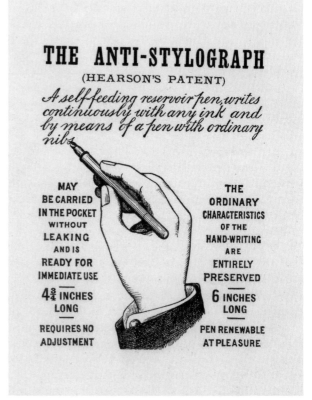

An invention by a Mr. Hearson, a member of a whole family of Hearsons who attended the School, and who went on to grace the engineering profession.

'EDMUND MANATON CARPENTER OMMANNEY was gazetted as a Second Lieutenant in the Royal Marine Light Infantry on 1st September, 1888, and was promoted to the rank of First Lieutenant on 27th September, 1889, Captain on 23rd September, 1897, and Major on 1st November, 1906. On 13th December, 1905, he was appointed Instructor of Musketry at Plymouth.' [Note the brother above – it has to be a brother, with a name like that.. The three Hearsons too. Time and again one finds brothers following similar occupations. There were two Abells in this list as well.]

'WESTCOTT STILE ABELL [Here's one of them.] entered the Royal Naval Engineering College at Keyham in 1892 … On the occasion of Queen Victoria's Diamond Jubilee in June, 1897, and shortly after his final examination at Keyham, he met with a severe accident, resulting in the loss of his right hand. Returning to Exmouth with a picnic party from Chudleigh Rocks, he was burning coloured lights at the end of the break when the contents of one of the tins exploded, shattering his hand from the wrist and inflicting severe wounds in his thighs and throat. His face luckily escaped damage, in spite of the fact that the front of the crown and of the rim of his straw hat were sheared off as if by a knife. He had to walk about half a mile before he could find a doctor, and then, being late at night and no trains running, he drove in a cab to Exeter, nearly eleven miles, retaining consciousness until he arrived at the hospital in that city. He remained in the hospital three weeks, and then, the Admiralty having given permission for the continuance of his studies at the Royal Naval College, Greenwich, he learnt to write with his left hand before the commencement of the college course in September. At the end of the session he was first on the list, and at the final examination in 1900 he gained a 1st class professional certificate, having obtained more than 80 per cent of full marks.' [See 16th August and 21st September.]

'THOMAS BERTRAND ABELL [Here's the other.] entered the Royal Naval Engineering College at Keyham in 1895 as an Engineering Student, and two years later he was selected as a Naval Construction Student. In 1900 he was appointed to the Royal Naval College at Greenwich for the course in Naval Architecture, and in 1903 he joined the Royal Corps of Naval Constructors as an Assistant Constructor, having, like his brother, obtained a 1st Class professional certificate. After serving a short time in Devonport Dockyard and at the Admiralty, he was in June, 1904, attached to the staff of the Admiralty Experiment Works at Portsmouth. [See 6th June.]

'JOHN DAVEY HENWOOD … entered the Navy as a Surgeon on 30th September, 1876, being first in order of merit among the successful candidates … On 17th November, 1906, he was placed on the retired list, with the rank of Deputy Inspector-General of Hospitals and Fleets.'

'WILLIAM STRADLING … graduated as B.A., being placed in the Senior Optime division of the Mathematical Tripos [the final honours degree examination at Cambridge; 'Senior Optime' meant second class] … In March, 1904, he was appointed as Assistant Master at the Royal Naval College at Osborne.' [Another headmaster of West Buckland – Harries' successor, Lt.-Comd. R.V.H. Westall – was trained at Osborne, and a third, G.B. Smith, was an instructor at Osborne. Both could easily have known Stradling. See also 26th/27th August.]

Saturday, 9th February.

Football – FIRST XI. (BOYS) v. KING'S COLLEGE, TAUNTON.
Lost 6 – 1.

Played at Taunton … in a veritable quagmire. This, and the heavy balls (three were used) very much handicapped our light team, who, nevertheless, played pluckily and were only down 1 goal at half-time.

King's pressed continuously during the second half and won easily, as the score shows.

Tuesday, 12th February.

The Reading and Debating Society.

The 104th meeting was held. [The Minutes actually say '12th Feb.', but the *Register* prints '11th'. Monday was indeed the usual day for meetings, but there was the occasional Tuesday gathering – see Tuesday, 5th March. Mr. Fry, who seems to have read and checked the Minutes as a matter of course, did not see fit to correct it, so he presumably agreed.]

G.C. Fry Esq. [was] in the chair. There were 10 members present. The minutes having been read and confirmed, L.K.V. Job proposed "that on the whole newspapers do more harm than good". The Hon. Member said that newspapers introduce much slander, & much ill feeling. They are often the cause of quarrels, & … there is information about the people concerned in law-suits, not – in several cases – fit for anyone to read, and there are lives laid bare that would never have got to the Public, had it not been for the Papers.

A short time ago, the Hon. Member went on to say, some papers stated that in the event of war between France & Germany, England would help France with a 100,000 men. Whether this was a rumour or not, it caused much enmity between England and Germany.

H.J. Harris, opposing, said that by reading newspapers one keeps in touch with things going on in the outer world. If it were not for newspapers, how would anyone know anything about the terrible disasters which occur outside our own country; or, supposing there is a war, how would any news get over the country.

Reading papers makes one quick at finding mistakes, & trains the brain, so that one can remember things better.

Concluding he thought that a boy who is not well up in general knowledge is not cultivated.

G.C. Fry Esq. thought that the better class of weekly papers do good, but local papers contain such a lot of advertisements of quack medicines etc. that from an advertisement point of view they do a great deal of harm.

The Hon. Member went on to say, that the Californian press had announced that Japan had sent an ultimatum to the United States. This however was not correct, & naturally led to ill-feeling between the two countries.

S. Bendall said that the reason why General Buller did not succeed in Natal was because he feared the newspapers & what they would say. "Tremendous losses, 5 killed, 2 wounded." This was the case after Spion Kop. [This only shows that anyone can get it wrong – and right. Modern figures give the losses at about 1,500 killed and wounded. So the papers were right with the 'tremendous'. And Bendall was right with the hounding that Buller suffered from the press. However, Buller never lost the loyalty of the men under his command, whose welfare was always his first concern. He was a brave man too – holder of the Victoria Cross. He was born in Crediton, and attracted strong loyalty in the West Country, where it was felt that he had become a scapegoat for others' mistakes. There is a huge statue to him in Exeter.]

He then referred to the Thaw case as an example of the evil that one can read in newspapers. [Whoever 'Thaw' was.] The Hon. Member thought that it would be better if there was one paper, controlled by the Government.

<u>H.H. Jones</u>. referring to Mr. Harris' speech, suggested that war news could be spread by means of the telegraph.

<u>W. Saunders</u>. said that weekly papers get all their news from the daily ones. He thought that the best way of obtaining reliable news, would be to wait a few months & then read it from a book.

<u>W.L. Armstrong</u>. said that papers are always devoted to sentional [sic] events, & tales & leave out all Political news. Then again, several papers are entirely devoted to betting news.

<u>J.B. Harris</u>. was of the opinion that Mr. Jones' idea would be a very expensive one. He thought that there were papers giving only betting news. [It looks as if there were a vital negative missing here, after the previous speaker's remarks.]

<u>C. Lewis</u>. said that papers say they get the news from their own correspondence [sic] , when more often than not they take it from other papers.

<u>H.J. Harris</u>; summing up, said that if some disaster occurred in our Colonies, the Government would leave it out of the paper. It would take several books, he thought to get in all the news of some months. He also thought Mr. Jones' idea was a very expensive one.

<u>L.K.V. Job</u>. in conclusion said that another instance that papers do more harm than good, is that really good papers, which do not contain anything about murders etc. are losing their circulation. He went on to say that papers are very misleading. One paper reported that a certain ship had met with very bad weather between two inland towns.

The House then divided and and the motion was won by 6 votes to 4.

The House adjourned at 8.30 p.m.

[The punctuation is inconsistent in this entry; so it was in the Minutes.]

Wednesday, 13th February.

Football – FIRST XI. (WITH MASTERS) v. TAUNTON
Y.M.C.A.
Lost 6 – 1.

As was expected, we were unable to avenge our beating of last term, and again had to admit a defeat this time by 6 – 1. We went to Taunton with a fairly strong team (C. Saunders and F. Vicary again turning out for the School), but we found our opponents even stronger than when they came down to us. It was a hard and very tiring game all through, but for once in a way we had a dry ground to play upon.

Friday, 15th February.

Many Old Boys will learn with great regret that Mr. J.G. SHAIN, who was a Master from 1869 to 1888, died [today] at Buntingford, Herts.

Saturday, 16th February.

Football – FIRST XI. (BOYS) *v.* CHITTLEHAMPTON.
Won 4 – 0.

This match was played on the School ground ... and resulted in a well-deserved win for the School by 4 goals to nothing. Taking advantage of playing with the wind, the School put on 3 goals during the first half, and added another after change of ends. The visitors, who were assisted by two or three of the South Molton players, played a hard rushing game, but were quite out-classed by the passing of the School forwards. R. Maynard deserves special mention for the fearless way in which he played; and P.J. Were also played well.

Old Boys' Social.

[This was another of the series of social gatherings started in the autumn of 1906, some to be held in Exeter, as here, and others to be held in London, as on 1st February.]

At the Exeter meeting of the Association ... W.C. Vallance presided, and among those present were:- The Revd. J.H. Copleston (Governor), and E.C. Harries (Head Master); Dudley J.C. Bush, J.P. (a Governor under the new scheme [the School was changing from a private shareholding company with directors to a private fee-paying school with governors, and Bush was to serve as Governor for another twenty-seven years]), G.J. Abell, E. Batting, F.R. Boatfield, J.F. Bowden, G.G. Branscombe, A. J. Carter, J. Cobley, A.J. Force, W.S. Goff, M. Holladay, F. Horsford, A.M. Hutchings, F. Lee, E.T. Loram, L.D. Martin, A.J. Mortimer, E.G. Otton, W.J. Otton, W. Plumpton, L. Pollard, H.S. Potbury, W.H.C. Pratt, H.T. Roberts, H.K. Thorne, W.S.W. Tilley. A. J. Tucker. J.F. Vallance, W.C. Wheeler (Hon. Sec.)

The toast of "The School" was proposed by the Chairman, who assured the Governors that the Association would do its utmost, collectively and individually, for the School. Mr. Dudley J.C. Bush, J.P., as a future Governor, responded, and expressed the hope that the undeniable advantages and magnificent situation of the School would secure it a brilliant future. Mr. H.S. Potbury, in proposing "The Head Master Elect", said that when, in July, 1904, in the name of the Old Boys then assembled at the School, he wished Mr. Harries "God speed" on his departure for Blundell's, he little thought he should ever have the pleasure of welcoming him back as Head Master. The Rev. E.C. Harries, in responding, briefly outlined his proposals for the future conduct of the School, and dwelt on the advantages of boarding-schools as opposed to day-schools. The Chairman, in responding to the toast of his health, paid a tribute to the good work done by the retiring Head Master during the eleven years he had been at the School.

An excellent musical programme greatly contributed to the enjoyment of the meeting.

Monday, 18th February.

The 105th meeting of the Reading and Debating Society was held, G. Fry Esq being in the chair. There were 11 members present. The minutes of the previous meeting having been read & confirmed, G.C. Fry Esq. read a very instructive paper on the "Birth of Chemistry". The Hon member first dealt with some of the early theories of the Greeks, especially Thales, Democritus, & Empedocles, on the composition of matter; he then described the practical knowledge of chemical arts possessed by the ancients, chiefly in connexion with metallurgy, painting, dyeing & glass-making.

The growth of alchemy & its introduction into Europe by the Arabians were then described, with some account of the more famous alchemists, e.g. Albertus Magnus, St. Thomas Aquinas, & Roger Bacon; ending with Paracelsus, who represents the end of the alchemical period & the beginning of the period of medical chemistry, in which he made some important reforms.

S. Bendall after congratulating the Hon member, asked him if he could explain how the pyramids were built.

G.C. Fry Esq replying said that nobody knew how the pyramids were built, but the stones were probably pushed on rollers up a very slightly inclining plane, & then put in their places.

The House adjourned at 8 – 30 p.m.

Wednesday, 20th February.

Football – SECOND XI. (BOYS) *v.* SOUTH MOLTON UNITED SCHOOLS.
Won 4 – 0.

[This match is undated, but comes in the record between reports of matches on 16th February and 6th March, so it must have been on a Saturday or Wednesday in between.]

Our opponents in this match did not confine themselves to present members of the Schools, and came out fully intending to win. They were a heavier team than ours, but by superior play all round we penetrated their defence four times, and at the same time kept our goal intact.

Friday, 22nd February.

Football in the Past.

[R.P. Chope being busy again – and the editor too no doubt (see 8th February).]

It will probably cause a shock of surprise to most readers of the *Register* to be told that football, as it is now played under either Association or Rugby rules, is quite a modern game, and a still greater shock to be told that thirty years ago the D.C.S., like Eton, Harrow, and Winchester, played under its own code of rules … [This, and what follows, is another example of the work of Mr. R.P. Chope – see the article on Old Boys in the Admiralty Service, 8th February. One is tempted by the uncharitable thought that he was so intelligent, academic, and hardworking that he understood only one literary style – encyclopaedic. Like those courageous editors of the *Register* a century ago, I have cut him a bit.]

When I first went to the D.C.S. in 1874, the game played was similar in some respects to the great game described in "Tom Brown's Schooldays". There, as at Rugby, no limit was placed on the number of players on each side, and every boy in the School – except a few of the youngest, called "the kids", who might run the risk of injury – joined in the game. Great ingenuity was shown in dividing the School into two sides of approximately equal strength. For example, we played Monitors v. School, Devon v. The World, First half of Alphabet v. Second, Oxford v. Cambridge (the boys could select whichever they liked, but could not change), West Buckland v. East Buckland (the dormitories then were so situated that about half the boys slept in each parish).

The match between the Monitors and the School was a great favourite, and in this the Masters generally took part, being divided between the two sides. Mr. Thompson [Headmaster from 1858, the year of the School's foundation, till his retirement in 1888] himself frequently acted as goalkeeper for the Monitors …

When we played football against strangers, such as Barnstaple or South Molton, the numbers were, of course, limited, but, as we compelled our opponents to play according to our Rules, they were severely handicapped and were rarely victorious. Unfortunately, this requirement sometimes led to serious disagreement, for it could hardly be expected that a team could exactly follow our code without previous practice. Perhaps our greatest game was played against "All Comers", without limit of numbers on either side. The "Nappers", as we called them, were captained by the Rev. J.H. Copleston, [almost certainly the 'Rev. J.H. Copleston' of Offwell Rectory, Honiton, a Governor of the School! – see December, 1906. Chope also remarked that he was Rector of West Buckland in the 1870's, again almost certainly in succession to the founder, the Revd. J.L. Brereton, who left to take up his father's living in Norfolk, on the latter's death in 1867. Copleston was moreover a talented cricketer] and the furious encounters between that gentleman and Mr. Thomas [another long-serving master, 1864-88] were almost Homeric.

Saturday, 23rd February.

The Annual General Meeting of the Shareholders… [was] convened by the Secretary, and held at the *George* Hotel, South Molton. [The School was a private company, financed by shareholders and run by directors – though not for much longer. See the Minutes for 30th May and 15th June.]

Present. Earl Fortescue (in the chair), Messrs. G.C. Smyth-Richards, C. Pearce, D.J.C. Bush, A Taylor and The Revs. J. Newman & J.H. Thompson. (Messrs. J. Sanders, W.P. Hiern and Comer Clarke were also present.)

1. The Minutes of the last General Meeting were read and confirmed.
2. Lord Fortescue proposed and Mr. Thompson seconded that the Governors' Annual Report and Statement of accounts be received and adopted. The same was carried unanimously.
3. Mr. John Mothersdale wrote saying that as he had now left North Devon, he felt compelled to resign his position on the Board of Governors. His resignation

was therefore accepted. The Secretary was instructed to write to Mr. Mothersdale, and on behalf of the Governors and the Shareholders to thank him for the many services he had rendered to the School both as an Ordinary Governor and as a Member of the Management Committee.

4. Mr. Pearce proposed and Mr Thompson seconded that Mr. Wilkin and Mr. Smyth-Richards be re-elected. Carried unanimously.

5. Other vacancies were left over to the next Meeting of Shareholders.

6. The Medical Officer's Report was read and considered very satisfactory. Proposed by Lord Fortescue & seconded by Mr. Bush that the same be received & adopted. Carried nem. con.

7. The election of Auditor was postponed to the next meeting of the Shareholders.

An Ordinary Meeting of the Governors [was] convened by the Secretary [Mr. Taylor, the teacher, who, among his many other duties, kept the minutes in meticulously clear handwriting. As Secretary to the Governors, he also drew up the balance sheets – see 31st July and 31st December.] and held at the *George* Hotel, South Molton (immediately after the Annual General Meeting).

<u>Present</u>. Earl Fortescue (in the chair), Messrs. C. Pearce, G.C. Smyth Richards, J. Sanders and W.P. Hiern.

1. The Minutes of the previous meeting were read and confirmed.

2. A discussion took place as to the new Head Master's salary. Lord Fortescue gave a report as to the arrangement made by him and Mr. Snell with Mr. Harries, and undertook to forward details of the same to the Secretary for insertion in the minutes. [For details of HM's salary, see Masters' Biographies.]

3. The Board of Education Inspectors' Report for the year 1906 was read, and also a letter from the County Council Education Committee relating thereto. With reference to the heating of certain rooms, which was the subject of the Board's Report and the County Council letter, the Secretary was instructed to write to the County Council explaining what the existing arrangements were, and to say that deficiencies would be remedied as early as possible.

4. A letter was read from Mr. Harries thanking the Governors and the Trustees for his unanimous election to the post of Head Master.

5. Circular letters to the Parents relative to the change in Headmaster, both from the Secretary and Mr. Harries, were read and approved.

6. Sanction was given for [an] abridged prospectus to be printed; it was noted that Mr. Harries would pay for the same if necessary. [This would appear to confirm the deductions, or most of them, offered in the 'Prospectus' chapter – p13.]

7. A sum of £15 was authorized to be expended on School advertisements during the Easter vacation; the same to be arranged by Mr. Harries and Mr. Taylor.

8. Cheques to the value of £232 " 18s " 4d were presented and signed.

9. The Governors decided not to waive their claim for a Term's notice of removal in the case of J.L. Buckingham, not sufficient grounds being given by the Trustee of the Late William Buckingham.

10. The Secretary was instructed to write to Mr. F.W. Matthews of Hayle, Cornwall, thanking him, on behalf of the Governors, for the Challenge Cup which he had presented to the School. [See 8th January.]

11. Mr. Burridge's request for his son to continue as a boarder at the School free of Tuition Fees was not acceded to, unless his son qualified to gain the Board of Education grant. [The boy left at Easter.]

12. The Secretary was instructed to write again to Mr. J.C. Carter of Exmouth, and press for payment of his School account. Unless payment was made within a fortnight, it was decided to put the matter in the hands of Messrs. Crosse, Day & Wyatt. [The Carter family were, ironically, loyal providers of sons for the School. There were four Carter boys in the 1890s and 1900s, three of whom died in the First World War. The survivor sired a son who attended between the wars, and who fathered another Carter who became a Physics teacher at the School – though he did not in fact attend as a boy. He in turn produced four sons, all of whom attended the School. There were also three or four cousins at the School, the Wakefields, two of whom died in the Second World War. The honour of the Carter family was partially redeemed by a margin note in Earl Fortescue's handwriting, that 'Secretary reported that £75 had been paid to date – about £40 being still owing'.]

13. Respecting the remuneration to be paid to Mr. Knight for the expenses he had had in repapering and redecorating the Head Master's House, the Secretary was instructed to find out what Mr. Knight would accept & then leave to the Management Committee to settle. [Another marginal note said 'settled at £15, 15/5/07'.]

14. It was decided that £300 should be the maximum amount to be allowed for the salaries of Assistant Masters excluding the Science Master.

Monday, 25th February.

The Reading and Debating Society.

The 106th meeting of the Reading and Debating Society.

There were 11 members present. After the minutes had been read & confirmed, the evening was devoted to "Readings".

	Programme
<u>H.J. Harris</u>	Nevada Nabobs in New York.
<u>S. Bendall</u>	Christmas.
<u>W.L. Armstrong</u>	Dodge-mud and how to play it.
<u>W.M. Burridge</u>	Jean's Cricket Match.
<u>C. Lewis</u>	Barbers I have met.
<u>J.B. Harris</u>	A Sleepless Night.
<u>W. Saunders</u>	Free Speech.
<u>L.K.V. Job</u>	"Goodness it was the car".

The House adjourned at 8 - 30 p.m.

Wednesday, 27th February.

In Memoriam
WILLIAM THOMAS

On the day when the School was reopened after the Midsummer Holidays, now nearly 43 years ago, a young master made his first appearance there. He had previously for a short time held a mastership in a Grammar School, and had been chosen from some seventy candidates for the D.C.S. post.

Slim then in figure, and young in years, he was still more youthful in appearance. In those days there were in the School a good many big boys of 17 or 18 or thereabouts. The youthful master went to the matron's room. The matron talked with him for a few minutes: then, having other duties to perform, she said to him, "And now you can go and play with the other boys." … Some old boys who may read these lines may perhaps remember how in later years he would laughingly tell the tale.

That was the beginning of a mastership destined to last for twenty-four and a half years, [which] would be interwoven with the story of almost every event of importance in the School record for that quarter of a century …

Devoted to his work, a born teacher, an excellent disciplinarian, how ever ready he was to spend any number of hours of unremitting toil, over and above the hours of his ordinary school work, in getting his boys forward, or promoting their success in any pending examination! And out of school, who more enthusiastic than he on the cricket ground or the football field! In the earlier years of his mastership he was an exceedingly good bowler, and he was always a good batsman and a skilful captain … And his interest was almost as great in football … Mr. Thomas was a friend of Gould, the most famous, perhaps, of all the famous Welsh Internationals … Gould arranged with Mr. Thomas for a match to be played at Newport, Mon., between D.C.S. Past and Present, and the famous Newport Club. "You must bring a *very* strong fifteen," wrote Gould, but there were several strong players among the D.C.S. Past, and the School was not dismayed. [Note 'fifteen'. It is hard, in study of the early days of the School, to be sure which type of football is being referred to – Association, Rugby, or the School's own version – see the entry for 22nd February. We do know that one old boy, Harry Packer (1883-86), went on to play rugby for Wales.]

Just, however, before the final arrangements had been made, Mr. Thomas's wife died, so the match was indefinitely postponed, and in the result was never played.

When Mr. Thompson resigned the Head Mastership of the D.C.S., Mr. Thomas was chosen from among upwards of ninety candidates for the Head Mastership of the Bovey Tracey Grammar School. Then past and present united in subscribing a substantial sum in recognition of his devoted and long-continued work, and this was presented to him at the Old Boys' Dinner in London in January, 1889.

For a time there was every likelihood that his work at Bovey Tracey would be successful. Unhappily evil days came which ended only with his life. We need not dwell upon them, nor speak of the kindness with which so recently the Old Boys came to his aid: sufficient for the present purpose it is to remember and recognise the fact that to the D.C.S. he gave heartily and ungrudgingly the best energies of the best years of his life.

End of February entries.

March

Friday, 1st March.

An Old Boys' informal social meeting was held at the Baronial Hall at the City of New York Restaurant, 47A Bedford Row, Holborn, presided over by Bullen Spicer, Esq., the well-known Army "coach". [See also 3rd August.]

Tuesday, 5th March.

The Reading and Debating Society.

The 107th meeting was held, G.C. Fry Esq being in the chair. There were 12 members present. After the minutes of the previous meeting had been read & confirmed, the meeting was given up to Impromptu Speeches. The following is a list of the subjects spoken on by the various members.

S. Bendall "Are the popular magazines bad for the intellect?"

W. Saunders "Is it better to be a bigger fool than you look, or to look a bigger fool than you are?"

H.J. Harris "Should military service be compulsory?"

J.B. Harris The best way to spend a summer holiday.

W.M. Burridge "Should the death penalty for murder be abolished?"

W.L. Armstrong "Is novel reading bad for the intellect?"

L.K.V. Job "What part of the world would you choose to live in if you were quite independent?"

E.H. Trudgian "Town and country life."

H.H. Jones "Is the British race deteriorating?"

C. Lewis "Women's suffrage"

R.T.H. Hooper "Is war ever justifiable?"

Obituary.

Henry David Turner (1868-1872) died, aged 52.

Wednesday, 6th March.

FIRST XI. (BOYS) *v.* SOMERSET COUNTY SCHOOL
(1ST XI.)
Lost 8 – 4

Played at Wellington. It was a curious match all through and resulted in no less than 12 goals being scored, and unfortunately the balance was very much against us. The forwards on both sides played well – H.J. Harris (2), A. Pearce and R.W. Seldon scoring our goals – but our defence was weak, particularly the goal-keeper. No doubt, the better side won.

[Somerset County School, at Wellington, was a similar foundation to the Devon County School, and was part of the overall national system tirelessly advocated by the inexhaustible Revd. Brereton.]

SECOND XI. (BOYS) *v.* SOMERSET COUNTY SCHOOL
(2ND XI.)
Won 3 – 1

This was a splendidly contested game on the School ground, the same day that the 1ST XI. was at Wellington.

There was very little to choose between the teams, and our win was a slight solace for the beating the first team experienced.

Thursday, 7th March.

THE TUCK RUN

BRERETON		COURTENAY	
W.L. Armstrong … …	18	A. Pearce … … …	20
T. Williams … … …	16	T.H. Richards … …	19
S. Bendall … … …	14	J.B. Harris… … …	17
P.J. Were … … …	13	W. Saunders … …	15
W. Elworthy … …	1	A.P. Moor … … …	12
J.I. White … … …	9	A.O. Parker … …	11
	—		—
	80		94

Courtenay won by 14 points.

Monday, 11th March.

The Reading and Debating Society.

108th Meeting of the Reading and Debating Society. G.C. Fry was in the chair. There were 12 members present. After the minutes had been read & confirmed R.T.H. Hooper proposed that this House does not approve of Professionalism in sport.

The Hon. Member said that games might easily be played without professionals, who play merely for money, & not for love of sport. The ancient Greeks & Romans managed to reach a high stage in sport without professionals & we can do the same. He thought that if a match were played between professionals & amateurs, the amateurs would show a more sportsmanlike spirit than the professionals.

H.H. Jones, opposing said that nearly all outdoor games required professionals & most large schools have professionals to teach the boys the game; besides if there were not any professionals the games would lose all interest. He went on to say that jockeys were professionals, & they rode for old gentlemen who perhaps could not ride themselves, but who took an interest in racing all the same.

S. Bendall thought that professionalism took away the real spirit of the game, & led to much bribery and corruption. Very often teams are bribed to lose a match, & jockeys to lose races.

W. Saunders thought that Professionalism improves all sports by making them more scientific. He went on to say that a man can be paid for his services & yet be a sportsman. The Hon. Member did not agree with Mr. Hooper, in his statement that the Gladiators were not paid. The conquerors he said, always had purses of money etc given them after the fight.

G.C. Fry Esq said it was hard to give a correct definition of Sport, but according to Chambers dictionary, it was anything that caused amusement.

The Hon. Member thought that if territorial teams were formed, football or Cricket etc, would be much more interesting. There is now a regular market for Pros, & the same Pro. perhaps plays for some Northern team one season, & for a Southern the next. The names of a County or Town in sports originally had some meaning but now they had none, as men playing for these towns come from all over the country. The amateurs, he went on to say, still hold their own in jumping and running, & whatever pros. have done for football & cricket, they have done nothing to improve running & jumping.

L.K.V. Job, remarking that he did not know much about the subject, on the whole thought that Professionalism could be done away with.

J.B. Harris, W.M. Burridge, W.L. Armstrong and H.J. Harris also gave their opinions on the subject.

H.H. Jones, summing up, said that if Pros were not paid to play Cricket or Football, we should lose the best players, because they could not cover their expenses. He said there were instances where amateurs had preferred to turn pros. If the Spectators who watch the matches played themselves, the leagues would get overcrowded. He concluded by saying that billiards would not have created any interest if it had not been for Roberts, Stevenson, & Dawson. [These were recent and contemporary national champions, and clearly household names. Roberts hadn't won since 1885, but he was known to a Devon schoolboy in 1907.]

R.T.H. Hooper, in conclusion, said there was a difference between being paid for your services & receiving presents for your success. As the Ancients were not payed [sic] but received presents he thought it was not right to term them professionals.

He went on to say that Chambers's explanation of the term "sport" was very vague, as he did not think that one … [word omitted – 'needed'?] … to be paid for playing with a toy. He also thought it was very bad for jockeys' constitutions to be compelled to eat certain food.

The House then divided & the motion was won by 6 – 5.

The House adjourned at 8 - 30 p.m.

Wednesday, 13th March.

[It said 'May' in the *Register*, but this has to be a misprint; the next match played, and reported *after* this one, was in April.]

FIRST XI. (BOYS) *v.* BARNSTAPLE WAVERLEY.
Won 4 – 1.

Played at Barnstaple in Rock Park … and resulted in an excellent win for the School. Play in the first half was exceptionally good, and caused quite a large crowd of spectators to congregate, who had previously been watching other matches in the Park. But for the smallness of the ground our score would have been much greater. One and all played well, and C. Lewis in goal quite justified his selection.

Saturday, 16th March.

[This piece – about R.P. Chope – was reprinted in the *Register* from the *Western Weekly News*, of this date. (See 11th January, 8th February, and 22nd February.) Mr. Chope was inexhaustible. He commuted between London, where he worked, and Hartland, where he lived - a committee man, journalist, author, antiquarian, J. P., and landowner. The occasion of the article, as can be seen, was his elevation to the position of president of the Old Boys' Association.]

Mr. R. Pearse Chope, this year's president of the Old Boys' Association – a portrait of whom is here given – is the eldest son of the late Mr. Thomas Chope, of Farford, Hartland, North Devon. After a short course of study at the local academy he went to the County School, and when only 15 years of age he was head of the school. At the Cambridge Local Examination he was first in all England, and won the University prize. In 1881 he entered Trinity College, Cambridge, where he was awarded a major scholarship. In 1884 he obtained first-class honours in the mathematical tripos, and graduated as B.A. Shortly afterwards he was selected by competitive examination as an assistant examiner in the Patent Office in London; early in 1903 he was appointed a deputy examiner, and since then he has been promoted to the important post of principal of the abridgments and printing branch of the office. In 1891 Mr. Chope wrote an account of the dailect of Hartland for the English Dialect Society, and has

Mr. Chope again – he was a devoted attender at every Old Boy function, and always managed to get himself on the front row of every photograph.

since assisted the Professor of Comparative Philology in the "English Dialect Dictionary".

Monday, 18th March.

The Reading and Debating Society.

109th meeting. G.C. Fry Esq. was in the chair. There were 12 members present. After the usual reading of the minutes, <u>W.L. Armstrong</u> read a most instructive paper on James Watt. The Hon. Member began his paper by saying that James Watt was born on the 19th of Jan 1736, at Greenock on the Clyde. In his youth he was delicate & sickly, & his attendance at school was hindered by his almost continuous ailments. At School he showed a decided taste for mathematics & this decided his trade of mathematical instrument maker, in which business he set up at Glasgow at the age of 19. He was given a shop in the University buildings & here he came in possession of the Newcomen model, which he was destined to make so famous. He started experiments on the steam engine & entered into negotations with Dr. Roebuck, who financed him, but Dr. Roebuck becoming insolvent, he was obliged to find some other partner. He at length lighted on Matthew Boulton of Birmingham, & the two set up the firm of Boulton & Watt. They turned out the first successful engine for an ironfounder at Broseley in 1780, & from that time Watt's fame was assured, & the business after many difficulties & very many disappointments flourished. Watt was very inventive, & he invented the statuary copying machine, the present method of copying letters & various other things.

He was also very interested in Chemistry, & after several experiments he concluded that water was a compound of hydrogen & oxygen, a result which Cavendish arrived at, at the same time.

The partnership between Boulton & Watt expired in 1800, & for 19 years longer Watt lived in comfort & happiness & reaped the full benefit of his years of toil, in the direction of the steam engine. Watt died on Aug 19th 1819, at the age of 83, & was buried in Handworth Church.

The paper was illustrated with lantern slides.
The House adjourned at 9 – 15 p.m.

Wednesday, 20th March.

THE LONG RUN

BRERETON		COURTENAY	
N.K. Pearce	16	A. Pearce	20
M.R. Roberts	14	R. Maynard	19
R.W. Seldon	12	H.J. Harris	18
L.G.H. Major	7	L.K.V. Job	17
___	0	W. Saunders	15
___	0	A.S. Ayres	13
	___		___
	49		102

Courtenay won by 53 points.

Monday, 25th March.

THE SHORT RUN

BRERETON		COURTENAY		JUNIOR FORTESCUE AND DAY BOYS.	
J.I. White	15	C.G. Harris	20	L.W.E. Grant	18
E.A. Adams	14	R.T. Hooper	19	S.D.S. Cradock	17
R.M. Read	9	V.J. Battershill	16	W.W. Owbridge	10
A.H. Austin	6	A.P. Moor	13	E.H. Southcombe	7
T. Bendall	1	W.E. Ayre	12	E. Pearcey	3
___	0	H.C. Batting	11	J.L. Carter	2
	___		___		___
	45		91		57

Courtenay won by 34 points.

[Only two fifth-formers and three fourth-formers won points in this race, so it looks as if it was intended to give the juniors a chance to see what they could do. It was, after all, a 'short' run.

This is the first reference to a third house, Fortescue. I have been unable to find a reference in any contemporary document to the setting up of it. Since it says 'Junior', it would appear that the house was pretty new, and that the authorities intended to fill it gradually with new, young boys. But, mysteriously, I can find no reference to it in the *Registers* of 1908 or 1909. In the records of the *Exmoor* race of 1911, there is a mention of the fact that boys of the Fortescue ran in it for the first time as a separate group. Incidentally, a fourth house, Grenville, was created in 1918 – we do have a reference to that.]

The Reading and Debating Society.

<u>110th meeting.</u> G.C. Fry was in the chair. There were 12 members present. The minutes of the previous meeting having been read & confirmed, G.C. Fry made a short speech in which he welcomed Mr. J. Britton. The Treasurer was then called upon to read the statement of accounts.

<u>Statement of Accounts (Lent Term 1907)</u>

	£. s. d.		£ s. d.
To cash in hand	2. 12. 11.	By lantern slides	
Subscriptions	14	on James Watt;	3. 6.
		on Crusade	4. 0.
		By balance	2. 19. 5.
	_____		_____
	£3. " 6. " 11		£3 " 6 " 11

W.M. Burridge then read a very interesting paper on the Crusades, which was illustrated by lantern slides. The Hon. mem. commenced his paper by saying that Constantine the Great was the originator of the custom for pilgrims to go to Jerusalem. During the 10th century Robert the Magnificent & many others paid visits to the Holy City, & made pilgrimages very popular.

In 1092, Peter the Hermit, having visited Jerusalem, decided to make the awful condition in which Jerusalem & the Holy Sepulchre were, known to the princes of Europe. Two meetings were held at Clermont, & as a result 150,000 french [sic] pilgrims set out for the Holy

Land under Walter the Penniless. The main hosts were decided [sic] into five distinct bodies, under different leaders. These bodies met at Constantinople. The first battle between the Turks & Crusaders took place at Dorylaeum, & the Turks were utterly defeated. After a desperate struggle Antioch was captured, & on 6th June 1099 the Crusaders arrived before Jerusalem. On 12th July Jerusalem was taken, & Godfrey de Boillon was made king of the city. Godfrey died a year later & Baldwin became king. He fought several battles, among them being Jaffa, Ramleh, & Tiberias. He died whilst on an expedition to conquer Egypt. Baldwin de Bourg succeeded him, & was in his turn succeeded by Fulk. The early years of his reign were occupied with the affairs of Antioch, & owing to the ignorance of his guides he was defeated by Zangi.

A second Crusade was now made but ended miserably.

Saladin now conquered Egypt, & began to trouble the Crusaders. He captured Aleppo, & in 1187 Jerusalem was again in Moslem hands.

This roused the Western princes again & in 1190 another expedition set out under Richard I & Philip. In 1191 Acre was captured, but even in the hour of victory the princes quarelled [sic] & Leopold of Austria returned home. Richard now entered into negotiations with Saladin & a truce was concluded for three years. Richard returned home & soon after Saladin died.

The 4th & 5th Crusades did not do much to alter the position in Palestine. Mohammedans & Christians now united to crush the Charismians. A battle was fought & the Cristian [sic again] army was almost annihilated. This disaster was fatal to the power of the Christians in Palestine, & from this moment even the semblance of the Christian kingdom began to fade away.

Looking at the Crusades from the general standpoint of the world's history, we can pass a favourable opinion. It was imperative that the advance of the Turk should be stayed, & this is what the Crusades did. They were the crowning glory of political achievement of the middle ages, the central drama to which all other incidents were in some degree subordinate.

G.C. Fry Esq, after congratulating the Hon. member on his paper, said that after so much fighting it seemed strange that Jerusalem should still be in the hands of the Turks [which, in 1907, it was].

J. Britton Esq., said that nothing gave him greater pleasure than to see the Reading & Debating Society still flourishing. He asked Mr. Burridge if the Flemmings [sic once more] took part in the Crusades.

Mr. Burridge answered in the affirmative & the House adjourned.

[John Britton had been a founder member, and first secretary, of the Society in 1903. He had had a brilliant career at the School, culminating in a scholarship in Mathematics at Corpus Christi College, Cambridge in 1905. Despite a deformed leg, he had won his cricket colours, he played fives and football, and he became Head Prefect. It seems here that he had dropped in just to see how the old place was getting on. See 3rd June, 2nd October, and 13th December.]

John Britton, celebrated ex-pupil, who came back frequently – here as a member of the Old Boys' Cricket team in 1906. Despite a deformed leg, he played a lot of sport.

Officers for Christmas Term.

President   S. Bendall
Treasurer   W.L. Armstrong
Secretary   W. Saunders
[The Society did not meet in the Summer Term.]

Tuesday, 26th March.

An Old Boys' informal social evening was held at the Baronial Hall at the City of New York Restaurant, 47A, Bedford Row, Holborn, and was presided over by G. William Hill, Esq., M.D., B.Sc., the eminent throat and ear specialist of St. Mary's Hospital.

A good number of visitors were present, and these contributed largely to the entertainment. Special mention might be made of the wonderful sleight-of-hand tricks by Mr. Charles Garland, who has performed at Maskelyne and Cooke's and is one of the very best of present-day conjurors. Other excellent "turns" were provided by Mr. Horatio J. Bostock, the well-known Shakespearean reciter, Dr. W. Alexander (Irish songs and tales), R. Garrett (song – "Drake's Drum"), L.H. Page (song – "Glorious Devon"), Rev. C.H. Roberts (song – "The Village Blacksmith"), T. Vine (comic songs – "A Tipperary Christening", "The Parson and the Clerk"), A. Holmes (comic songs – "French at Breakfast", "A Trip to Paris", "The Conversazione"), L.A. Smith (song – "Drinking"), G.M. Sanderson (song – "The Skipper"), and A. Podmore (recitation – "How they brought the good news") Among the Old Boys who assisted in the entertainment, special mention should be made of the songs of … Harold H. Hilton [Open Golf Champion in 1892 and 1897], and the Devonshire dialect recitations of A Small ("The Electric Light Scheme") and R.P. Chope ("Pixie-led") [the tireless Mr. Chope]. J.E. Messenger and T.R. Potbury gave valuable assistance as accompanists. It is to be hoped that all Old Boys will do their best to make these meetings known among their friends, and that the next series will be even more successful than the last.

Wednesday, 27th March.

SCRATCH SIXES.

[This looks like an impromptu six-a-side football tournament. It is not dated, but I have interpreted it as being intended probably as a bit of fun near the end of term, and designed to include as many boys as possible, not just the 'real' players. I have accordingly placed it near the end of term, shortly before Easter and the great event of the *Exmoor*.]

Eight teams competed in the "Sixes" this year, namely:

(1) S. Bendall (Capt.), T. Bendall,   [There were four Bendall brothers all told, two of whom had already left, and at least two Bendall sisters. One of these sisters later married the Headmaster, Harries, and the other married Harries' brother. See 29th May, and biographies.] L. W. E. Grant, H. F. Lovell, R. Maynard, T. H. Richards.

(2) W. M. Burridge (Capt.), E. B. Driver, H. E. Hicks, W. G. Jewell, E. H. Southcombe, T. Williams.

(3) H. J. Harris (Capt.), V. J. Battershill, L. G. H. Major, N. K. Pearce, F. E. Sanders, A. L. J. Youings.

(4) R. W. Seldon (Capt.), W. L. Armstrong, H. G. Hopper, R. D. Medland, M. R. Roberts, P. J. Were.

(5) W. Saunders (Capt.), J. H. Harris [a misprint for 'J.B.'], C. G. Harris, R. T. H. Hooper, A Pearce, H. J. Richards.

(6) A. E. Preston (Capt.), W. Elworthy, W. F. Kingdon, A. P. Moor, J. I. White, S. J. Widgery.

(7) H. H. Jones (Capt.), A. S. Ayres, C. M. Barnecutt, L. K. V. Job, C. Lewis, H. G. Woolaway.

(8) E. H. Trudgian (Capt.), J. L. Carter, S. D. S. Craddock, C. E. Drake, F. S. Lee, A. O. Parker.

FIRST ROUND

Saunders beat Bendall, 6 – 2:
Seldon beat Burridge, 1 – 0;
Jones beat Trudgian, 5 – 0;
Harris beat Preston, 1 – 0.

SECOND ROUND

Jones beat Saunders, 2 – 0;
Seldon beat Harris, 1 – 0.

FINAL

Jones beat Seldon, 4 – 1.

Thursday, 28th March, Maundy Thursday.

The Library.

We acknowledge with thanks the following gifts to the Library:-

From R.P. Chope (1874-1881) [there he is again] –
  "The Story of the Iliad", by A.J. Church.
  "The Story of the Odyssey", by A.J. Church.
  A stereoscope, and set of views of "British Wild Life".

From W. Bendall (1900-5) [an elder brother of Sidney, the Head Prefect, and Tom, in the Second Form – see the Scratch Sixes above] –
  "The Black Tulip", by Alexandre Dumas.
  "A Tale of Two Cities", by Charles Dickens.
  "A Monk of Fife", by Andrew Lang.
  "The Rob Roy on the Jordan", by J. Macgregor.

The stereoscope presented by Mr. Chope is constantly in demand at the times when boys frequent the Reading Room. Gifts of additional stereoscopic views, on natural history or general subjects, would be welcome.

End of March entries

April

Monday, 1st April – Easter Monday.

THE *EXMOOR* RUN

This, the forty-ninth *Exmoor* Run, was held … in glorious weather. The start was made from Five Barrows, near the Somersetshire border.

The hares, Messrs. A. Taylor, G.C. Fry, and E.B. Waite, started to lay the track about 1.30, and the boys were started in batches an hour later, at intervals of about five minutes.

The route from Five Barrows lay across Fyldon Common into the Mole valley, as far as the old Heasley Copper Mines. From there the road was followed to North Molton Clump. A bee line was then taken westwards to Popham Cross and River Bray, which was crossed at New Bridge. Here the road was again left, and a straight line across country led to the School.

[The *Exmoor* – pure and simple - as it had always been called, was in fact a sort of glorified paper chase, and had been like that ever since its inception in 1859. It is the oldest institution in the School. Records of runners go back to 1864, when the *Register* recorded that the Run took place on a half-holiday granted at the request of the Archbishop of Canterbury, who had visited the School in 1863 to present the prizes. It was not unknown in the early days for the Headmaster himself, the Revd. Thompson, to be among the hares. The end of the race was just outside the School fives court. There was a charming aura about it of village fetes and sack races and muddy plimsoles and ad-hoccery in general. Immediately after the race, as Harries wrote in the School's giant 'Athletic Records' book, 'Tradition then prescribes hot soup, followed by baths.'

The following year, 1908, Harries, as a new Headmaster, changed it to a formal cross-country race, and a proper, fixed course was laid down under the supervision of the ever-present Mr. Taylor. Perhaps Harries wanted to do something memorable to celebrate the golden jubilee of the School. More likely, he wanted to do something to give the School a more modern look, to revamp the bumpkin image, to engender a more fashionable, public-school air. The *Exmoor* has continued into the twenty-first century, and has been cancelled only twice in nearly 150 years – once in the appalling winter of 1947, and once in 2001, because of the foot and mouth outbreak. But back to 1907: this race, on Easter Monday, 1907, was the last of the old village-fete chases.]

The hares were caught more than 3 miles from home by H. C. Batting, who therefore becomes the holder for the year of the *Exmoor* Challenge Cup, and also receives a silver medal. He did the course of about 10 miles, over very hilly country, in 1 hour 35 minutes. W.W. Owbridge came in second, about 4 minutes after Batting. C.G. Harris and M. R. Roberts were respectively third and fourth. [Ten miles! And there were about six miles to be covered to get from the School to the start at Five Barrows. So – paper chase or no paper chase – it was no event for fainthearts. The race continues to this day. The School likes to claim that it is the longest, oldest, toughest, regular, scheduled, *compulsory* cross-country run in the curriculum of any school in the country.]

BRERETON			COURTENAY		
M.R. Roberts	…	17	H.C. Batting	…	20
R.M. Read	…	16	C.G. Harris	…	18
N.K. Pearce	…	14	R. Maynard	…	15
H.H. Jones	…	13	H.J. Harris	…	6
E.H. Trudgian	…	12	———		0
R.W. Seldon	…	10	———		0
		82			59

Brereton won by 23 points.

[Owbridge, who came second, received no points. As the writer in the 'Athletics Records' book observed, this was 'presumably' because he had 'received a handicap'.

The School's weather records show that this was the warmest day of the year right up to the middle of July.]

Tuesday, 2nd April.

Shooting.

The highest aggregate scores during the Lent term were made by A.E. Preston, R.D. Medland, W. Saunders, A.J.E. Helps, J.B. Harris, and L.K.V. Job. There were two Dormitory Competitions, of which Courtenay won the first by 10 points and Brereton the second by 12 points. In both competitions L.K.V. Job made the highest individual score, and therefore won both the silver spoons presented by Mr. W.L. Miles. [See 8th January.]

We hope that our Rifle Club will soon be supplemented by a Cadet Corps [it was – in 1909, with the Headmaster as its fervent commander], and that the wilds of Exmoor will be the scene of exciting and instructive field days, when the Courtenay and Brereton Companies will practise mutual annihilation. The military experience gained by Mr. Harries at Blundell's and at Aldershot will be of inestimable value to the future Corps.

The following are the scores in the Dormitory Competitions:-

I.

BRERETON			COURTENAY		
A.E. Preston	…	36	L.K.V. Job	…	42
S. Bendall	…	35	W. Saunders	…	36
N.K. Pearce	…	33	J.B. Harris	…	35
R.D. Medland		29	H.J. Harris	…	30
		133			143

II.

BRERETON			COURTENAY		
A.E. Preston	…	36	L.K.V. Job	…	37
A.J.E. Helps	…	35	W. Saunders	…	34
R.D. Medland	…	33	R. Maynard	…	27
W.M. Burridge		29	A.O. Parker	…	23
		133			121

Wednesday, 3rd April.

FIRST XI. (BOYS) *v.* SOUTH MOLTON
Y.M.C.A.
Lost 4 – 1.

It was a great pity that this match was played so soon after the Exmoor Run. The fellows had not nearly recovered from their exertions two days before, and the result was a decided defeat for us. Our opponents had much improved since the beginning of the season, and on the day's play deserved their victory.

Thursday, 4th April.

The Library.

During the Lent term 385 books were issued. In the corresponding terms of 1906 and 1905 the numbers were respectively 302 and 185.

Friday, 5th April.

Weather.

The first term of of 1907 was remarkably dry, the total rainfall being only 6.35 inches, as compared with 11.42 inches and 10.46 inches in the first terms of 1905 and 1906 respectively. March, 1907, had an average temperature no less than 6 degrees higher than March, 1906, and was actually warmer than April. This was almost entirely due to the rainless very hot period which extended from March 21st to April 1st inclusive.

Football.

It cannot be said that the past football season was a success. Since Christmas, 10 matches [have been] played, of which 4 were won, 5 lost and 1 drawn.

The complete summary for the whole season is as follows:

	PL	W.	L.	D.	GOALS F.	A.
Masters' XI.	6	1	4	1	9	22
1st XI.	12	4	6	2	26	42
2nd XI.	5	4	0	1	16	1
Non-Colours XI.	1	1	0	0	4	1
Totals	24	10	10	4	55	66

This is not a very flattering table except so far as the 2nd XI. is concerned. Keenness was not lacking, nor ability (except in some instances), but weight, and this, of course, will come in time. Ordinary practice games were well contested, and much bodily good must have resulted.

Colours were awarded to J.B. Harris, H.H. Jones, R. Maynard, and A.E. Preston.

A. Pearce, F.E. Sanders, and P.J. Were also played in one or more First XI. matches.

The following boys left at Easter:-

A.S. Ayres	H.J. Harris	E. Pearcey
F.W. Balman	W.G. Jewell	R.M. Read
C.M. Barnecutt	H.H. Jones	F.E. Sanders
W.M. Burridge	R. Maynard	E.H. Trudgian
C.E. Drake		

Saturday, 6th April.

[In the evening] a presentation was made by past and present boys and masters to Mr. Knight, on his retiring from the Head Mastership of the School. The present included a complete riding outfit – saddle, bridle, crop, etc., – and also a fishing rod. Mr. A. Taylor, who has been a colleague of Mr. Knight for about twelve years, presented the gifts on behalf of the subscribers, and said that when it became known that Mr. Knight was about to resign his post, it was the unanimous and spontaneous wish of past and present boys and masters to express to him their esteem and regard for him personally, and their sense of the great services he had rendered to the School during his twelve years' connexion with it. He hoped that Mr. Knight would have much sport with the articles now presented to him, and wished him every happiness and prosperity in the future.

Mr. Knight, the leaving Headmaster. The School was down to 31 pupils when he took over in 1900, and he hauled it up to the sixties. He spent 27 hours a week in the classroom, which even the inspectors thought was a bit high.

The School team (with masters) of 1906-07. Knight, the Headmaster, was a very keen footballer and cricketer.

Mr. Knight, in returning thanks, said that Sir John Tenniel, at a dinner given in his honour, rose to respond to the toast of his health, and was so overcome by his feelings that he sat down again without speaking a word. That unuttered speech would probably, had he been able to give it, have been the most eloquent speech he ever made. It was so with him (Mr. Knight) now. He heartily thanked all those who had so kindly thought of him on this occasion, and hoped that he might be able in the future to render some service to his hearers, who, he trusted, looked upon him as a personal friend.

Hearty cheers were given at the end for Mr. and Mrs. Knight.

[Although Mr. Knight had indeed been at the School for nearly twelve years, he had been Headmaster for only seven. He had come as an assistant master with the previous Head, Mr. Challen, in 1895, along with Mr. Taylor, and became Headmaster himself on Challen's departure in 1900.]

Monday, 8th April.

A Garden of Strong Men.

[This article appeared in the April, 1907 number of the magazine *Health and Strength*.]

Let us now praise famous men.
Men of Glorious Devon.

This couplet was not included in his list of eulogies by the author of *Ecclesiasticus*, but the omission is probably due to the fact that he felt it to be superfluous. Like good wine, the men of the gallant shire need no bush. For, are not their deeds written plainly, the world over? Assuredly no section of Great Britain can claim to occupy a larger place in its history. The most glorious chapter in our annals, the spacious reign of "Great Elizabeth", is adorned on every page with the name and deeds of some Devonian. Indeed, it would not be too much to say that, but for her Devon subjects, the Virgin Queen would have had but little claim to greatness.

Men of Devon had almost as large a hand in the early history of the New World as their great rivals and enemies the Spaniards. North, South, East and West, throughout the world, have they left the marks of their passage, and it has even been alleged that the first Barbary Corsairs, those fierce sea wolves who filled Europe with dread, hailed from the Western country.

Only one race, the Scots, can claim to have spread their influence so widely, and these same Scots alone can claim to rival Devonians in the possession of that true clannish spirit, which is, after all, a common recollection of great deeds accomplished, a racial heritage which impels all its possessors to guard against the present failure of any member of the clan, a failure which may dim slightly the honour of their country or their shire.

We cannot all be Scotsmen, nor can we all be Devonians born, but many of us can at least ensure that our sons may become something more than foster-children of the glorious shire.

For is not a man's old school, dearer to him even than the kindest and best of nurses. Well named Alma-Mater,

45

The undefeated School football team of 1903-4, featured in an article of the April, 1907 number of Health and Strength.

the buildings, the play-ground, the class-rooms and the associations generally, make up a vague personality which has exercised probably more influence on his life than that other personality which has become for him the embodiment of home itself. All the great schools have this prerogative, and can number their scattered children by the thousand, but even their personality is a purely local one, and it is to be regretted, therefore, that the desire of the late Prebendary Brereton to institute "County Schools" throughout the kingdom, should not have enjoyed a greater success. Several, certainly, were founded, but of these but few remain, and in Devon alone can the movement be said to have become firmly rooted. Opened at West Buckland, in 1861, by Earl Fortescue and the Rev. Prebendary Brereton, it has perhaps alone, of all its imitators, preserved the true county spirit, which recognises its limitations rather by the voyagings of its children, than by the geographical limits of the shire. There, wherever a Devonian stands, be it in Africa, Asia or America, is a bit of old Devon, while the sea of course from the days of Drake has always been included within its boundaries. [The main building was opened in 1861; the School was founded in 1858.]

Truly, have the seeds of the county school been sown in good soil, its fruits have been scattered wide and far, winning recognition and appreciation in every branch of life. But then no finer spot for a school could have been selected. On the hills of North Devon, 650 feet above sea level, with 25 acres of playing fields adjoining, and all Exmoor and all Dartmoor at hand, there can be little

wonder that the scholars from West Buckland have been famed far and wide for their athletic prowess, nor that in such bracing atmosphere the original cobwebs have been speedily blown out of their brains.

At Association football the school holds a unique record, its three elevens having gone through an entire season without defeat, only two drawn games breaking the sequence of their victories, while their record of goals, viz., 100 to 20 is ample evidence of their superiority over their rivals. Of their Rugby prowess it is only necessary to mention that the school turned out such famous players as Harry Packer, the famous Welsh International, Leonard Heard, another member of the great Newport team, and many great county players. With the splendid swimming facilities provided, there is littler wonder that the list of its celebrities is a long one, while not a few of its old boys have distinguished themselves on the cricket field and with the rifle. The only amateur golfer, who has twice succeeded in winning the open golf championship, as well as being twice the winner of the amateur championship, Mr. Harold Hilton, is another old boy.

But the greatest glory of the school lies, perhaps naturally, at cross-country running. It certainly possesses unique opportunities for the practice of this most health-giving and enjoyable pastimes, as apart from the ordinary cross-country run, the boys enjoy the opportunity of following both fox-hounds and stag-hounds on foot, over some of the finest country in the world. We all know what the Exmoor air did for the Doones, and how it bred an even mightier man than that family of giants, so it is no surprise to find that the Devon county school is an easy first in turning out specimens of physical prowess.

It is at school after all that the foundations of the Man are laid: and I do strongly advise all boys who read these lines, to make the best use of the playground, the gym, and the swimming bath – as well as the study and the schoolroom. They will never regret it.

Harold Hilton, twice Open Golf Champion. (But he did not learn his golf at school.)

Harry Packer, the School's first rugby international.

[The article was illustrated by pictures of Harry Packer, the School's only – then - rugby international; Harold Hilton, its sole golf champion; and the School football team – inexplicably the team of 1903-04. Either the article had languished in a drawer of the Editor's desk for three years, or the journalist had only just heard about the team's feat three years later, and still thought it worth inclusion. Incidentally, although the School did indeed produce a lot of good football players – in both breeds of the game - the 'long list' of 'celebrities' in swimming is curiously absent from the record in the relevant numbers of the *Register*. Even the encyclopaedic Mr. Chope could find only one goodish swimmer: a certain F.W. Grenfell won 'the Gold Medal as Amateur Champion of Scotland', four silver cups as Amateur Champion at Plymouth, and a two more at Devonport – hardly 'celebrity' status, one would think. Oh – and in America he won 'a Gold medal with one thousand dollars for swimming and saving life'. One is driven to suspect that the journalist, a clear partisan of his magazine and its philosophy, allowed himself to be somewhat carried away by his own rhetoric. Some of his punctuation was a trifle idiosyncratic too.]

Saturday, 13th April.

[The Western Weekly News published another portrait of an Old Boy of the School.]

The subject of this week's portrait and sketch is Mr.

J.W. Shawyer, the hon. secretary of the London Section of the Devon County School Old Boys' Association. Son of Mr. John Shawyer, of Exford, North Devon, Mr. Shawyer won the Elsworth Scholarship two years in succession (1882-3), and completed his education at the County School (1885-8). He is an all-round athlete. He came to London in 1890, becoming a member of the Institute of Actuaries in 1897. He is well-known in insurance circles, having held important positions in the Security company (chief accountant and cashier), Ocean Accident and Guarantee Corporation (manager of the Burglary Insurance Department), and the Law Union and Crown Fire and Life Office (head-office inspector). He is now the West-end Inspector for the Life Association of Scotland.

Tuesday, 16th April.

Mr. Duke was appointed to the Staff, on probation.

Friday, 19th April.

Mr. Knight wrote to the Editor of the *Register:*

Bittescombe Manor,
Wiveliscombe.

Dear Sir, - May I be permitted, through the medium of the *Register,* to express my most heartfelt thanks to all those who subscribed towards the very handsome presents given me on my leaving the School? Both my wife and I shall always value the gifts very highly, as, in addition to their intrinsic value, they shew conclusively that many of my old colleagues and pupils think kindly of me. It has been my good fortune, during my stay of nearly twelve years at the Devon County School, to be able to further the interests of many with whom I have had to deal, and I should like to repeat what I said on the occasion of the presentation – that if I can, at any time, do any of my friends, who have been at the School, a good turn, I shall be truly delighted to do anything in my power.

With renewed assurances of gratitude,

I am, Dear Sir,

Yours faithfully,

W. A. KNIGHT.

Saturday, 20th April.

More than one inch of rain fell today. [Remember the School was 650 feet above sea level. Yet the Easter Term had been 'remarkably dry' – see 5th April. Exmoor, as is its wont, was now making up for it.]

Saturday, 27th April.

[The *Western Weekly News* published a 'sketch' of an old boy of the School who was also a local worthy.]

[Mr. A.J. Pride was] born in 1878, the son of Mr. Joseph Pride, of Thorverton, near Exeter. Mr. Pride was educated at the Devon County School, and afterwards at King's College, London. Ever interested in sport, he was a member of the school cricket elevens in 1893-4-5, and of the football team in 1894-5. He entered the Civil Service in 1896, and after three years in the Post Office he went into the service of the London County Council, at present being connected with the educational branch of that body's work. As the hon. Secretary and treasurer of the London Devonian Athletic Club Mr. Pride is the pride of all the members.

[The Editors of the *Register* added a note about the recent political success of Mr. F.A. Coon (1879-81), who had been] recently returned unopposed for the third time to the Cornwall County Council as a representative for St. Dennis and Roche. [The *Western Weekly News* had published an article about him too, claiming that] the growth and development of St. Austell during the last twenty years have been largely due to the varied activities of Mr. Coon.

Tuesday, 30th April.

The total rainfall for 1907 up to the end of April was exactly 5 inches less than the rainfall of the first four months of 1906, the two totals being 11.51 and 16.51 inches.

End of April entries.

May

Wednesday, 1st May.

The Lower Civil Service.

[You will not be surprised to be told that the author of this article was the *Register's* most assiduous contributor by far, R.P. Chope. Between 1905 and 1908, for instance, he offered the besieged editors no fewer than fifteen monographs. All the other contributors could muster only eight between them. In this piece, printed in the summer number of the magazine, he produced not only more of his ponderous statistics and relentless facts, but also some reflections.]

Before making any attempt to set down my own opinion of the Civil Service as a calling, I thought it would be well to obtain that of some member of the Lower Division, under which designation I include all branches that can be considered within the reach of school-boys. The reply I got was startling:- "Tell them to avoid it like poison. It is far better to be a village butcher, baker, or grocer." Although I believe this is a somewhat exaggerated view, I agree that in many cases the best counsel to be given to those about to enter the Civil Service is the well-known advice of *Punch* to those about to marry – "Don't!" Unless a youth is prepared to fling aside ambition, to sink his individuality, and to become a mere spoke in the wheel of a complex machine, he will probably do better elsewhere. In the Civil Service he is always fettered with red tape, he is told – as Robert Burns was told – that his duty is to work and not to think, and he is frequently disappointed at seeing that promotion really goes by seniority and luck, and only nominally by merit. The common idea that Civil Servants resemble the fountains in Trafalgar Square, because they *play* from 10 to 4, is applicable only to a very small proportion of the total number. The majority have to scorn delights and live laborious days, and probably work at least as hard as any other body of men. Unfortunately, the work is very unevenly distributed, and there is no elasticity. If a man is ill or on holiday, his colleagues have to do his work. It is practically impossible to get any relief, however great the pressure; and the work has to be done by the same staff, whether it is much or little.

However, if a person would be contented with a moderate salary, in consideration of the permanence of his employment, and wishes to be free from the cares and anxieties of a professional or commercial life, the Civil Service has much to recommend it. The treatment of those who are unfortunately obliged to absent themselves on temporary sick leave is exceedingly generous; and a pension is granted on permanent retirement, either on the ground of age or of ill-health, equal to as many sixtieths of the retiring salary as the number of years the officer has been on the permanent establishment.

The following are the principal situations which may be regarded as open to competition to boys of the Devon County School:-

Situation.	Limits of Age.	Limits of Salary.
Boy Clerks	15 – 17	15/- to 19/- weekly.
Second Division Clerks	17 – 20	£70 to £350.
Assistants of Excise	19 – 22	£85 " £250.
Assistants of Customs	18 – 21	£70 " £250.
Admiralty Supply and Accounting Departments	18 – 20	£100 " £350.
Assistant Surveyors of Taxes	19 – 22	£100 " £380.

[And so on – for another three and a half pages in the *Register*. Heaven knows how long the original piece was, before the Editor got to work.

[Mr. Chope, by the way, was a civil servant. He worked in the Patent Office all his professional life. For twenty years he was head of the Abridgments and Printing Branch. During the course of his service, he published not only thousands of full specifications of new inventions patented, but over 100 *volumes* of illustrated shortened versions – well, it was the Abridgments Department.

In his spare time, apart from that recorded on 16th March, he was an active philologist, churchwarden, benefactor of his local church, author of over 200 'Notes of the Past' for the *Hartland Chronicle*, historian, archaeologist, founder and patron of his local theatrical company, and giver of recitals in the Devon dialect all over the county.

The miracle is that he never seems to have found the time to come and speak at the Reading and Debating Society. Well, he didn't in 1907.]

Friday, 3rd May.

[The Revd. Ernest Harries formally began his work as Headmaster on this day. An editorial in the *Register* for June, 1907 equally formally recognised the fact. However, the Staff Records Book states that Harries' appointment became 'definitive' two days later - see below.]

Another chapter in the history of the School [has] opened … We trust that the chapter may be a long and very successful one. [It was.]

The following biographical sketch was taken from *The Western Daily Mercury*:- "The Rev. E.C. Harries was born at Shrewsbury, and educated at the famous school there, under Prebendary Moss. He was at that school six years, and left at the end of 1886. Mr. Harries took his B.A. degree at Trinity College, Dublin, and was second master at the Wellington (Somerset) County School until 1900. He was then appointed second master and chaplain at the Devon County School, where he remained till 1904, when he became assistant master and chaplain at Blundell's School, Tiverton, a position he has just relinquished to take over his responsible duties at West Buckland. Mr. Harries has those sporting instincts which appeal so strongly to West Country folk. Whilst at Wellington he played Association Football regularly for Somerset, and was president of one of the football districts in the county. He also played the Rugby game for Wellington, and in the season was a prominent cricketer.

The new Headmaster, the Revd. E.C. Harries. He had previously served at the School, between 1900 and 1904, as Deputy Head and Chaplain.

Since he has lived at Tiverton, Mr. Harries played regularly for the South Molton Football Club up to this season."

That the work Mr. Harries has done at Blundell's during the last three years was not unappreciated is shown by the fact that he received separate parting gifts from the School, the Day Boys' House, and the Junior House; while the following extract from the March number of *The Blundellian* speaks for itself:- "In speaking of the Cadet Corps one may justly refer to the loss it will sustain in the removal of the Rev. E.C. Harries to his new sphere. [He didn't waste much time in setting one up at West Buckland. The Archive has a photograph of Harries, in full uniform, in front of his first contingent in 1909.] During his three years at Blundell's Mr. Harries has identified himself with almost every feature of the school life, and he will be much missed, not only in the Corps, the great improvement of which has been largely due to his untiring efforts, but in many other departments. We would wish him all success in his head-mastership."

Saturday, 4th May.

During the Easter holidays a considerable improvement was effected in the Second Form class-room by converting the old doorway from the quadrangle into a window, and opening a new doorway in the west wall. The room now has three windows instead of two, and all the light comes from the left.

The new Reading Room has also been made much more comfortable by a flooring of linoleum and matting.

The hours of evening preparation have been so arranged that, instead of going to bed directly after supper, boys now have three-quarters of an hour of leisure for reading, music, or games. The change has been much appreciated.

The cricket pavilion is at last complete, and makes a very handsome addition to the ground.

Mr. W.L. Miles has continued to encourage shooting by presenting silver spoons to the winners of the monthly competitions.

Earl Fortescue is this year's President of the "Society of Devonians in London," of which an Old Boy, Mr. R.O. Hearson, is Hon. Sec.

The Rev. J. H. Thompson, M.A., Head Master from 1858 to 1888, has been elected Rural Dean of the Deanery of South Molton, and has accepted the living of Warkleigh with Satterleigh.

We acknowledge with thanks the receipt of the following contemporaries: - *The Blundellian, the Tauntonian, The West Somerset County School Magazine.*

The next *Register* will be published about the second week in October. All contributions should reach the Editor before the end of September.

Thanks principally to Mr. R.P. Chope, the Editor found himself in the happy position of having to choose from an embarrassment of riches in making up the present number of the *Register*, and some articles have had to suffer severe condensation. [Poor Mr. Chope – see 8th Feb., 22nd Feb., 1st May, 3rd June, 10th June, 1st October, 7th October, 29th October.]

Extra copies of the *Register* can be obtained from the Editor at 6d. each.

The triennial inspection of the School by the Board of Education is to take place during the week ending June 22nd.

Sunday, 5th May.

The appointment of Revd Harries as Headmaster was made definitive.

The appointment of Mr. Duke, who joined the Staff on probation on 16th April, was also made definitive.

Mr. Walter Longueville Giffard, late of Durston House School, Ealing, was appointed to the Staff on probation. [For his unusual second name, see Staff Biographies.]

W.L. Armstrong was appointed Prefect.

[The *Register* of the Summer Term also recorded the successes obtained by scholars the previous December in the Cambridge Local Examinations]

Cambridge Local Examinations.

SENIOR.

Honours, Class III. – J.B. Harris, South Molton.
Passed. – S. Bendall, Bristol; W.M. Burridge, Bratton Fleming.

JUNIOR

Honours, Class I. (with distinction in French and Mathematics). – W.L. Armstrong, Shipley, Yorks.
Honours, Class III. – H.J. Harris, South Molton. [He had left at Easter – see 5th April.]
Passed. – F.T. Miller, Filleigh; J.R. Reynolds, Cullompton. [These two boys had left by the start of 1907. There is no mention of them in School lists of that year. Alas, there is no record of their leaving, because the publications of School lists did not begin until this year – 1907. Another sign of Harries making an early mark.]

Monday, 6th May.

The following boys entered the School:-

FORM IV.	FORM III. B.
G.H. Dawe, Barnstaple	H.J. Dixon, Filleigh
S.A. Loram, Exeter	G.G. Garland, Filleigh
W.H. Pugsley, Barnstaple	T.P. Isaac, Barnstaple
W.J. Squire, Barnstaple	
W.J. Yeo, West Buckland	

FORM III.A	FORM II.
V.J. Loram, Exeter	R.B. Boatfield, Torrington
E.W. Oakey, Bristol	C.E. Brooks, East Buckland
C.H. Petherick, Bude	

Saturday, 11th May.
Cricket
SCHOOL *v.* LANDKEY.

Played at home. Landkey won the toss and had the advantages of batting first on a sodden pitch. To their total of 72 the School could only reply with 28, but succeeded in dismissing 8 Landkey men in their second innings for 35 runs. Pearce took 11 wickets for 40.

SCHOOL.		LANDKEY.	
A. Pearce, c Thomas b Lock	11	E S. Slack, b Pearce	4
A.E. Preston c Slack b Saunders	1	A. Bowden, b Pearce	4
S.Bendall, b Lock	6	C. Saunders, b Pearce	0
J.H. Harris, b Thomas	1	W.Thomas, c Parker b Pearce	17
R.W. Seldon, b Thomas	0	E. Braddick, run out	0
W. Saunders, b Thomas	0	W.W. Head, b Pearce	3
A.O. Parker, b Lock	0	N.K. Pearce, b Elworthy	6
C. Lewis, run out	1	G. Lock, b Elworthy	14
P.J. Were, not out	4	F.Thorne, b Elworthy	8
W. Elworthy, b Lock	0	M.R. Roberts, b Harris	5
A.L.J.Youings, b Thomas	3	F.Thomas, not out	3
Extras	1	Extras	8
Total	28	Total	72

A new teacher, Mr. Walter Longueville Giffard. He was only twenty years old.

[It looks as if two members of the Landkey team did not turn up, because familiar names from the School roll – N.K. Pearce and M.R. Roberts – appear in the Landkey batting order.

Details of the Landkey second innings were not published. This omission often occurs in the record.]

Wednesday, 15th May.

An ordinary Meeting of the Governors…[was] convened by the Secretary and held at the School.

Present. Earl Fortescue (in the chair), The Rev. J.H. Copleston, Messrs. C. Pearce, M.B. Snell & W.P Hiern.

1. The minutes of the last Meeting were read and approved.

2. Respecting the Headmaster's stipend, Earl Fortescue forwarded to the Secretary a copy of the letter dated January 2nd, stating that the fixed salary should be £100, and capitation fee £2 per boarder. This with the Chaplaincy, which Mr. Harries was asked to accept, would bring his salary up to about £220 a year to start with. These terms, which were formulated by Lord Fortescue and Mr. Snell and based on the lines of the new Scheme, Mr. Harries accepted.

3. The Secretary was instructed to draw up a letter of sympathy to be adressed [sic] to the widow and family of the Late Mr. John Mortimer, expressing condolence in the bereavement and appreciation of the great services which Mr. Mortimer had rendered to the School as a Shareholder, Governor and member of the Financial and General Management Committee.

4. The following Resolution was proposed by Mr. Pearce and seconded by Rev J.H. Copleston and carried unanimously
   "That Debentures for an aggregate amount of £3000 bearing interest at the rate of 3 per cent per annum and ranking pari passu, be, and are hereby created; that the form of Debenture submitted to the Meeting and for the purpose of identification initialled by the Chairman be, and is hereby approved, and that the seal of the company be affixed to Debentures in favour of the persons whose names are set out at the foot hereof, for the amount set opposite hereof, for the amount set opposite their respective names.
   £1000   The Right Honorable [sic] Hugh, fourth Earl Fortescue, of Castle Hill, Devon: Peer.
   £1350   Michael Bowden Snell, of 5 Copthall Buildings, Tokenhouse Yard, London E.C. Esquire.
   £500   William Hobbs Adams, of 17, Throgmorton Avenue, London. E.C. Esquire.
   £150   Richard Pearse Chope, of the Patent Office, Southampton Buildings, London: Esquire.

5. The Rev. J.H. Copleston proposed and Mr. Snell seconded that the Seal of the Company be affixed to the Deed of Release of part of the Mortgage Debt. The same was carried unanimously, and the Deed was accordingly sealed and signed.

6. The following resolution was proposed by the Rev. J.H. Copleston and seconded by Mr. M.B. Snell, and carried unanimously:

"That a hearty vote of thanks be accorded to Earl Fortescue for the generous manner in which he had helped the financial position of the School, by cancelling £892 " 15 " 0 [see Prospectus – Fees] of his Mortgage Debt, and then agreeing to take in place of the remaining balance of £3000 Mortgage Debt, £1000 of Income Debenture 3% stock, and £2000 as a First Mortgage and fixed charge at 3% on the School buildings and assets; at the same time reducing the rate of interest from 3½ to 3% per annum.

"The Governors also wish to record their appreciation of Lord Fortescue's generosity in making the reduced rate of interest retrospective for the years 1905 and 1906."   [In short, the Fortescues, with assistance from Messrs. Snell, Adams, and Chope, bailed the School out, and not for the first time. For Snell, see also 3rd August, 2nd October, 2nd November. For Mr. Chope, look anywhere you like; he is ever-present.]

7. The Secretary was instructed to send out notices to all the Share and Debenture Holders, convening the First Extraordinary General Meeting, for the purpose of voluntarily winding up the the Company, the same to be held at The George Hotel, South Molton on Thursday, May 30th at 12 o'clock (noon).

8. On the recommendation of His Majesty's Inspector – T.W. Phillips Esq: – the Governors decided to make application to the Board of Education for permission to change the date on which the "School Year" ends from December 31st to July 31st, so as to bring the Devon County School into line with other Secondary Schools in the County. The Secretary was instructed to make the formal application for the change, subject to a proportional amount of grant for the first two Terms of 1907 being paid.

9. It was decided that the 3 vacancies in the Day Boy Studentships should be filled up by the commencement of the Christmas Term.

10. Mr. Harries gave a general statement of the present and future prospects of the School, his views as to the best means of making the School more widely known by means of small prospectuses meeting with approval.

11. The boarding charge for Mr. Harries's Mother and Aunt was fixed at 10/- each per week.

12. The Secretary was instructed to write to Mr. J. Pearcey of Silverton saying that the Governors did not see their way to allow his son to continue at the School at the lower fees, unless he would give guarantee that his son remained at the School a sufficient time so as to earn the Government grant. A period of at least 2 years was suggested.

13. A statement of the receipts and expenditure for the year 1906, drawn up in accordance with the requirements of the Board of Education [the meticulous Mr. Taylor missed a comma here] was presented for the general approval of the Governors. Since the same had not been verified as correct by the Auditors, the Secretary was instructed to send it to the Board with being signed. [Presumably he means 'without'.]

14. Cheques to the amount of £270 " 12 " 2 were presented and signed, and payment thereof ordered.
    [Quite a meeting!]

Monday, 20th May. Whit Monday.

The Athletic Sports.

The third and last day [the others had been on 15th and 18th.] On this day, there were present a considerable number of relatives and friends of the boys. The weather, though fine, was grey and rather cold.

There were no very striking times or distances recorded, though many of the races were very closely contested, and the open half-mile was a dead heat between S. Bendall and A. Pearce. The jumps, with the exception of the open long jump, which was very poor, were an improvement on those of last year.

The Open Championship Cup went to A. Pearce (Courtenay), who scored 33 points, J.B. Harris (Courtenay) coming second with 25. The Junior Cup (under 15) went, for the first time in its history, to a day-boy, D. Squire, with 36 points; R.W. Seldon (Brereton) being second, with 16 points. [Harries, the Headmaster, was a great believer in the ethos of boarding, and almost – one feels – regarded day-boys as second-class citizens – not quite 'full' pupils because they could not benefit from the whole range of attractions that boarding could offer. 'Deprived', in modern terminology. This athletic success of a day-boy, therefore, was somehow thought worthy of mention – as if the Mile Race had been won, for the first time, by a boy with one leg.]

Dormitory points were reckoned for all the events except handicaps, and Courtenay proved victorious, with 112 points, against Brereton's 102. Dr. Wiliam [sic] Hill's Dormitory Cup was presented to the Courtenay Sports Captain. [Dr. Hill, a pupil at the School from 1870 to 1874, had donated the cup quite recently, and this was the first presentation of it.]

The hearty thanks of the Committee are due to the following, who kindly contributed to the Prize Fund: - [There followed an exhaustive list of generous donors, headed, inevitably, by Earl Fortescue, the Earl of St. Germans, Viscount Clifden, Sir Thomas Acland – all Directors – and including numerous staff, parents, old boys, and neighbours.]

The prizes were distributed after the Sports by Mrs. Harries [the Head's mother, not his wife. He was a bachelor.]

OPEN CHAMPIONSHIP.

100 YARDS. –	1st, J.B. Harris;	2nd, S. Bendall.	12 secs.
QUARTER-MILE. –	1st, J.B. Harris;	2nd S. Bendall.	61 4/5 secs.
HALF-MILE. –	1st, S. Bendall and A. Pearce (dead heat)		2 min. 24 1/5 secs.
MILE. –	1st. – A. Pearce;	2nd, S. Bendall.	5 min. 52 secs.
HURDLES. –	1st. – J.B. Harris;	2nd, W.L. Armstrong.	22 ½ secs.
LONG JUMP. –	1st, A. Pearce;	2nd, A.E. Preston.	15ft. 1in.
HIGH JUMP. –	1st, A.E. Preston;	2nd, A. Pearce.	4 ft. 6 ¼ in.
CRICKET BALL. –	1st, A. Pearce;	2nd, L.K.V. Job.	73 yds. 2ft. 9in.
STEEPLECHASE. –	1st, A. Pearce;	2nd, S. Bendall;	3rd, W.L. Armstrong.

JUNIOR CHAMPIONSHIP (UNDER 15)

100 YARDS. –	1st, A.O. Parker;	2nd, D. Squire.	
QUARTER-MILE. –	1st, D. Squire;	2nd, A.O. Parker.	66 4/5 secs.
HURDLES. –	1st, D. Squire;	2nd, W. Elworthy.	
LONG JUMP. –	1st, R.W. Seldon;	2nd, W. Elworthy.	15ft 3in.
CRICKET BALL. –	1st, D. Squire;	2nd, A.O. Parker.	73 yds. 11in.
STEEPLECHASE. –	1st, D. Squire;	2nd, R.W. Seldon;	3rd, N.K. Pearce.

HANDICAPS, ETC.

HALF-MILE. –	1st, S.A. Loram;	2nd, H.G. Woolaway;	3rd, E.W. Oakey.
120 YARDS. –	1st, A.E. Preston;	2nd, S. Bendall;	3rd, J.B. Harris.
HIGH JUMP (under 5 ft.). –	1st, R.W. Seldon;	2nd, H.J. Richards and V.J. Loram (equal).	
220 YARDS (under 14). –	1st, A.O. Parker;	2nd, E.W. Oakey;	3rd, V.J. Loram.
220 YARDS (under 13). –	1st, F. Hooper;	2nd, C.G. Harris;	3rd, W.J. Squire.
HURDLES (under 13). –	1st, M.R. Roberts;	2nd, C.G. Harris.	
YARDS (under 13). –	1st, C.G. Harris;	2nd, C.E. Brooks;	3rd, M.R. Roberts.
100 YARDS (under 11). –	1st, J.L Carter;	2nd, R.B. Boatfield.	
TUG OF WAR. –	Courtenay.		

SCHOOL RECORDS.

EVENT.	TIME OR DISTANCE.	HELD BY	YEAR.
100 Yards	10 four-fifths secs.	G.C. Collyer	1888
Quarter Mile	56 two-thirds secs.	R. Sanders	1900
Half Mile	2 min. 18 one-fifth secs.	W. Bendall	1905
Mile	5 min. 11 secs.	T.H. Watts	1903
Hurdles	18 secs.	J.R. Barber	1902
High Jump	5 feet	R.A.W. Barfoot	1884
Long Jump	20 feet 2 inches	J.R. Barber	1903
Cricket Ball	105 yards 3 inches	T.H. Watts	1903

[A hundred yards in 10.8 seconds, in 1888, more than likely in plimsoles, seems pretty good. So does a long jump of over 20 feet in 1903. And there probably aren't that many schoolboys today, or club cricketers for that matter, who can throw a cricket ball over a hundred yards. Watts was a gifted footballer too; see 1st February.]

Saturday, 25th May.

HOUSE MATCH.
BRERETON *v.* COURTENAY.

The wicket was very soft, and Brereton's score was good under the circumstances. Courtenay, on the other hand were far too anxious to score, and this accounted to a great extent for their defeat.

BRERETON		COURTENAY	
P.J. Were, b Pearce	1	L.K.V. Job, b Elworthy	0
R.W. Seldon b Pearce	17	A. Pearce, b Elworthy	0
A.E. Preston, b Pearce	1	C. Lewis, c. Were b Preston	0
S. Bendall, b Pearce	0	J.B. Harris, c. Were b Elworthy	3
N.K. Pearce, b Pearce	4	W. Saunders, b Preston	2
M.R. Roberts, b Pearce	13	A.O. Parker, c. Bendall b Preston	5
W. Elworthy, b Pearce	0	T.H. Richards, run out	0
S.A. Loram, b Harris	4	C.G. Harris, b Elworthy	0
A.L.J. Youings, b Pearce	11	H.E. Hicks, c Bendall b Elworthy	0
J. White, run out	3	H.C. Batting, b Preston	2
V.J. Loram, not out	2	L.W. Grant, not out	0
Extras	5	Extras	2
Total	61	Total	14

[The match was left incomplete – for all its low scores – on 25th May. As the pitch was 'very soft', it seems reasonable to cast the weather as the culprit.]

Monday, 27th May.

The House match between Brereton and Courtenay was completed. [With the second innings amassing all of fourteen runs, it must have been a cliffhanger.]

Wednesday, 29th May.

SCHOOL (WITH MASTERS) *v.* SOUTH MOLTON.

Played at home. The School won the toss, but were all out for the paltry total of 55. South Molton did much better, their score finally reaching 161.

SCHOOL		SOUTH MOLTON.	
A Taylor, b Southcomb	5	H.J. Harvey, c Giffard b Pearce	1
Rev. E.C. Harries, c Harvey b Elworthy	8	C. Taylor, c Harris b Pearce	34
J.B. Harris, c C. Southcomb b Elworthy	3	C. Southcomb, s Giffard b Preston	13
W.L. Giffard, c Harvey b C. Southcomb	4	W. Southcomb c Harries b Pearce	37
C. Bendall, run out	0	T.H. Vicary, c Job b Pearce	14
L.K.V. Job, c C. Southcomb b Elworthy	0	M.H.G. Pallin, not out	29
R.W. Seldon, b Elworthy	15	P. Vicary, c and b Taylor	2
S. Bendall, b C. Southcomb	2	H.H. Beardsley, c C. Bendall b Harries	14
A. Pearce, c Taylor b C. S'comb	4	F.S. Johnson, b Harries	0
A.E. Preston, not out	13	W. Terraneau, c Giffard b Taylor	5
A. O. Parker, b Elworthy	1	J.S. Elworthy, c C. Bendall b Taylor	0
Extras	0	Extras	12
	55		161

[Taylor, Harries, and Giffard were the Masters in this case. All the others were pupils, except 'C. Bendall', a brother of Sidney Bendall, the current Head Prefect. This was Charles, the eldest Bendall brother, who left in 1904. William left in 1905. The youngest, Tom, in Form II in 1907, left in 1913. All four served in the War, and, blessedly, survived. Moreover, two Bendall sisters married Harries and his brother – see biographies. I have recently come across yet another Bendall in a cricket team of 1935, and it is not altogether too fanciful to see a family likeness.]

Thursday, 30th May.

An Extraordinary General Meeting of the Devon County School Company, duly convened by the Secretary, [was] held at the *George* Hotel, South Molton. <u>Present</u> Earl Fortescue (in the Chair), Revs. J.H. Thompson, J. Newman, Messrs. J.F. Wilkin, C. Pearce, D.J.C. Bush [a later, long-serving Chairman, from 1908 to 1934], J.F. Sanders, A E. Shapland and A. Taylor.

1. The minutes of the last Extraordinary General Meeting were read and confirmed.
2. Mr. Bush proposed and Mr. Newman seconded that Mr. Joseph Kingdon be re-elected School Auditor, at the same remuneration as before, namely £5 a year. Carried unanimously.
3. The following resolutions were proposed by Earl Fortescue, seconded by Mr. A.E. Shapland and carried unanimously:
   (i) "That the Company be wound up voluntarily, and that Mr. Frederick Bullen Wyatt, Solicitor of South Molton, Devon, be, and he is hereby appointed Liquidator for the purpose of such winding up."
   (ii) "That the remuneration of the Liquidator for his services in the winding up be fixed at the sum of Two Guineas." [£2.10]
   (iii) "That the Liquidator, be, and he is hereby empowered to settle or arrange with all Creditors of the Company not already settled or arranged with."
   (iv) "That the Liquidator do as from the date of the confirmation of these Resolutions hold the site, buildings and contents of the School and all other property of the Company, (subject to the Mortgage in favor [sic] of Lord Fortescue to secure £2000 and interest at the rate of £3 per cent, per annum), upon trust for a Secondary School to be conducted in accordance with a Scheme to be made by the Board of Education, and to execute a Declaration of Trust and make an application to the Board of Education for a Scheme, and to do all other Acts which may be necessary to establish the Scheme accordingly."
4. It was decided to hold the Second Extraordinary General Meeting, to consider, and if approved, pass the above Resolutions as Special Resolutions, on Saturday, June 15th 1907, at 12.15 (noon) at The *George* Hotel, South Molton.
5. A hearty vote of thanks was accorded Earl Fortescue for presiding at the Meeting.

[So there it was – the great transmogrification. The Devon County School Company was going to be laid to rest, and West Buckland School was going to rise in its place.]

May 30ᵗʰ 1907.

At an Extraordinary General Meeting of the Devon County School Company, duly convened by the Secretary, and held at the George Hotel, South Molton on Thursday, May 30ᵗʰ 1907:

<u>Present</u> Earl Fortescue (in the Chair), Revᵈˢ J.H. Thompson, J. Newman, Messrs J.F. Wilkin, C. Pearce, D.J.L. Bush, J.F. Sanders, A.E. Shapland and A. Taylor.

1. The minutes of the last Extraordinary General Meeting were read and confirmed.

2. Mr Bush proposed and Mr Newman seconded that Mr Joseph Kingdon be re-elected School Auditor, at the same remuneration as before, namely £5 a year. Carried unanimously.

3. The following resolutions were proposed by Earl Fortescue, seconded by Mr A.E. Shapland and carried unanimously:

(i) "That the Company be wound up voluntarily, and that Mr Frederick Bullen Wyatt, Solicitor of South Molton, Devon, be, and he is hereby appointed Liquidator for the purpose of such winding up."

(ii) "That the remuneration of the Liquidator for his services in the winding up be fixed at the sum of Two Guineas."

(iii) "That the Liquidator, be, and he is hereby empowered to settle or arrange with all Creditors of the Company not already settled or arranged with."

(iv) "That the Liquidator do as from the date of the confirmation of these Resolutions hold the site, buildings and contents of

Handwritten minutes of the Governors' Meeting which changed the status of the School. The Secretary to the Governors was the ubiquitous Mr. Taylor ('Judy' Taylor), who wrote this. [See overleaf, also.]

1907 (cont?)

the School and all other property of the Company, (subject to the mortgage in favor of Lord Fortescue to secure £2000 and interest at the rate of £3 per cent, per annum), upon trust for a Secondary School to be conducted in accordance with a Scheme to be made by the Board of Education, and to execute a Declaration of Trust and make an application to the Board of Education for a Scheme, and to do all other Acts which may be necessary to establish the Scheme accordingly".

4. It was decided to hold the Second Extraordinary General Meeting, to consider, and if approved, pass the above Resolutions as Special Resolutions, on Saturday June 15th 1907, at 12.15 (noon) at The George Hotel, South Molton.

5. A hearty vote of thanks was accorded Earl Fortescue for presiding at the meeting.

Fortescue

15th 1907.

At the Second Extraordinary General Meeting of the Devon County School Company, duly convened by the Secretary, and held at The George Hotel, South Molton, on Saturday, June 15th 1907.

Present   Earl Fortescue (in the chair),
Messrs G.C. Smyth-Richards, D.J.C. Bush, J.F. Wilkin, C. Pearce, J.F. Sanders, A. Taylor, A.E. Shapland and The Rev. J.H. Thompson.

End of April entries.

June

Saturday, 1st June.

Cricket.

SCHOOL *v.* KING'S COLLEGE, TAUNTON.

Played at home. The School undoubtedly had the worst of the luck in losing the toss, as the wicket was very soft to begin with, and at the end of our opponents' innings was little less than a quagmire. For their total of 123 for 7 wickets, King's were mainly indebted to the brothers Rippon, who accounted for 99 runs between them. The School could only reply with a total of 40, and seemed to find great difficulty in playing Mathews, who took 7 wickets for 11 runs.

SCHOOL.		KING'S COLLEGE.	
C. Lewis, c Spicer b Harris	4	Rippon II., c Bendall	
		b Harris	45
R. W. Seldon, c Keeling b Mathews	8	Salt, b Preston	1
A.E. Preston, b Mathews	0	Mumford, b Preston	6
S. Bendall, c and b Mathews	1	Rippon I., run out	44
J.B. Harris, lbw Mathews.	0	Bucknall, b Harris	6
L.K.V. Job, c Mumford b Harris	4	Gaylard, b Job	9
P.J. Were, c Cotgrave b Mathews	4	Mathews, not out	10
W. Saunders, b Mathews	6	Harris, b Job	3
A. Pearce, not out	10	Cotgrave, not out	0
A.O. Parker, run out	1	Keeling did not bat	
W. Elworthy c Gaylard b Mathews	0	Spicer did not bat	
Extras	2	Extras	1
Total	40	Total (for 7 wkts.)	123

[An eagle-eyed scorer will notice at once that the College score was in fact 125, not 123. And that the brothers Rippon joint score was 89, not 99.]

Marriage.

BARRINGTON – JULIAN - at Lyford Parish Church, by the Rector, the Rev. George S. Thorpe, Alfred Edward Barrington (1870-2), of Tor Royal, Prince Town, to Sophie Fanny Julian, only daughter of the late Henry Archer Julian, of Pico Tosquiado, The Azores.

Monday, 3rd June.

Head Boys.

[This title needs a little explanation. It goes without saying, of course, that the article was written by the tireless Mr. Chope. In this context, 'Head Boy' did not mean 'Chief Prefect' – or, as they said in those days, 'Head Monitor'. At the Devon County School, 'Head Boy' meant the boy who had performed best in public examinations.

Just as the editors of the *Register* had often felt compelled to condense Mr. Chope's contributions, so I am equally guilty; what follows is only a tithe of what Mr. Chope wrote.]

Up to 1877 the School year was divided into four quarters – and there were two School Examinations annually [internal ones] – at Easter and Michaelmas – while the Oxford and Cambridge Local Examinations were held at Midsummer and Christmas respectively. In 1878 the School year was first divided into three terms, and from that date there was only one general School Examination in each year. . . . [Later on the School dropped the Oxford exams and concentrated on the Cambridge ones.]

W.S. Abell is a member of the Royal Corps of Naval Constructors … John Brewer, whose name appears first on the list, had the distinction of obtaining a larger percentage of marks than any boy has since obtained … John Luxton went from D.C.S. to Clifton College, whence he proceeded to St. John's College, Cambridge …

Leonard Rogers is now a Major in the Indian Medical Service, and, besides having the highest medical qualifications – F.R.C.S. Eng., M.D. Lond., and F.R.C.P. – he is the author of numerous official reports and other medical papers [Leonard Rogers, who first joined the School in 1879, went on to obtain a knighthood, was credited with discovering a cure for leprosy, and lived to attend the School's centenary celebrations in 1958.]

[In his closing reference list, Chope makes mention of J. Britton – see also 25th March, 2nd October, and 13th December - who was 'Head Boy' four years running, and of course of William Stradling, the son of a dairyman, who had the best public exam results *five* years running, from 1893 to 1897 inclusive, and who went on to become a Scholar of St. John's College, Cambridge, and, later, a teacher at the Royal Naval College, Osborne.]

Wednesday, 5th June.

Cricket.

SCHOOL (WITH MASTERS) *v.* 4th BATT. DEVON REGIMENT

[No date is given in the *Register,* but this report is placed between fixtures on 1st June and 8th June respectively, and there were several Wednesday fixtures at other times, so the guess seems reasonable.]

Played at home on a slow wicket. We batted first and were able to declare with the total at 95 for 8 wickets, with just enough time to get our opponents out. They lost 4 good wickets through trying to force the pace, and so win the match; while the defensive powers of the remaining members of the team were not strong enough to prevent the School winning just on the close of time.

SCHOOL.		4TH BATT. DEVON REGIMENT.	
A. Taylor, c Bramwell b Goodwyn	12	Col. Boles, b Saunders	3
Rev. E.C. Harries, b Bramwell	22	Capt. Goodwyn, c Harries b Taylor	22
C. Saunders, b Byrom	14	Capt. Bramwell, b Saunders	7
W.L. Giffard, b Byrom	9	Capt. Fernie, b Taylor	0
A.J. Pike, lbw Fernie	11	Capt. Grenville, not out	12
C. Bendall, b Fernie	1	W.S. Mitchell, b Taylor	7
J.B. Harris, b Goodwyn	7	L. Byrom, run out	2
R.W. Seldon, not out	5	C.W. Hodgson, b Saunders	0
L.K.V. Job, b Goodwyn	0	Capt. H. Chichester, c Job b Taylor	4
A.E. Preston, not out	0	F.D. Quicke, b Saunders	0
A. Pearce, did not bat		H.E. Pellew, c Giffard, b Saunders	0
Extras	12	Extras	5
Total (for 8 wkts.)	95	Total	60

[There still seems to be something amiss with the Editor's arithmetic; the scores of *both* sides are wrong this time.]

Thursday, 6th June.

Marriage.

ABELL – BROOK. At Christchurch, Ryde, Thomas Bertrand Abell, R.C.N.C. (1892-5) to S. Brook.

[T.B. Abell, like his elder brother, W.S., was a graduate of the Royal College of Naval Constructors. A strong connection seems to have been built up between the School and the technical side of the Royal Navy. See the entry for 8th February.]

Saturday, 8th June.

Cricket.

SCHOOL (WITH MASTERS) v. DULVERTON.

Played at home. The School batted first, and the innings closed for 94, the top scorer being the Rev. E.C. Harries with 26. Dulverton had lost 6 wickets for 40 when stumps were pulled up, the result being a draw in our favour.

SCHOOL.		DULVERTON.	
A. Taylor, b Wright	3	F. Cartman, c Job b Taylor	7
Rev. E. Harries, c Cartman b Hawkins	26	A.B.S. Roberts, b Giffard	6
J.H. Harris, run out	9	C. Lugg, b Taylor	0
W.L. Giffard, b Brooke	18	Rev. A. Spicer, b Taylor	2
R.W. Seldon, c Gage b Brooke	4	G. Baker, lbw Pearce	4
L.K.V. Job, lbw Brooke	0	A. Hawkins, not out	6
S. Bendall, not out	17	E.G. Brooke, b Pearce	3
A. Pearce, run out	9	C. Parkhouse, not out	4
A.O. Parker, b Brooke	0	W. Gage Did not bat	
A.E. Preston, b Cartman	2	H. Wright Did not bat	
W. Saunders, b Brooke	2	W. Elworthy Did not bat	
Extras	4	Extras	8
Total	94	Total (for 6 wkts.)	40

[The fact that stumps were not simply 'pulled' but 'pulled up' gives the action a decisive air of finality. Clearly no argument was going to be brooked.]

Monday, 10th June.

The Bucklands in Domesday Book.

[One of R.P. Chope's many, and lengthy, articles which the polite editors felt they had to include in the *Register* concerned the history of East and West Buckland villages, with special reference to their inclusion in the great land survey of Norman England in 1086 which is known to all posterity as the Domesday Book. Nevertheless, the long-suffering editor admitted that he had had to inflict upon Chope's work some 'severe condensation' (see 4th May). In the same way, the present editor has had to inflict further surgery for the purposes of this book.

Mr. Chope began by mentioning that 'increasing attention' had lately been given to the study of local history, starting a process which had culminated in 'that grand project – the *Victoria County History* '. It had begun in 1900, and the first volume relating to Devon had only 'recently' been published.]

Now let us see what we can find out about our small and comparatively obscure parishes of East and West Bucklands [sic]. First, as to the name: Although they are now situated so near to the only region in England where the wild deer still survives, their name has nothing whatever to do with *bucks* , but is much more appropriate to a school, being *book*-land, an ideal spot in which to "read and reap". ['Read and Reap' was the School motto.] ... By "bookland" was meant charter-land, that is, land granted to an individual holder by a charter or deed, in contradistinction to "folkland" or land held by folk-right or custom ... There were many hundreds of these booklands in Anglo-Saxon times, but the majority were known by other names. At the time of the great Domesday Survey we find no less that 14 "Bochelands" in Devon without any distinguishing mark. These have since acquired a second name, usually that of the family owning it, for example, Buckland Filleigh (owned by the family of Filleigh, the predecessors of the Fortescues), Buckland Brewer ... Buckland Toutsaints ... [and so on]. Buckland Monachorum is, of course, Buckland belonging to the monks (of Buckland Abbey) ... *Our* Bucklands, forming a pair, have generally been distinguished merely as "East" and "West"...

The following entry [relates] to the chief manor of West Buckland:-

Baldwin (the Sheriff [of Devon], son of Count Gilbert of Brionne) has a manor called *Bochelant* which Alnot held when King Edward was alive and dead (that is, 1066), and it paid tax for one virgate [a unit of Saxon land measurement, often variable according to region, but most commonly about

58

30 acres]. Now Ansger holds it of Baldwin … There Ansger has 6 farmers, 4 cottagers (called *bordars*), 2 labourers (serfs), 12 cattle, 35 sheep, 36 goats, 24 acres of wood, and 4 acres of meadow. Worth 40s. [£2] a year, and was worth the same when Baldwin received it.

But this was not the only manor in West Buckland. Baldwin also held *Esnideleia* (Snidleigh, *alias* Stoodleigh) [it was in a farmhouse at Stoodleigh that the school had begun with 3 pupils – see 3rd February] , which Edric had previously held, and it also paid tax for 1 virgate…

In East Buckland there were four small manors, viz., East Buckland itself, two other "Bochelands" … and Brayley (the clearing by the River Bray). The three Bucklands were held by Geoffrey, Bishop of Coutances, with Drogo as his under-tenant. … Brayley was held by Odo, son of Gamelin … Altogether these four manors or holdings were taxed at 2 virgates and 3 ferdings [a ferding was a quarter of a virgate]… There were 3 farmers, 3 cottagers, 9 labourers, 8 cattle, 46 sheep, 15 goats, 36 acres of wood, 23 acres of meadow, and 95 acres of pasture. There were worth 40s. [£2.00] formerly 46s. [£2.30]. . . .

Wednesday, 12th June.

Marriage.

At St. Mary's, Woodstock, Cape Colony, EDWIN HERBERT CHARD (1891-2), second son of the late Edwin Chard, Cotham Park, Bristol, to Patsy, second daughter of Richard King, Cambridge Park, Bristol.

Wednesday, 12th June.

Cricket.

SCHOOL *v.* SOMERSET COUNTY SCHOOL.

[Somerset County School, later known as Wellington School, was one of several schools founded soon after the Devon County School, by way of response to and imitation of the original one in Devon. Others appeared in Dorset, Surrey, Sussex, London, Bedford, Gloucester, Suffolk, Norfolk, and Durham.]

Played at Wellington. Rain prevented any play at all before 3 o'clock. The School took first knock, and lost Pearce when the total had reached 14. Seldon and Harris then took the score to 41. When Seldon was run out for a patient 22, Bendall rendered material assistance, and with the total at 81 for 5 wickets, we were able to declare, leaving them about an hour in which to get the runs. They, however, failed in their object, as, when stumps were pulled up, they had lost 8 wickets for 69.

For the School Preston bowled well and was backed up by keen work in the field.

SCHOOL		SOMERSET COUNTY SCHOOL.	
A. Pearce; b Stevens	7	S.R. Price, b Preston	1
R.W. Seldon, run out	22	W.W. Ridler, c Saunders b Job	11
J.B. Harris, b Smith	23	J.N. Rawle, b Preston	0
S. Bendall, b Hancock	12	D. Hancock, b Preston	23
L.K.V. Job, b Rawle	2	L.C. Stevens, c Pearce b Elworthy	6
W. Saunders, not out	1	P.A. Haddon, b Preston	12
A.E. Preston, not out	6	W.J.C. Brown, b Elworthy	1
A.O. Parker did not bat		H.G.F. Brown, c Harris b Preston	12
P.J. Were did not bat		S.R. Davis, not out	2
C. Lewis did not bat		C.F. Smith, not out	1
W. Elworthy "		S.J. Ley, did not bat	
Extras	8	Extras	0
Total (for 5 wkts.)	81	Total (for 8 wkts.)	69

[Stumps were 'pulled up' again. One can almost see the umpire marching off.]

Saturday, 15th June.

The Second Extraordinary General Meeting of the Devon County School Company [was] duly convened by the Secretary, and held at the *George* Hotel, South Molton.

Present Earl Fortescue (in the chair)
　　　　Messrs G.C. Smyth-Richards, D.J.C Bush, J.F. Wilkin, C. Pearce, J.F. Sanders, A. Taylor, A.E. Shapland and The Rev. J.H. Thompson.

1. The minutes of the Extraordinary General Meeting, held on 30th May 1907 were read and confirmed.
2. Earl Fortescue proposed, and Mr. Shapland seconded that the Resolutions (for voluntarily winding up the Company) passed on 30th May 1907 be, and they are hereby confirmed as Special Resolutions. Carried unanimously.
3. It was resolved (i) "That the Company do apply to the Board of Education for an Order establishing a Scheme for the administration of the Devon County School Foundation as a Public Secondary School, and giving all necessary and proper directions in relation thereto" and (ii) That the Seal of the Company be affixed to a formal application accordingly." Carried unanimously.
4. A letter, dated 10th June 1907 addressed by the Board of Education to the School Secretary, was read with regard to varying the constitution of the Governing Body under the new Scheme, and requesting the views of the present Governing Body thereon. It was resolved that a meeting of the Governors be convened for the 29th June 1907 at the "George" Hotel, South Molton for the purpose of considering the same.
5. The Liquidator was instructed to defer sending the application for the Scheme until after the Meeting on the 29th inst.
6. It was resolved that the Seal of the Company be affixed to the Declaration of Trust of the property of the Company for a Secondary School.

[The final winding-up meeting was not held until 'Friday, the 24th day of May, 1912, at 3.30 o'clock in the afternoon' – according to the letter sent out by the official Liquidator, Mr. Fred. B. Wyatt, of 7, East Street, South Molton. Mr. Wyatt was to receive two guineas for his services - £2.10.]

Tuesday, 18th June.

HOUSE MATCH.
BRERETON v. COURTENAY.

Won by Brereton. Seldon played a good innings, and Roberts showed promise. . .

1st INNINGS.	BRERETON		2ND INNINGS.	
R.W. Seldon, c Job b Pearce	3		b Harris	28
P.J. Were, run out	6		run out	1
S. Bendall, c and b Pearce	10		b Harris	0
A.E. Preston, run out	2		b Harris	0
M.R. Roberts, c Saunders b Job	13		b Pearce	11
N.K. Pearce, b Harris	1		c Saunders, b Pearce	2
W. Elworthy, b Pearce	6		c Hicks b Pearce	3
S.A. Loram, b Job	0		c and b Pearce	3
V.J. Loram, b Pearce	1		c Job, b Pearce	0
J. White, b Job	0		not out	0
R.D. Medland, not out	2		b Pearce	0
Extras	11		Extras	2
Total	55		Total	50

1st INNINGS.	COURTENAY.		2ND INNINGS.	
A.O. Parker, c Were b Preston	2		b Elworthy	0
L.K.V. Job, b Elworthy	2		b Were	14
J.B. Harris, b Preston	7		c White, b Were	7
A. Pearce, c Were b Preston	7		c Seldon, b Elworthy	0
W. Saunders, lbw Elworthy	5		b Were	1
C. Lewis, b Elworthy	0		not out	6
L.W.E. Grant, b Elworthy	2		c Pearce b Elworthy	0
T.H. Richards, c Bendall b Elworthy	2		c Preston, b Were	0
C.G. Harris, b Preston	3		b Elworthy	0
H.E. Hicks, not out	2		run out	0
H.C. Batting, b Preston	0		b Were	4
Extras	3		Extras	1
Total	35		Total	33

[Note the engaging little inconsistencies with the commas.]

Wednesday, 19th June.

Cricket.

SCHOOL (WITH MASTERS) *v.* NORTH DEVON.

Played at Instow. North Devon [won] by 75 runs with 3 wickets in hand. The School batted first and made 145, of which Mr. Giffard scored 44 and Seldon 22. When North Devon went in, they lost 3 wickets cheaply and had lost 6 wickets for 100 when Horndon joined Henley, and the pair added another 120, being still together when stumps were drawn. [An over-eager editor, smiling at previous lapses of arithmetic, was about to jump in with the observation that, if they lost only six wickets, they must have had 4 wickets in hand at the end, not 3. He looked at the scorecard just in time; North Devon had only ten men. One up to the *Register*.]

SCHOOL.		NORTH DEVON.	
A. Taylor, c Mitchell b Jones	17	C. Mitchell, c Saunders b Taylor	9
R.W. Seldon, b Blackburn	22	L. Henley, not out	94
J.B. Harris, b Blackburn	3	C. Mercer, c Giffard b Saunders	7
W.L. Giffard, c Sealy b Blackburn	44	E.G. Jones, c Giffard b Taylor	0
C. Saunders, c Blackburn b Mercer	18	E.M. Lucas, b Preston	15
A.J. Pike, b Mercer	0	J.G. Blackburn, b Saunders	15
S. Bendall, b Mercer	0	Rev. R.W. Sealy, b Saunders	1
L.K.V. Job, b Mercer	0	D. Horndon, not out	42
A.E. Preston, lbw Mercer	2	Rev. H.W. Millet did not bat	
A Pearce, not out	7	W. Sealy did not bat	
A.O. Parker, c and b Blackburn	13		
Extras	19	Extras	47
Total	145	Total	220

[But they have done it again for all that – the North Devon total seems to come to 230, not 220. And stumps were 'drawn' this time – obviously a more easy-going umpire.]

[C. Saunders, the elder brother of W. Saunders, had been Head Boy the previous year. He left to become articled to Mr. G.C. Smyth-Richards, of Barnstaple, a School Governor. A.J. Pike was also, though this is only a reasonable guess, an Old Boy.

Clement Saunders was killed in the First World War, on 11th February, 1917.]

Thursday, 20th June.

Inspection.

Board of Education Report of Second Inspection of the Devon County School, West Buckland, Devonshire.

Inspectors: Mr. E.M. BATTISCOMBE, H.M.I., Mr. T.W. PHILLIPS, H.M.I., Mr. F. SUDDARDS, H.M.I. [The full report ran to 21 pages. So here, perforce, it has been edited.]

First Day –
Devon County School – in receipt of grants under the Board's Regulations for Secondary Schools. [So it was not completely independent.]

Assistant Staff – 6 (Regular – 4; Visiting – 2)
Scholars – 66 (Boarders – 55; Day Scholars – 11)
Scholarship Holders – 14.

Number of Scholars in 5 years preceding inspection: 1902 – 83; 1903 – 79; 1904 – 73; 1905 – 72; 1906 – 74. [Harries' predecessor, Mr. W.A. Knight, had taken over in 1900 at a time of crisis, when the pupil numbers had dropped to 31, in a school with accommodation for about 150. He hoisted them to 80, but they began to slip again – culminating in another crisis, which had ended, as just seen, in a voluntary dissolution of the original Devon County School Company, a transfusion of grants from the Board and of funds from generous Old Boys – and Fortescue, and a re-formation of the School under the auspices of the Board of Education on the one hand, and a new Board of Governors on the other. Harries had taken on a fearsome challenge. This inspection, coming almost immediately after his official substantive appointment in May, must have been a bit of a strain.]

Class of life and area from which the pupils are drawn:

[The Inspectors made seven divisions] – Professional and Independent, Merchants and Manufacturers, Retail Traders, Farmers, Commercial Managers, Service (domestic and other) and 'Postmen, etc, Artisans'. [Alas! They give no figures, and offer only the comment that there had been] no material change since the First Full Inspection of the School.

[As to locality], all 11 day boys came, [not unsurprisingly], from West Buckland. Of the Boarders, 30 came from 'Other Places in Devonshire', 22 from 'Other Counties in the United Kingdom', and 3 from 'Places Abroad'.

Nature and Scope of the School – the average age of entry is about 13 years and average duration of School life about 2 years. [This was a constant source of concern to successive headmasters: boys simply did not, on average, stay long enough. Harries was to improve considerably on this over the coming years.] Only 6% of the boys were under 12, and only 12% were over 16. After they leave School the majority of the boys enter commercial life or become farmers. [Well, that was the founder's idea – an education for the middle classes - and the School motto was 'Read and Reap'.]

Governing Body – The School has hitherto been the property of a Company, but negotiations have been proceeding for some time past with the object of transferring it to an Educational Trust. Matters have proceeded sufficiently far to make it clear that the School has some very good friends. [Fortescue and some Old Boys coming to the rescue, as explained above – 15th May.]

An Assistant Master [Mr. A. Taylor] has been acting as Secretary to the Company although recently the Head Master has been 'Correspondent' in communication with the Board of Education. It is now proposed that the Assistant Master referred to should act as Clerk to the new Governing Body and therefore the official Correspondent of the School. It is a somewhat anomalous arrangement for a member of the School Staff to be Clerk to the Governors but the way in which he has carried out the duties of Secretary to the Company has been so satisfactory [I should think so; his minutes are meticulous, and his balance sheets are works of art – see illustrations.] that it is not anticipated that any difficulty will arise from his acting as Clerk and Correspondent. If the arrangement is tried it is clearly important that the Governing Body should take every care that the superior authority of the Head Master is safeguarded. [It is a measure of Taylor's integrity and of Harries' trust in him that the arrangement continued, so far as I know, very smoothly.]

Finance. The chief items in the receipts for 1906 were for Tuition fees £496.19.6., Boarding fees £1470.19.10., Board of Education Grant £186 and Local Education Authority Grant £157 inclusive of a Special Grant of £17 for Workshop expenses. In expenditure,

salaries accounted for £692.19.5., Boarding expenses £1095.18.0. and the Estate Management Account (including interest charges) £418.6.3. On the Complete Account … there was a deficit of £41.7.6., which was met by a guarantee fund provided by Mr. Snell, an active supporter of the School [an Old Boy and ex-Head Prefect]. It has been the custom for some years to distribute a certain proportion of the Board of Education Grant among the Head Master and Staff as an addition to their regular stipends. The amount so received by any individual Master has not been large but the attention of the Governing Body is directed to the fact that the procedure is in contravention of the Regulations of the Board of Education …

Considering the class of boy who attends the School, it is open to question whether the Boarding fees might not be raised with advantage. [Harries wrote in the margin, no doubt referring to the previous paragraph, 'If we have to pay more in salaries this will be absolutely necessary.' [For old coinage values, see Prospectus – Fees, note.]

Scholarships and Exhibitions … On the question of Entrance Scholarships it would be wise to arrange if possible that they should be tenable for four years if the holders are worthy, for more real good is done by awarding a smaller number for four years than a larger number for two or three years. [An attempt, perhaps, to address the problem of the shortness of the average stay of boys in the School.]

Premises and Equipment. The situation of the School is excellent and the Buildings on the whole satisfactory. Most unfortunately, the various additions that have been made from time to time were not carried out on a well considered and uniform plan, the result being that in many particulars the premises are very inconvenient in design. [There follow detailed references to individual rooms and buildings, together with suggestions about setting up a Gym., a Sixth Form room, and an Art room. The lack of heating in laboratories and Reading Room was mentioned. Nor could the inspectors miss the fact that the School could easily accommodate many more boys than were actually present at the time of the report.] The School has admirable playing-fields, a good fives court and an excellent open-air swimming bath which is supplied by a constantly running stream of fresh water.

Staff. The Head Master … has quite recently been appointed … with the whole hearted support, not only of the Governing Body, but also of the most prominent of the Old Boys who are in such a marked manner rallying to the support of the School. The Head Master is full of energy and enthusiasm and is most earnest in his schemes for the development of the School. He seems quite the right kind of man for the post, and, if he is given a fair chance, is likely to ensure the future success of the School. [He did. In the course of the next twenty-seven years, the School went from strength to strength, and he was to acquire a legendary reputation.]

One Assistant has been at West Buckland for the past twelve years and though not highly qualified academically is unquestionably a most valuable member of the Staff. In School work he takes Drawing, Singing and Geog-

Devon County School – Staff and Prefects. Standing, L. to R. – W. Saunders, J. Britton, W.L. Giffard, S. Bendall, W.M. Burridge, W.L. Armstrong, J.B. Harris. Seated, L. to R. – C.G. Fry, Revd. E.C. Harries, A. Taylor. There was a music master, Mr. Watson, but he does not appear in Staff photographs before 1913. (See Staff Biographies.)

raphy and on the administrative side has for some years acted as Secretary to the Proprietary Company. [This was Adelbert Taylor – 'Judy' Taylor to generations of boys.]

The Science Master [Mr. G.C. Fry – see Masters' Biographies] is the only member of the Assistant Staff who holds a degree. The other two masters were quite recent appointments [Giffard and Duke – see Masters' Biographies], the engagement of one of them being of a strictly temporary character. [Duke was to leave in August.]

In addition to the regular Staff the School has the services of the County Instructors in Manual Work and Modern Languages.

It is suggested that in making [future] appointments special regard be had for the claims of Mathematics, French and English. [Harries underlined 'French', and wrote in the margin, 'Am putting this right this term. Mathematics will have to wait. My own qualification will suffice for the English.']

[One curious gap shows here. In the Record Book of Staff appointments, the name of a Mr. Watson appears, who, according to the book, taught Music for 42 years, from 1896 to 1938. He was the musical mainstay of Harries' prodigious run of annual Gilbert and Sullivan performances from about 1915 to the mid-thirties. He is often mentioned in the *Register*, but does not figure here. Nor does he appear in many of the Staff photographs for the early years of the century. Is this an overhang of the old attitude that musicians don't really 'count', or, if they do, they rate little above tradesmen? Yet 'Watto' was a School institution. Odd.]

Old Boys' News.

From the *North Devon Journal*: At the North Devon Volunteer Rifle meeting at Okehampton ... the Dawson plate was won by Capt. Potbury, of Sidmouth, with a score of 67. [This was F.J., one of four Potbury Old Boys, from the 1870's and 1880's. There were six brothers altogether; two, mysteriously, did not attend the School. See 7th January, 4th December, and 14th December.]

Friday, 21st June.

Second Day of Inspection.

CURRICULUM.

The timetable is on the whole satisfactory. Its most doubtful feature is the arrangement by which Mathematics is taken during the whole of two afternoons a week, when all the School takes it at the same time.

[Harries wrote in the margin, 'Cannot be altered until increased number allow us a Maths Master.'] ...

In regard to Class work, one general comment is called for. Throughout the School, it was noticed that chorus answering was very general. Questions were asked of the Class as a whole and answers came from anybody who felt inclined to give them. The result was that the smarter boys in the Class were doing all the work whilst the weaker ones had no reason to exert themselves at all. [Harries said he was stopping this practice, adding tartly that it had been 'caused largely by the French Inspector'.]

English. The teaching of English is in a transitional stage and is not as yet fully organised. [Poetry and Literature were suffering at the hands of Grammar, especially in the upper school, though there were plenty of essays being set. Various suggestions for improvement were put forward.] It is very desirable that as soon as possible a Master should be appointed with special qualifications to teach English Subjects. [Harries noted, 'I propose taking it myself.']

History. ... Text-books ... at present in the School are hardly suitable for the purpose [almost certainly shortage of money again] ... It is hoped, too, that the careful grading of the Course will receive careful attention and that a special point will be made of securing that the work of each Form is suited to the age and capacity of the boys composing it. [There was encouragement for more précis-type notes, more historical maps, and more historical essays.]

Geography. The work is exceptionally careful and methodical, and the attention of the boys during the lessons was well maintained. The instruction is on traditional lines and it may be suggested that the lessons would gain in value if more attention were paid to modern theories which have profoundly affected the methods of Geographical teaching in Schools ... The possession of a good text-book would obviate the necessity for long dictated notes and tabulated summaries. [Money again.]

French. There is at present no Master on the Staff with special qualifications in French, though it is understood that one will shortly be appointed. In these circumstances, the teaching must be regarded as being in a transitional stage. [Nevertheless] text-books are very suitable ... teaching in the Lower Forms was vigorous and interesting ... [and] .... boys in Form IV were able to read and translate fluently ... Up to the present the ground covered is not very wide, but what has been learnt has been well understood, and there is every reason to anticipate a successful development of the work in the future.

Latin. ... New text-books based on modern theories of Latin teaching are gradually being introduced and the whole of the work is in the hands of a single Master who is new to the School this term. [Giffard.] It is too soon as yet to judge ... the oral teaching is vigorous and there can be no doubt as to the interest displayed by the boys ... the standard of attainment in the Upper Forms is undeniably low. The causes of this weakness must be sought in the past history of the School ... [Work should be] more suitably graduated to the attainments of the scholars ... all written exercises should be carefully examined and revised, and boys should be required to submit ... corrections of all the errors which they have committed.

Mathematics. It was not possible to see much of the Mathematical work of the School at the time of the Inspection, but sufficient was seen to make it clear that the standard attained in the middle of the School is not a high one though reasonably good work is done in the top Form. [The previous Headmaster, Mr. Knight, had been a gifted and successful Maths teacher.]

Science. The whole of the Science work of the School is in charge of the Science Master [Mr. G.C. Fry] who is a well qualified and careful teacher and who has organised the course of instruction on sound lines. Generally speaking a satisfactory standard is attained thoughout though unquestionably Forms V and VI would benefit if they could be taken separately and not together as is now the case on account of limitation of staff. The practical work ... was intelligently done ... Test questions ... set by the Inspector during both practical and theoretical lessons made it clear that the boys had an intelligent knowledge of what they were doing. The note-books throughout were methodically kept and well corrected. [Fry was a clearly a diligent teacher. The Minutes of the Reading and Debating Society, which he was in charge of, carry his annotations and corrections in the margin – though even his eagle eye missed a few things. Small wonder, if he was busy marking all those Science note-books as well.]

An interesting development ... is to be seen in the keeping of a regular set of meteorological records. This is an excellent side of the work and is very well done.

In general, the Science work of the School can be said to be in a distinctly healthy condition. [There is no substitute for a properly-qualified, conscientious teacher.]

Art. [This] is given by a member of the permanent Staff [Taylor again], who, though not possessing high certificate qualifications, is an experienced and methodical teacher, and has made very good use of the knowledge which he possesses: he is keenly interested in the subject and has devoted a considerable amount of his leisure to further Art study with the object of improving his qualifications. [There is little substitute for a keen, methodical, interested, experienced teacher either.]

The Course is, so far as it goes, sound in character and is carefully graded. The work of the scholars is throughout distinguished by very careful and accurate workmanship, and testifies to the earnestness of the teaching and to the thoroughness with which the subjects included in the course have been dealt with.

[There followed so many details, comments, and recommendations that one can not but conclude that one at least of the inspectors was an Art specialist.]

Manual Instruction. Manual work is well taught by the County Instructor in a room which is suitably fitted for the purpose.

INTERNAL ORGANISATION OF SCHOOL.

The Entrance Examination is qualifying rather than competitive, the object being to determine the Forms that should be joined by the new boys ...

Preparation work is carefully arranged according to a definite Time-Table and thus a check is exercised upon any tendency to over-pressure.

The School has a Lending Library and a Reference Library... adjoining the School Reading Room ... The rooms would be more widely used if they were properly heated.

CORPORATE LIFE OF SCHOOL.

There is a regular Morning Assembly ... attended by boarders and day boys ... There are four prefects ... , who are responsible for the discipline of the dormitories and for part supervision of evening preparation. They also read the lessons at Morning Prayers not only in School Assemblies, but also on Sundays at the Parish Church which the boys attend.

Games are compulsory [for] every boy unless exempted for medical reasons. A special feature of West Buckland physical activity consists in cross country running ... Colours are awarded for running as for Cricket and Football, and there is keen rivalry between the dormitories ... Swimming is actively encouraged, the excellent Swimming Bath proving a most valuable asset.

A Shooting Club has been formed and is under the management of the Science Master [Fry – so it was bound to be well run] ... A Cadet Corps is also contemplated, and if one is founded it ought to be quite successful, as the Head Master has for several years held a commission in connection with the Corps at Blundell's. [It was founded in 1909, and was indeed successful. The Corps Commander – Harries,

of course, minus dog collar – was so keen that during the First World War he took a course in Bayonet Combat.]

A commendable feature in the social life of the School is the active encouragement that is given to Singing. In addition to the ordinary Class Singing ... there are fornightly concerts during the winter and special Choir Singing in connection with the Church Services. [Taylor was Choir-master and Organist at East Buckland Church, and Harries, who was crazy about Gilbert and Sullivan, used to stage a full comic opera every year for twenty years – starting in the middle of the First World War!]

The Literary and Debating Society is a flourishing organisation whilst the School Magazine is a distinctly good publication.

The Old Boys' Association is ... very strong and active ... . There is indeed nothing more striking in connection with West Buckland than the active interest which the Old Boys take in the School. [Maintained, the Headmaster tells me, to this day.]

CONCLUSIONS AS TO GENERAL EFFICIENCY.

The School has during the last few years passed through a troublous time and there seems at one period to have been a serious intention to close it. Instead ... the new administration is to be established and a special effort is to be made to restore to the School some of its former prosperity. It has many promising features, but much depends on finance ... Provided that the Governing Body have funds at their disposal to maintain

The School servants. The only one I can name is George Balment, the general handyman, who served the School for 58 years, right from its foundation.

a strong and well qualified Staff, there seems no reason why the wishes of the many supporters of the School should not be realised.

[It would have been easy in this summary to pick out only the 'nice' bits or only the 'nasty' bits, and, no matter how hard an editor tries to be fair, any summary is bound to be imperfect. Let it be said that the Inspectors found plenty to criticise, but when they found things to praise – and they were by no means few – they were generous in their encouragement. They offered constructive suggestions too, and they were well aware – and said so - that, because of the School's recent difficulties, remedying any of the faults was going to be primarily a problem of lack of finance rather than lack of awareness or of willingness.]

Saturday, 22nd June.

Cricket.

SCHOOL v. BRATTON FLEMING.

Bratton Fleming were sent in to bat on a wicket which looked as though it might improve, and they evidently found it difficult, as they were all dismissed for 27 runs. For their total of 76 the School were mainly indebted to Were (20) and Saunders (19). Bratton Fleming did much better at their second attempt [which was not printed], the feature of the innings being some fine hitting by W.M. Burridge. [This looks like the ex-prefect Burridge, who had left at Easter – same initials. He came from Bratton Fleming.]

SCHOOL		BRATTON FLEMING.	
R.W. Seldon, c Johnstone		F. Lavercombe, c and b	
b J. Britton	10	Preston	1
L.K.V. Job, b J. Britton	6	F.G. Barrow, b Elworthy	12
J.B. Harris, lbw J. Britton	7	J. Britton, b Harris	2
S. Bendall, b J. Britton	5	R. Britton, c Lewis b Harris	3
A. Pearce, c Webber			
b R.Britton	0	W.M. Burridge, c and b	
		Preston	0
W. Saunders, b Sprye	19	Capt. Sprye, run out	0
A.E. Preston, b J. Britton	5	H. Webber, b Pearce	6
A.O. Parker, c and b J. Britton	0	G. Lavercombe, b Elworthy	0
P.J. Were, not out	20	W.M. Burridge (Jr.),	
		c Pearce b Elworthy	0
C. Lewis, run out	2	H. Parkin, b Pearce	0
W. Elworthy, b R. Britton	1	A. Johnstone, not out	0
Extras	1	Extras	3
	76		27

Saturday, 22nd June, contd.

Old Boys' News.

From the *Western Weekly News*: Mr. R.O. Hearson, the new secretary of 'Devonians in London" [sic – the commas], ... is a son of the late Mr. Thomas Hearson, of Barnstaple, and was born 57 years ago. He is a Devon County School "Old

Boy", of which school Earl Fortescue, this year's Devonians' president, is chairman of governors. He commenced business as a printer and stationer in the City in 1874, but three years ago the business was incorporated with the well-known firm of Wertheimer and Co. A churchman, Mr. Hearson was for fifteen years an overseer and a churchwarden, and was for eleven years a member of the Court of Common Council. On the latter he was a for a twelve month chairman of the Library Committee. He is a Freeman of the City, and a member of the Livery Company of Curriers. [Look it up; I had to.] He is a prominent Freemason; a P.M. [Past Master] of Chiltern Lodge (1475), P.Z. [Past Zerubabel – equivalent to Head of Chapter] of Chiltern Chapter, and P.P.G.P. [Past Provincial Grant Pursuivant – well, that's what I was told by a mason] of the province of Bedfordshire. A member of the executive of Devonians in London since their inception twenty years ago, Mr. Hearson is a member of the executive of Barumites, and was their president in 1905. He has become a member of the committee of the Three Towns Church Extension movement.

[Is this the sort of thing that the Revd Brereton had in mind when he set up his new school to provide a middle-class education? It would seem difficult to think of anybody much more solid or respectable.]

Thursday, 27th June.

Old Boys' News.

In the annual Athletic Sports of the Royal Naval Engineering College, Devonport, Engineer Cadet A.E.F. Orchard was 1st in Throwing the Cricket Ball (95 yards), 1st in Hurdle Race Handicap (19 sec.), and 2nd in High Jump (winner 5ft.¾in.)

Saturday, 29th June.

A Meeting of the Governors [was] duly convened by the Secretary, and held at The George Hotel, South Molton.

Present Earl Fortescue (in the chair), Messrs G.C. Smyth-Richards, M.B. Snell, G.A.W. Thorold, J.F. Wilkin, C. Pearce, W.P. Hiern & The Rev. J.H. Copleston (Governors)

Also The Revs. J.H. Thompson, J. Newman, & D.J.C. Bush Esq
The Rev. E.C. Harries (Head Master) & F.B. Wyatt Esq (Liquidator). [Note the presence of the 'Liquidator', Mr. Wyatt – continuing the process of changing the style and identity of the School, which involved voluntary liquidation of the original company – see 15th June.]

1. The minutes of the last Ordinary meeting were read and confirmed.
2. A letter from the Earl of St. Germans was read desiring that his name be withdrawn as a candidate for a Governorship of the School under the new Scheme. [He had been a Director under the old scheme.]

3. The County Council wrote informing the Governors that W.P. Hiern Esq: and J. Sanders Esq: had been re-appointed as the County Council Representatives on the School Governing Body, to hold office until the 31st March 1908, and thereafter until a fresh appointment has been made by the County Council.

4. In reply to the Governors' application to the Board of Education for permission to change the School Year, a letter was read from the Board granting permission "that the School Year may terminate on the 31st July instead of on the 31st December as heretofore". Also that "Grant for the Interim Period of 7 months, January – July, 1907, will, subject to compliance with the regulations for Secondary Schools, be allowed, **pro rata**, on the basis of the grant allowed for the 12 months of the School Year 1906".

5. The minutes of the Conference between H.M. Inspectors and the School Governors, held on 21st June, were read and approved.

6. A letter from the Board of Education, dated June 10th 1907, respecting the constitution of the new Governing Body, and suggesting that the new Scheme be drafted on undermentioned lines, so that the School might reap the benefit of an increased Government Grant, was read and fully discussed. The following resolution was proposed by Earl Fortescue and seconded by Mr. Snell and carried unanimously:

"The Governors have carefully considered the "letter of the Board of Education of the 10th "June, and do not think it would be advisable to "make any such alterations as are therein "suggested in the Draft Scheme E.E. 0771 dated "29th December 1906, inasmuch as it was on "the faith of the said Draft Scheme that the "Debenture Holders consented to surrender "their Debentures – the Governors having "received notice from some of the Debenture "Holders withdrawing their consent to surrender "their stock in view of the proposed alterations".

7. At Mr. Snell's suggestion it was proposed that the School buy in the Debenture Stock of the two ladies who had refused to voluntarily surrender the same, if there was sufficient money to do so after all the liabilities had been met.

8. The Liquidator was instructed to make the formal application to the Board of Education for the new Scheme. [So the decisive step was taken.]

Saturday, 29th June contd.

Cricket.

SCHOOL *v*. TAUNTON SCHOOL.

Played at Taunton. The School won the toss and sent Taunton in to bat. They made a bad start, losing 2 wickets for 4 runs, but, thanks mainly to some steady batting by Maitland-Jones, and useful scores by Rook and Hopkins, the score had been brought to 196 by the time the last wicket fell. The School could only raise 65, Seldon being top scorer with a splendid 29, while Preston gave good assistance with 19. Our fielding throughout was good. In a second innings [not printed, perhaps mercifully] the School only made 45, and were thus beaten by an innings and 86 runs.

SCHOOL.		TAUNTON SCHOOL.	
R.W. Seldon, b Jones	29	A. Maitland-Jones,	
		c Parker b Elworthy	62
P.J. Were, b Jones	1	B.S. Clark, b Harris	0
J.B. Harris, run out	0	J.C. White, b Harris	2
S. Bendall, b J.C. White	2	F. White, run out	14
W. Saunders, lbw Jones	1	N. Homer, c and b Harris	16
L.K.V. Job, c J. White b Jones	0	H.C. Rook, lbw Were	38
A. Pearce, b Jones	0	E.L. Hopkins, not out	34
A.E. Preston b Jones	19	W. Shapland, b Elworthy	5
A.O. Parker, b Jones	0	J. Ashford, c and b Were	0
C. Lewis, run out	4	T.C. Kidner, b Preston	13
W. Elworthy, not out	3	J.B. Hill, b Were	3
Extras	6	Extras	9
Total	65	Total	196

End of June entries

July

Tuesday, 2nd July.

[An odd day for a cricket match. It was normally Wednesday or Saturday.]

Cricket

SCHOOL *v.* TAUNTON SCHOOL.

Played at home … The School won the toss and batted first, but were only able to make 39. J. White was responsible in a large degree for this result, as he bowled well, but the batsmen treated him with far too much respect, and seemed afraid even to hit any of the short balls he sent down. When Taunton School went in, it was soon seen that they were in a merry mood for scoring, and they gave the School as much fielding as the keenest of them could desire for the rest of the afternoon.

SCHOOL.			TAUNTON SCHOOL.	
R.W. Seldon, c Kidner b J. White	6		A Maitland-Jones,	
			c Harris b Job	73
P.J. Were, lbw Maitland-Jones	0		J.C. White, b Preston	13
J.B. Harris, b Maitland-Jones	2		B.S. Clark, run out	10
S. Bendall, c and b J. White	4		H.C. Rook, b Elworthy	96
W. Saunders, b J. White	0		F.W. White, c Harris b Job	0
L.K.V. Job, b J. White	6		N. Homer, not out	35
A. Pearce, b J. White	8		E.L. Hopkins, not out	11
A.E. Preston, c Homer b J. White	0		T.C. Kidner did not bat	
A. O. Parker, c Hopkins b J. White	5		J. Ashford did not bat	
C. Lewis, not out	0		W. Shapland did not bat	
W. Elworthy, b J. White	2		J.H. Hill did not bat	
Extras	6		Extras	8
Total	39		Total for 5 wickets	246

[It seems that Taunton School's team was almost a two-man affair, certainly in the bowling department. In the two matches between them and the School, Maitland-Jones and White accounted for 18 of the twenty wickets that fell – and the other two were run out. White opened the batting as well in one game, and Maitland-Jones in both, scoring a total of 135 runs in both matches. Though Rook was also no mean performer – he made 134 in both games.]

Wednesday, 3rd July.

The Choir.

The following boys formed the School Choir during the Summer Term:-

E.A. Adams, A.H. Austin, G.H. Dawe, E.B. Driver, C.G. Harris, A.J.E. Helps, H.G. Hopper, L.G.H. Major, A.P. Moor, E.W. Oakey, H.J. Richards, M.R. Roberts, R.W. Seldon, J. White, A.L.J. Youings.

FESTIVAL. – Owing to the great number of Choirs which are now affiliated to the North Devon Choral Union, no Church in North Devon was sufficiently large for one big Festival this year, so a series of Festivals was held, the one the School selected to attend being held at South Molton. The less said about it the better. It was a shockingly wet day, and only a matter of half a dozen choirs took part in the service; while the congregation was "next to nothing". [sic] The singing was only fair, and there was a complete lack of "go." [sic again] By no stretch of the imagination can it be said that the Festival was a success. From our point of view especially, this was most unfortunate, for the special preacher was the Rev. J.H. Thompson [the first Headmaster of the School, who had retired in 1888], who preached a most appropriate sermon.

Thursday, 4th July.

General Knowledge Paper.

SET FOR THE CHOPE PRIZE, 1907.
[The questions were, of course, set by that polymath workaholic, Mr. Chope himself.]

1. – Give the latitude and longitude of the School. Show by a diagram of radial lines, with the School as centre, the directions of the North Pole, London, New York, Paris, Edinburgh, Cork, Bristol, Gibraltar, Exeter, Plymouth, Barnstaple, and South Molton, and state the distance of each.

   What is the geological formation of the School site? What formations adjoin it? Would you expect to find coal there? Say why.

2. (a). – What are the meanings of:- A blue, the blues, the Blues, Prussian blue, laundry blue, bluebell, bluebottle, blue-book, bluestone, bluecoat, blue stocking, Bluebeard, blue-john, blue-peter, blue-betsy, blue-mould, blue moon? Or,

   (b). – What meanings would you give to the word *bull* in connexion with: - Devon, Ireland, Bisley, the Stock Exchange, Rome, and a china shop? Explain the phrases: "Cock and Bull Story," [sic] "Bull and Mouth." Why is the name John Bull given to the typical Englishman? What is the difference between bull-fighting and bull-baiting?

3. (a). – Name 12 great inventors, and say what they invented. Or,

   (b). – Name 12 famous Devonians, and say why they are famous. Or,

   (c). – Name 6 living persons distinguished as politicians, artists, authors, actors or actresses, singers, and soldiers or sailors.

4. – What is the difference in principle between (*a*) a steam engine and a petrol engine, (*b*) weaving and knitting, (*c*) the telegraph and the telephone, (*d*) a dynamo and a dynamometer, (*e*) an electromotor and an electrometer, (*f*) photography and X rays? (Not more than two to be attempted.)

5. – Name (*a*) 20 birds, or (*b*) 15 trees, or (*c*) 40 flowers observed by you in the neighbourhood.

6. – Name the 12 books you like best, and say what you know about their authors. (Not more than 3 lines about each.)

7. (*a*). – Name 8 of the chief departments of the Government, and say who are the present political heads. Or,

   (*b*). – Who are the present Bishop of Exeter, Lord Chief Justice of England, Viceroy of India, President of the French Republic, Lord-Lieutenant of Devon, Chancellor of the Exchequer, Mayor of South Molton, Governor-General of the Commonwealth of Australia, Premier of Cape Colony, M.P. for the Barnstaple Division, Chancellor of the University of Cambridge, and Lord Mayor of London?

8. – What do you understand by the following terms:- Mikado, matador, stevedore, battledore, sirdar, rajah, stock-broker, stock-breeder, prima donna, belladonna, kaffir, coffer?

9. – What do you know about Alexander the Great, Peter the Great, Marco Polo, Paul Jones, John Cabot, James Cook, Benvenuto Cellini, Michael Angelo [sic], Hernando Cortes, Florence Nightingale, Rosa Bonheur, George Washington?

10. – Explain the formation of dew, hoar-frost, snow, and hail.

11. – From what plants, and from what parts of the plants, are the following products obtained:- Sugar, starch, ginger, beer, cider, cotton, linen, tea, cocoa, sago, tapioca, cornflour?

12. – Render into English one of the following specimens of Devonshire dialect [Chope couldn't resist this; he was an acknowledged expert in local dialect, and gave frequent recitals]:-

   (*a*). – "The puggen end of the linney neist to the pegs-looze geed way and was ruseing down; maister was standing by the tallut when the cob-wall sluer'd away all to wance, and made such a sture that a come heal'd bust and grute."

   (*b*). – "I don't drill time in thease gude place.
   Wanged or no mine's tutwork pace,
   Zo ott's this hackle for?
   Chewers ban't gwain to crick my back,
   Britting o' thick and crazing thack,
   But 'eet I'll do my coure."

[We have no information – alas! – as to how many pupils saw fit to sit this fearsome test, or even whether they had any choice about it. Nor do we know what sort of marks they obtained. We know that there must have the usual crop of schoolboys howlers among the answers, because Chope made a collection of them, and now and again published the 'best' of them – where else? – in the *Register,* thanks to the indulgence, or the weary patience, of the Editor.

We know also the name of the winner of the General Knowledge Prize, presented on Speech Day – see 29th July. One cannot help but feel that if ever a prize was richly deserved, this was it.

Chope's passion for facts, and his fearsome command of them, must have provided plenty of food for comment in the School, because in 1917 the *Register* printed a parody of the famous General Knowledge Test. It was allegedly composed by a member of staff, Mr. Inniss. He had left in 1915. So perhaps he set off the idea, and the collection grew as each member of the Common Room mischievously put in his two penn'orth, till somebody thought it worth publishing two years later. One can only hope that Mr. Chope saw the funny side of it. For a look at Mr Inniss' 'Major-General Knowledge' Test, see my earlier book, *The Natural History of a Country School*, p. 109.]

Saturday, 6th July.

The Choir Outing.

If the Festival was not a success, the Outing certainly was … We drove to Lynton, and except for a storm of rain just as we started, and another one while we were having lunch (under cover), the weather was beautifully fine. By permission, we drove by the private road through Six Acre Farm to Lee Abbey and the Valley of the Rocks, and thence walked to Lynton and Lynmouth and on to Watersmeet. At "Myrtleberry" we had a most sumptuous tea (Will those strawberries and cream ever be forgotten?), and all too soon the time arrived for driving back. School was reached soon after nine o'clock, most of us being tired out from our twelve hours' trip. Without doubt it was the very best Choir Outing for many a long day.

Wednesday, 10th July.

Cricket.

SCHOOL *v.* SUMMERLAND STRAGGLERS.
Played at home … The Stragglers won the toss and batted first, but a rot set in, and they were all out in half-an-hour for 20 runs. Preston bowled well, taking 7 wickets for 8 runs, while Seldon batted steadily.

SCHOOL.		SUMMERLAND STRAGGLERS.	
R. W. Seldon, c J. Pearce b Britton	30	J. Britton, b Preston	5
J. B. Harris, b Britton	2	R. J. Buckingham, c Were b Preston	1
S. Bendall, run out	4	J. Eddy, b Harris	0
A. Pearce, b Saunders	5	W. L. P. Hole, b Preston	0

W. Saunders, b J. Pearce	3	C. Saunders, b Preston	2
A.E. Preston, b Saunders	2	J. Pearce, b Preston	5
L.K.V. Job, st. Buckingham b Britton	8	C. Pearce, b Harris	0
P.J. Were, c Burbage b Eddy	12	J. Walters, b Preston	4
A.O. Parker, b Saunders	4	G.R.E. Williams, b Preston	0
C. Lewis, run out	8	W. Burbage, lbw Harris	1
W. Elworthy, not out	6	E. Newcombe, not out	0
Extras	8	Extras	2
Total	92	Total	20

[The J. Pearce and C. Pearce of the Stragglers were probably Arthur Pearce's elder brothers, who had not long since left. Or perhaps C. Pearce was the Governor father of Arthur. C. Saunders was almost certainly the brother of W. Saunders, and J. Britton was equally probably the recently-left ex-secretary of the Reading and Debating Society. See also 25th March, 3rd June, 19th June, 2nd October, and 13th December. It seems that Old Boys simply could not stay away.

Interesting how the School's innings is always mentioned first, no matter who wins the toss or who goes in first.

Charles Lewis made a habit of getting run out. In the course of the season, the School lost ten wickets by run-outs, and Lewis was the victim of five of them. He was either incredibly unlucky, or he was a shocking judge of a run. How he must have looked forward to the football season, when he could display his prowess as the best goalkeeper the School ever had.]

Wednesday, 17th July.

Cricket.

SCHOOL (WITH MASTERS) *v.* SOUTH MOLTON.

Played at home … The School batted first, and, thanks mainly to a capital innings by Seldon, ran up the total of 130 for 8 wickets before declaring. South Molton were left about an hour and a quarter to get the runs, and had lost 8 wickets when stumps were drawn, the match thus ending in a draw greatly in favour of the School.

SCHOOL.		SOUTH MOULTON. [sic]	
A. Taylor, b Pallin	23	C. Taylor, b Taylor	27
Rev. E.C. Harries,		H.H. Beardsley, c Parker	
b C. Southcomb	8	b Taylor	14
R.W. Seldon, c Taylor b Pallin	53	W. Southcomb, b Harris	15
W.L. Giffard, b Harvey	2	C. Southcomb, run out	0
J.B. Harris, b Pallin	0	W.G.H. Pallin, b Harris	9
P.J. Were, b C. Southcomb	5	T.H. Vicary, not out	7
L.K.V. Job, lbw Pallin	15	P. Vicary, b Harris	5
A. Pearce, not out	1	E. Huxtable, c Harris b Taylor	0
A.E. Preston, b Pallin	0	S.V. Horton, c Elworthy b Taylor	2
A.O. Parker, not out	4	W.J. Harvey, not out	1
W. Elworthy, did not bat		T.H. Johnson, did not bat	
Extras	19	Extras	16
Total for wickets [sic]	130	Total for 8 wickets	93

[That gremlin in the scorebox again – look at South Molton's total score. A nice dab of irony – J.B. Harris was bowled by Pallin, and Pallin was bowled in the other innings by Harris.]

Marriage.

At the Parish Church, Barnstaple, REGINALD H. SMYTH (1895-98) , of l, Halsdon Villas, Pilton, Barnstaple, to Eustace Dening. [sic – Eustace as a girl's name is new to me.]

Saturday, 20th July.

A portrait and biographical sketch of the late J.L. Squire appeared in the *Western Weekly News.*

Cricket.

SCHOOL (WITH MASTERS) *v.* DULVERTON.

Played at Dulverton, resulting in an easy win for the School by 100 runs. For the School, the Rev. E.C. Harries hit hard for 32, and A. Taylor took 7 wickets for 25 runs.

SCHOOL.		DULVERTON.	
A. Taylor, b Lugg	21	F. Cartman, c Parker b Taylor	6
R.W. Seldon, b Spicer	7	A.B.S. Roberts, b Preston	0
W.L. Giffard, b Lugg	15	G. Pryce, c Parker b Taylor	0
J.B. Harris, b Spicer	19	Rev. A. Spicer, not out	29
Rev. E.C. Harries, b Pryce	32	W. Allen, b Preston	0
P.J. Were, c Parkhouse b Spicer	9	E.G. Brooke, c Harris b Taylor	0
L.K.V. Job, lbw Spicer	3	H. Wright, b Taylor	7
S. Bendall, b Pryce	5	C. Parkhouse, b Taylor	0
A. Pearce, b Pryce	0	C. Lugg, st Giffard b Taylor	0
A.O. Parker, not out	6	W. Gage, c Preston b Taylor	0
A.E. Preston, c Allen b Pryce	5	B. Tarr, c Seldon b Preston	0
Extras	24	Extras	4
Total	146	Total	46

Today was registered the highest shade temperature of the year [so far] – 79°. Up to the middle of this month, the warmest day of the year had been [the day of the Exmoor Run on] April 1st. [This temperature later proved to be the highest in the whole year.]

Tuesday, 23rd July.

Swimming.

The competitions for the Dormitory Swimming Cup, presented by Mr. F.W. Matthews, were held. Brereton won both the Open Races and the Relay Race, but Courtenay had it all their own way in the Junior events, and by getting second places in the Open events secured the Cup.

The following were the events and winners. "B" indicates Brereton, and "C" Courtenay.

OPEN.

Long Race (8 lengths). - 1st, S. Bendall (B.); 2nd, W. Saunders (C.)

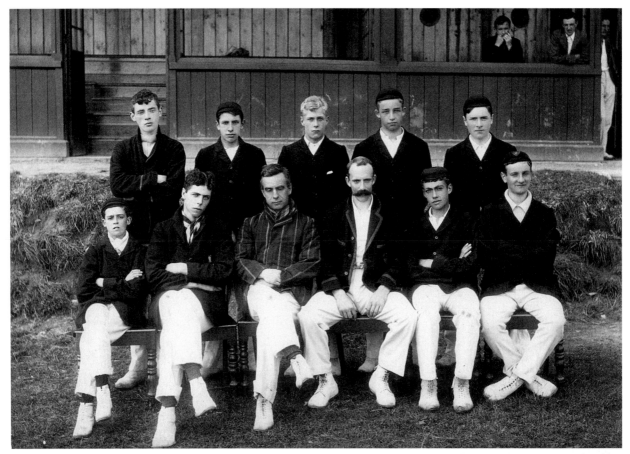

The School (with Masters) Cricket team – July, 1907. Standing, L. to R. – A. Pearce, P.J. Were, A. O. Parker, A.E. Preston, L.K. V. Job. Sitting, L. to R. – R. W. Seldon, W.L. Giffard, E.C. Harries, A. Taylor, J.B. Harris, S. Bendall.

Short Race (2 lengths). - 1st, S. Bendall (B.); 2nd, W. Saunders (C.)

Relay Race. - Brereton Team (S. Bendall, E.A. Adams, A.E. Preston, A.L.J. Youings) beat Courtenay Team (W. Saunders, L.W.E. Grant, A.P. Moor, S.J. Widgery).

JUNIOR (under 14).
Short Race (2 lengths). - 1st, L.W.E. Grant (C.); 2nd, A.P. Moor (C.)

Long Race (4 lengths). - 1st, L.W.E. Grant (C.); 2nd, W.W. Owbridge (C.)

Courtenay won the cup by 32 points (2 firsts and 4 seconds) to Brereton's 24 points (2 firsts and the Relay Race. [Second bracket omitted. Tut-tut.]

S. Bendall won the silver medal for swimming.

Thursday, 25th July.

Cricket.

SCHOOL (WITH MASTERS) *v*. BARNSTAPLE BANKS.
Played at home. The ground played much faster than it had done before, and consequently a high-scoring game was witnessed. The Banks batted first and lost their first wicket for 7, but Penhale and Hallett then added over 100 before they were separated, and the innings was finally declared closed with the score at 184. The School did practically as well in reply, as they had scored 127 for the loss of two wickets at the close of play, the chief feature of the innings being a fine display by Mr. Taylor.

SCHOOL.		BARNSTAPLE BANKS.	
A. Taylor, not out	74	M.H. Toller, c Parker b Taylor	2
R.W. Seldon, b Fielder	34	P. Penhale, run out	58
W.L. Giffard, b. Penhale	0	C. Hallett, not out	75
J.B. Harris, not out	10	E.S. Turner, not out	21
Extras	9	Extras	27
Total for 2 wickets	127	Total for 2 wickets	184

[Once again, the School scorer will not win any Maths prizes; the Banks' total was 183.]

Saturday, 27th July.

Old Boys' Gathering.

[This was probably the biggest event in the School's regular calendar, and was spread over four or five days, as a glance at today's entry and those following will show.]

The first gathering of Old Boys under the régime of the new Head Master, the Rev. E.C. Harries, M.A., assembled.

The following were present during the whole or part of the Old Boys' Gathering:-

The School Swimming Pool. There was originally a pond. Then, in response to some rather cutting remarks from the inspectors about the relative lack of facilities, the School bestirred itself, and in the next few years produced a laboratory, a shooting range, and a swimming pool – which remained open to the elements until the 1970's.

F.R. Boatfield, J.F. Bowden, J. Britton, R. Britton, P.W. Buckingham, R.J. Buckingham, G.E.L. Carter, H.R. Champion, G.S.W. Chapple, A.H. Chard, J.A. Chope, R.P. Chope, Comer Clarke, W.E. Grills, T.J. Holmes, J.C. Johnson, E.O. Lisle, Rev. G.T. Llewellin, E.T. Loram, V.C. Martyn, A.F.C. Martyn, F.T. Miller, A.C. Milton, G.B. Oerton, J.F. Orchard, J.C. Pearce, E.R. Pearce, H.S. Potbury, T.R. Potbury, H.T. Roberts, C. Saunders, J.W. Shawyer, A. Small, M.B. Snell, Rev. J.H. Thompson, R.P. Wheadon, and W.C. Wheeler.

At the Annual General Meeting of the Old Boys' Association the Rev. J.H. Thompson, M.A., first Head Master of the School, was elected President for the ensuing Jubilee year [the School had been founded in 1858], and Professor T.A. Hearson, M.Inst.C.E., and Comer Clarke, J.P., were elected Vice-Presidents.

Cricket.

SCHOOL (PAST AND PRESENT) *v.* NORTH DEVON.
Played at home. The School had the help of two or three of the best Old Boys [four, actually – see below], and, mainly by their assistance, easily defeated a fairly representative North Devon team. The visitors, who batted first, did not succeed in making much of a score, only two of them reaching double figures. Their total of 73 the School passed with 6 wickets in hand, while the century was hoisted when 5 wickets were down, the innings finally closing for 138. In their second innings North scored 168 for 3 wickets, Mitchell being responsible for 86 and Lucas 44.

SCHOOL		NORTH DEVON.	
R.W. Seldon, b Millett	8	H. Trott, b Taylor	11
A. Taylor, c Lucas, b Trott	16	C.R.G. Mitchell, c Giffard, b	
		Saunders	9
H.S. Potbury, run out	17	Rev. R.W. Sealy, b Wheadon	9
W.L. Giffard, b Trott	22	E.M. Lucas, c Wheadon, b Taylor	7
R.P. Wheadon, c Mitchell,			
b Horndon	4	E.G. Jones, b Saunders	5
J.H. Harris, b Jones	27	D. Horndon, c Wheadon, b Taylor	12
C. Saunders, run out	14	E. Sealy, b Taylor	2
P.J. Were, c Trott, b E. Sealy	1	J. Pike, c Harris, b Saunders	1
A. Small, c R.W. Sealy,			
b E. Sealy	5	Rev. W.H. Millett, b Taylor	4
S. Bendall, c and b Jones	0	A.B. Searle, not out	3
A.E. Preston, not out	4	L.K.V. Job, run out	1
Extras	20	Extras	9
	—		—
Total	138	Total	73

[The Old Boys 'lent' Potbury, Wheadon, C. Saunders, and Small to the School, and the School had to 'lend' L.K.V. Job to North Devon to make up their numbers. C. Saunders was brother to W. Saunders, the prefect, and Potbury was one of four brothers to attend the School. Just in case you didn't read the other explanatory notes on 19th June and 4th December.]

Sunday, 28th July.

Special services were held in East Buckland Church.

In the morning a most appropriate sermon was preached by an Old Boy, the Rev. R. Sealy Genge, M.A., vicar of Christ Church, Wolverhampton, who took for his text *Eccles. xii.*, 1, "Remember." The sermon in the evening was preached by the Head Master from the text in *II Thessalonians* ii., 15, "Therefore, brethren, stand fast, and hold the traditions which ye have been taught, whether by word, or our Epistle."

Special lessons were read in the morning by R. Pearse Chope, B.A., and M.B. Snell, J.P., and in the evening by J.W. Shawyer and W.C. Wheeler. The Old Boys' hymn, "Once again in glad reunion" (S. Childs Clarke) was set to music for the occasion by Mr. A. Taylor, organist and choir-master of the School.

Monday, 29th July.

Cricket.

SCHOOL 2ND XI. *v.* OLD BOYS (AN XI).

This match between the older Old Boys and the 2nd XI was begun on the morning of the Speech Day. The younger generation, who batted first, gave a very tame display, with the exception of Elworthy and White. The Veterans, with apologies to Carter and Chapple, showed us that they retained sufficient skill to inflict a fairly decisive defeat.

SCHOOL.		OLD BOYS.	
C. Lewis, run out	4	G.E.L. Carter, run out	0
M.R. Roberts, c Chard, b Grills	4	F.R. Boatfield, b Youings	34
A.L.J. Youings, b Lisle	0	S. Chapple, b Elworthy	18
W. Elworthy, c Chapple, b Boatfield	19	H.R. Champion, c Youings, b White	18
N.K. Pearce, c and b Chapple	7	J.W. Shawyer, b Elworthy	4
J. White, c Sub., b Chard	15	A.H. Chard, b White	2
T.H. Richards, c Lisle, b Shawyer	3	J.A. Chope, c Roberts, b Elworthy	1
L.W. Grant, c Chapple, b Carter	4	E.O. Lisle, not out	3
H.E. Hicks, c Chapple, b Boatfield	3	W.B. Champion, b White	4
C.G. Harris, c Lisle, b Boatfield	0	R.P. Chope, b White	0
S.A. Loram, not out	2	W.E. Grills, absent hurt	0
Extras	2	Extras	10
	63		94

[Poor Charlie Lewis – run out again. See 10th July.]

An ordinary meeting of the Governors [was] duly convened by the Secretary, and held at the School:

<u>Present</u>. Earl Fortescue (Chairman), Messrs. G.C. Smyth-Richards, G.A.W. Thorold, C. Pearce, J. Sanders, W.P. Hiern, and M.B. Snell.

Also: The Rev. J.H. Thompson, Mr. R.P. Chope (Governors elect), and the Rev. E.C. Harries (Headmaster).

1. The minutes of the last meeting were read and confirmed.
2. The Headmaster read his Report for the Term, which was duly received and adopted. Arising out of the said report, it was decided that the salaries for the assistant masters should stand as they are for the present.
3. Regarding the urgent necessity, as represented by His Majesty's School Inspector, of heating the east wing of the School by means of hot air or hot water pipes, Mr. Harries informed the Governors that an experienced engineer had inspected the premises and was preparing a Report on the proposed work. A Committee, consisting of Messrs G.C. Smyth-Richards, C. Pearce and J. Sanders was appointed to receive and consider the Report.

    The Secretary was instructed to write to Mr. J.F. Young, the organising Secretary of the Devon County Council, as to the possibilities of the County giving a grant towards the cost of the work. He was also instructed to write to the Board of Education for permission to be granted Lord Fortescue and Mr. Snell to realize a certain amount of Capital to meet the expense.
4. The Governors being informed that the Old Boys had subscribed or promised a sufficient sum of money to provide 3 additional "Old Boys' Scholarships", a cordial vote of thanks to the Old Boys was proposed by Mr. Sanders, seconded by Mr. Pearce, and carried unanimously.
5. The question of changing the name of the School, was deferred to a later meeting of the Governors. [The 'Devon County School' became 'West Buckland School' in 1912.]
6. On the strong recommendation of the Government Inspector, Mr. Smyth-Richards proposed and Mr. J. Sanders seconded that all new boys purchase their own text-books. Boys who are already in the School to be subject to the old conditions. Carried unanimously.
7. Respecting the constitution of the Board of Governors under the new Scheme, the Secretary was instructed to write to the Board of Education, and submit the following names of gentlemen, who are willing to act in the capacity of Governors, for the Board's approval: <u>Life Governors,</u> The Lord Bishop of Exeter, vice the Earl of St. Germans – resigned. George A.W. Thorold, vice John Mortimer – deceased. and The Rev. Preby. Richard Martin, whose name was inadvertently left out of the Published Draft Scheme. [Punctuated as the Secretary wrote it.]
    <u>Ordinary Governors:</u> William Fisher, of Pottington, vice G.A.W. Thorold (Life Governor), and Robert

Alfred Holt, South Molton, vice John Mothersdale, resigned.

8. Cheques to the value of £978 – 10s – 3d were presented and signed.

The Governors afterwards attended the Annual Prize Distribution.

The annual Prize Distribution took place in Big School [the largest classroom in the original main building] ... and was attended by a large company of parents, Old Boys, and friends. Earl Fortescue, Lord Lieutenant of the County, and Chairman of the Board of Governors, presided, and was supported by several other Governors. Mr. A.L. Francis, M.A., (Head Master of Blundell's School), distributed the prizes and gave an address.

Before the speeches the Choir sang the School Song, written by the late Prebendary J.L. Brereton, and set to music by Mr. Hubert Bath. [Mr. Bath, born in Barnstaple in 1883, achieved some fame both as conductor and as a composer – anything from cantatas to comic operas. Later in life, he wrote music for films, most notably *Cornish Rhapsody*. See also 11th January.]

The HEAD MASTER announced the receipt of letters from Sir Thomas Acland, the Bishops of Exeter and Crediton, and Canon Edmonds, regretting inability to be present. He was gratified to state that the health of the boys had been wonderfully good, in spite of the weather. Perhaps the wet weather was a very good thing after all, inasmuch as it cleared away the dreadful germs which nowadays they heard so much about. The health of the boys was largely due to exercise, and their creature comforts were as well looked after as they ever had been in the past. As to the discipline of the School, he could only say that he had nothing to complain of. The discipline was excellent in every way, and credit for this attached primarily to the prefects, whom he warmly thanked. Turning to education, he said that the successes which they had to report were eminently satisfactory. Their old pupil, John Britton, was doing extremely well at Cambridge, and he hoped in the near future to be able to announce him as a wrangler, at any rate, as a person high up in the honours list of mathematics. [Britton returned to speak at the Reading and Debating Society – 25th March and 13th December – probably freed by college vacations.] He expected a very high honour next day at Oxford for another old pupil and friend, George Carter. A great number of the boys at present in the School were showing considerable promise, and he hoped that in time they would emulate the performances of those who had gone before them. He congratulated the Old Boys on the wonderful successes of their protégés – the winners of the Old Boys' Scholarships – who had distinguished themselves in the School prize lists. This year they had had the usual Board of Education inspection, and he trusted that the pleasure the inspectors apparently felt at what they saw and heard would be evidenced in their report, which had not yet been received. Speaking of improvements, Mr. Harries said they had provided a reading-room of really most respectable pretensions. They had improved one of the class-rooms out of all knowledge; they had

finished the bath and paid for it, and what was more satisfactory was that it was full of water. (Laughter.) He said that because a great number of people had prophesied that there would be no water. Their prophecy seemed likely to come off until the rain came, and an expert, not a water finder, confidently expected to find more water [that's what it says], thus supplementing the present supply. The pavilion had also been finished, and now added materially to the picturesqueness of the scene. In the near future he hoped, too, that a new room would be set aside for the purpose of drawing, that a new class-room would be provided, while the question of heating the eastern wing was to be taken in hand during the holidays. He hoped too, that the general supply of water would be improved in the coming year. The subject of education was, he thought, nearly thread-bare. He should like to point out to parents that it was quite impossible for him to do anything with a boy unless he had him under his care early enough. He must come at the age of 12 if he was to be of any use thereafter, and it was quite hopeless to expect a boy to show any signs of development until he was 16. It was only when he was 16 that he learnt the meaning of the word "responsibility", and it was not until he learnt the meaning of that word that a boy was going to be of the slightest use to the nation. He said this because the tendency on the part of the parents was to tell him that a boy must leave school early in order to be apprenticed at some particular business, but if a boy left school at 17, and served 3 years' business apprenticeship at his business, he was then but 20, and was not much more than a boy. He maintained that by taking boys away early from schools, parents sacrificed the best part of their education in order that they might learn some small technical thing. Boys who did not leave school until they were at least 16 years of age were the ones that did them credit, and those who came at 9, and left at 17, were the ones that distinguished themselves at the Universities. They often saw no result from the boy who came at 13 and left at 15½. Next year the Devon County School would attain its jubilee, and he should like to see it celebrated by the founding of a leaving scholarship, the conversion of the covered playground, which was rather an eye-sore, into a gymnasium, and the formation of a Cadet Corps. (Applause). [sic] They would be failing in their duties as Englishmen, if they did not have Cadet Corps, and perhaps Lord Fortescue, who was an expert and an enthusiast on matters military, might be able to suggest some plan by which the County Association would be prepared to help them. (Applause). [sic again] In conclusion, Mr. Harries cordially thanked the Governors and the staff for their co-operation, and the visitors for their attendance, and said that [in] another year he hoped to provide an additional attraction in the form of a small Shakespearean play. [As it turned out, it wasn't an entire Shakespeare play – not even a 'small' one. But it was Shakespeare – 'extracts' from *As You Like It*. There is a photograph in the School Archive.] He welcomed his old Head Master, Mr. Francis [Harries had been recruited from Blundell's, whither he had gone to serve after four years as DCS Chaplain], under whom for nearly three years he had the honour and pleasure to serve ...

Mr. Francis then delivered the prizes, as follows:-

FORM PRIZES.
II.   J.L. Carter.   "The Arabian Nights."
III. (a) C.H. Petherick.   "The Early Days of Christianity," by Farrar.
     (b) F. Chave.   "Stories from Greek Tragedy."
IV.   H. F. Lovell.   "The Life of Christ," by Farrar.
V.   C. Lewis.   Tennyson's Poems.

MATHEMATICS PRIZES.
III.   P.J. Were.
IV.   H. Matthews. "The Story of the Iliad," by Church.
V.   R.T.H. Hooper.   "The Life of St. Paul," by Farrar. [If other schools' prize lists were like this one, Mr. Farrar seems to have done rather well out of the process.]

SCIENCE PRIZES.
III.   C.H. Petherick.   "Stories of King Arthur."
IV.   H.F. Lovell.   "Stories from Virgil," by Church. [Mr Church doesn't seem to have done too badly either.]
V.   R.T.H. Hooper.   "Life of Cromwell," by Frith.

THE EDMONDS DIVINITY PRIZE.
J.B. Harris.   "Helps to the Study of the Bible."

THE ACLAND SCIENCE PRIZE.
J.B. Harris.   "Starland," by Sir R.S. Ball.

THE ACLAND MATHEMATICS PRIZE.
W.L. Armstrong.   "Pioneers of Science," by Sir Oliver Lodge.

THE MICHAEL SNELL ENGLISH PRIZE. [A former Head Prefect, Snell was one of the syndicate of affluent and generous Old Boys who had recently come to the School's financial rescue.]
S. Bendall.   "New Land," by Sverdrup.   2 vols.

THE CHOPE GENERAL KNOWLEDGE PRIZE.
W.L. Armstrong.
   "Alexander's Empire," by Mahaffy.
   "Chaldaea," by Ragozin.
   "Phoenicia," by Rawlinson. [Look at the Examination Paper (4th July); if ever a boy earned a prize, Master Armstrong did.]

THE HEAD MASTER'S LANGUAGE PRIZE.
J. B. Harris.   Shakespeare's Plays.

CAMBRIDGE LOCAL HONOUR PRIZES.
J.B. Harris, Senior, Class III. "Highways and Byeways in Devon and Cornwall," by Norway.
H.J. Harris, Junior, Class III. "Cranford," by Mrs. Gaskell.

The Dormitory Sports Cup, presented by a distinguished Old Boy, Dr. William Hill (1870-4), won by Courtenay (A. Pearce, captain).

The Dormitory Swimming Cup, presented by Mr. F.W. Matthews, won by Courtenay (W. Saunders, captain).
Silver Medal for Swimming, S. Bendall.

Silver Spoons, given by Mr. W.L. Miles [see 4th May], to the winners of the monthly shooting competitions, E.A. Adams, J.B. Harris, W. Saunders.

Cricket Bat, presented by another Old Boy, Mr. H. B. Squire, for the best cricket during the season, won by R.W. Seldon. [See 8th January.]

Mr. FRANCIS, who was well received, delivered an admirable and humorous address. He supposed that the reason he had been asked there was because he had had some experience. With one exception he was the senior head master. (Applause). [sic – regarding the the punctuation, that is, and several times below] First of all, he said, he had a personal remark or two to make, and recalled some interesting reminiscences of the Rev. J.H. Thompson as an undergraduate in his early Cambridge days of well-nigh forty years ago. Speaking of the reverend gentleman's remarkable deliveries in his cricket days, Mr. Francis said that he hoped all the members of the School who knew of his fame as a great schoolmaster would bear in mind that he was the father of that new style of bowling so effectively utilised by Mr. Bosanquet and others, and known in cricket as the "googly" – whatever that meant. (Laughter and applause). The present was a very anxious time for all the leading schools. This was the day of day schools, and as the British public could not think of more than one thing at a one time, there was a tendency to lose sight of the boarding schools. Of course, they were glad that the towns should have big day schools, but at the same time the education authorities must not forget that the boarding schools were a very vital point of the education of the country. (Applause). Never were they more so than now. (Applause). He was sure that Lord Fortescue, who had just returned from London, could give them some idea of the tranquility [sic – the editors, or the printers, have allowed an American spelling, the single 'l', to creep in – remarkably early. Perhaps the editors of the Oxford Dictionary might like to make a note of it] which existed there in regard to street noises. Education needed peace, and peace had fled.

"The motor cab, where're we go,
Pursues, an unrelenting foe,
While motor bike and motor bus
Conspire to make an end of us,
But bike and bus and hansom are
Mere mercy to the motor car."

(Loud laughter). If that was a faithful description of town life, there was a better chance of peaceful education to be found in the country (Applause). Therefore he was thankful that there were boarding schools such as this to which people in towns such as Bristol could send their boys. (Hear, hear). Oh, that they had more people from Bristol there that day to see that delightful spot, to feel that lovely breeze! Then they would think twice before they left their boys in the stuffy schools of the town. (Applause). These schools also afforded the great advantage of a better physical training, and the opportunities of such training in the School were to be added to by the gymnasium. (Applause). Anyone who looked ahead could not help realising that the nation must depend largely upon the physical training of her sons from childhood. (Applause). They hoped by next year to have a cadet corps started, and he wished it all prosperity. (Applause). Their public schools were the homes of patriotism. (Applause). Those schools formed a beautiful link between the life of the home and the life beyond, and in them was inspired that larger patriotism which was now essential to the welfare of the country. (Hear, hear). How valuable that intermediate training was, was never more strikingly shown than in the late war, when old public school boys flocked in thousands to the standard of their country in the time of great need. (Applause). [One gets an interesting perspective on events from this vantage point of 1907. To the speaker, and to the audience, the 'late' war was, of course, the Boer War. The 'time of great need' meant only one thing, as it means only one thing now – but a different thing.] And he knew this: that the sons of the Devon County School had been very forward in showing their affection – their presence that day proved it – for the place of their education during the anxious time through which it had passed, he trusted, in safety. (Applause). [He was referring, it seems, to the recent bad time in the School's finances, and to the rescue package put together by a syndicate of Lord Fortescue and some Old Boys. See 15th May.] Surely if there was any particular spot where patriotism could be taught, it was in the county of Devon that they could breathe it in, amidst the memory of Drake, of Raleigh, and of Grenville. (Applause). Nor must it be forgotten that although Devon was so far from the great centres of national life, it was in Devon, of all places, that the great education movement which had now culminated began. Let them not forget, least of all in that place, the names of such men as the good Earl of Devon, the old Sir Thomas Acland, the late Lord Fortescue, Lord Clinton, and Frederick Temple. (Applause). They would do well to remember that 50 years ago these men were awake and stirring in the cause of education before the nation as a whole had the slightest idea what the word meant, and before the great national movement of to-day. (Applause). It was by the noble work and self-sacrifice of such men as these that that school stood on the hills of North Devon, and long might it stand as a monument. (Applause). Long might it flourish, in the words familiar there, "for the promotion of God's glory, in the extension of useful knowledge upon the imperishable foundation of Divine truth." (Loud applause). Speaking for himself and for his old friend Mr. Thompson, and for his friend and late colleague – their able Head Master (Mr. Harries) – (applause) – for the sake of all the good work which had been done there, and for the memories of the wise men he had named, with all his heart he trusted that the governors, masters, and scholars of that School might receive from their education authorities the liberal support and encouragement to which they had so just a

claim. *Floreat Schola Devoniensis.* [Which is as near as he could probably get to saying in Latin, 'Long live the Devon County School'.] (Loud applause).

Mr. M.B. SNELL explained that as one of the oldest of the Old Boys present – he was sorry to see some of his schoolfellows getting really as old as he was! – (laughter) – he had been asked to propose a vote of thanks to Mr. Francis for coming there and giving them the beautiful address he had. The fact of Mr. Francis coming there struck a sympathetic chord between them both, especially as they had as head master one of the former masters at Blundell's. (Applause). He hoped that Mr. Francis would come to West Buckland a good many times. He asked the boys to join in giving three cheers for Mr. Francis for his kindness in coming to give them an address.

The response was of an unmistakably hearty character.

The Rev. J.H. Thompson proposed a vote of thanks to Earl Fortescue for presiding, and in doing so he remarked that his thoughts must need turn back to the past and to the very many occasions upon which Earl Fortescue's father had presided over similar gatherings. His memory also went back to at least one gathering which was presided over by the present Earl Fortescue's grandfather. So that the hereditary association of the Fortescue family with the school made it especially fitting that Earl Fortescue should preside over that gathering. (Applause). He should always remember one evening in October, 1858, when a young man, who was hardly more than a boy, appeared at Southmolton Road Station to inquire the way to West Buckland. He had been asked by Earl Fortescue's grandfather and by Mr. Brereton, whose name would always be held in reverence in that school – (hear, hear) – to come and take charge of the school, which many people said would never exist. The school opened in 1858 in a farmhouse in Stoodleigh. In 1859 he well remembered Earl Fortescue's grandfather taking the chair at a gathering in a large wooden room they had erected because the house itself did not afford sufficient accommodation. When the chairman expressed his satisfaction at the work which was being done he said he wished to make a present of the land to the school. (Applause). [Mr. Thompson's memory was not quite as reliable as he might have liked to think. It was Lady Fortescue who presided, as the contemporary record specified. The Earl was there, and indeed spoke, but, as the record was careful to state, it was he who 'supported' her ladyship, not she who 'supported' him. And his lordship offered to pay for the building, not make a present of the land.] He well remembered a bleak winter day in the year 1861, when Earl Fortescue's grandfather laid the foundation stone, using the memorable words which Mr. Francis had just quoted. (Applause). [Mr. Thompson's memory is letting him down again; the foundation stone was laid in October, 1860 – as the inscription bears out to this day. 4th October may not have been technically winter, but, knowing West Buckland, it could easily have been both bleak and wintry. One must remember, though, that by 1907 Thompson was seventy years old, and, as one of the founding fathers, he can, one feels, be allowed a little anecdotal licence.] Within a year his lordship fixed a day for the opening of the School, but on his way down from London only got as far as Exeter, where he died. Some little time afterwards the School was opened by Lord Fortescue's father, whom he well remembered standing at the front-door, formally turning the key, and declaring the building open. His lordship always took the greatest interest in the School, and they would always remember the earnest addresses which he gave on many different occasions. Mr. Thompson also recalled that Lord Fortescue as a Harrow boy laid the foundations of the covered playground - which had been spoken of in terms hardly respectful – and concluded by expressing the hope that for many years Earl Fortescue would continue to occupy his present position, which had been so well and worthily filled by his father, and before him by his grandfather.

Earl Fortescue, replying, thanked his hearers very much for the kind way in which they had acknowledged the very small services he had rendered to the School in presiding. In regard to the formation of the Cadet Corps and the suggested help from the County Association, that latter organisation was likely to be pretty fully occupied at first in making bricks with a very inadequate allowance of straw. They did not know yet really what they would have to do, or what means they would have of doing anything. So far as he was concerned, if it fell to his lot to take an active part in the proceedings of the Association, he was sure they would all do their best to make it a success, so that it might achieve the results for the country which the Secretary of State for War and the Government desired. He did not think there was any better object or one more deserving of encouragement than Cadet Corps in the various large schools throughout the country. (Applause). Of course, they all knew the old story attributed to the Duke of Wellington that the battle of Waterloo was won on the playing fields of Eton. It was exceedingly doubtful if the Duke said anything of the kind [very shrewd of the Earl], and, if he did, the playing fields of Eton in those days were used a great deal more for the purpose of single combat for individual boys than for cricket, which was then very much in its infancy. (Hear, hear). A manly exercise like cricket was a very good thing in its way, but swimming, rifle shooting, and drill were not only manly, but useful pursuits as well, and he believed if any future Duke of Wellington indulged in a reflection as to what had contributed towards winning a great battle in a national crisis, he would be more likely to attribute it to the existence of a Cadet Corps than to cricket. (Hear, hear). He hoped, if a Cadet Corps was formed there, that the County Association might be able to give assistance to it, and to all other similar institutions throughout the county. But the work of the County Association was likely to be very heavy, and likely to have a good many objects to which it would have to devote itself in its early stages, so it would be altogether premature for him to promise that at the celebration of the jubilee of the School there would be a large donation from any central source for the object mentioned. [The School got its cadet force finally in 1909, and still has it.]

Cheers were given for Lord Fortescue, the Head Master, visitors, and others, and the singing of the National Anthem terminated the proceedings.

In the evening, Mrs. Harries [the Headmaster's mother] was "at home" to the Old Boys.

Tuesday, 30th July.

Cricket.

SCHOOL (WITH MASTERS) *v.* OLD BOYS.

This two-days match was begun [today]. The Past were lucky enough to win the toss, and made a good start, having 60 on the board before the first wicket fell. The hundred was reached with 4 wickets down, and the score had been carried to 233 when the last wicket fell. The School then went in, and came out again, not even the most sanguine Old Boy being prepared for the absolute collapse which took place.

1ST INNINGS

OLD BOYS.		SCHOOL.	
J.F. Orchard, st Giffard, b Harries	36	A. Taylor, b Wheadon	9
H.S. Potbury, b Harris	71	R.W. Seldon, b Saunders	5
J.C. Johnson, b Harries	5	Revd. E.C. Harries, b Wheadon	4
G.E.L. Carter, b Taylor	1	J.B. Harris, b Orchard	2
R.P. Wheadon, st Giffard, b Preston	32	S. Bendall, c Carter, b Saunders	0
J. Britton, b Preston	0	W.L. Giffard, b Orchard	1
C. Saunders, c and b Taylor	7	L.K.V. Job, c Carter, b Orchard	1
T.R. Potbury, not out	38	P.J. Were, b Wheadon	1
A.F.C. Martyn, b Taylor	2	A.O. Parker, b Orchard	0
H.R. Champion, b Harris	14	A. Pearce, lbw Orchard	2
S. Chapple, b Taylor	6	A.E. Preston, not out	0
Extras	21	Extras	19
	233		44

In the second innings the School did much better; Mr. Taylor and Mr. Giffard put on 130 for the first wicket, [the final score was 211], and. . . the Old Boys were set to get 27 runs to win, with 9 minutes to get them in. . . .the winning hit [came] off the last ball of the match. [It's *Boys' Own Paper* stuff, isn't it?] [And, once again, the scores don't add up.]

[In the evening] an excellent concert was given, which was largely attended by visitors from the neighbourhood.

The following was the programme:-

1 – PIANO SOLO	March (*Sousa*)		A.H. AUSTIN
2 – SONG & CHORUS	"The Postillion"		THE SCHOOL
3 – SONG & CHORUS	"Queen of Angels"		A. TAYLOR
4 – QUARTETTE	"Sailors' Chorus"		[no performers given]
5 – SONG	"Mary"		J. WHITE
6 – GLEE	"Softly fall the Shades of Evening"		[no performers given]
7 – SONG	"Glorious Devon"		M. WATSON
8 – DUET	"What are the wild waves saying?"	{	A.H. AUSTIN / L.G.H. MAJOR
9 – CHORUS	"Old Towler"		THE CHOIR
10 – SONG	"The Lowland Sea"		Rev. E.C. HARRIES

The Past v. Present Cricket match.   Mr. Chope, of course, is in the middle of the seated row.

The Pavilion during the match.   It was story-book stuff; the Old Boys made the winning hit off the last ball of the match.   One became so familiar with some of these boys that one could name several of them here – sometimes by their stance alone, even at a distance.

'Big School', as it was known, where the prizes were presented. It is a couple of Modern Languages classrooms now.

Mr. Duke has left the Staff [after only one term], and will be replaced by Mr. E.M. Bagshawe, who was a student at Gloucester Theological College, and has since been a master on the training ship "Worcester," and at St. Anne's, Redhill.

W. Saunders [has] passed the Senior Cambridge Local Examination.

The following boys have left the School. The figures indicate the year and term of entering the School. Names in italics are those of day-boys:-

J. I. White, 1902 (2), South Molton
V. J. Battershill, 1904 (3), Exeter
F. J. Brooks, 1905 (2), East Buckland
R. D. Medland, 1906 (3), Bude
B. Webber, 1907 (1), South Molton

[So the average stay of these boys was less than 8 terms – a constant source of concern to the authorities at the time. See Harries' comments at Speech Day the day before.]

Shooting.

The Rifle Club numbered 29 boys during the Summer Term. Besides the usual weekly practice, three Dormitory Competitions were held, of whch the first was a tie and the other two were won by Courtenay. Mr. W.L. Miles, as usual, presented a silver spoon for the highest individual score in each of these competitions.

Mr. Miles has also laid the Club under a further deep obligation, by designing and presenting to the School a framework for disappearing targets, which can be controlled from the firing-point.

The following are the scores in the monthly competitions. Seven shots were fired by each competitor at 15 yards range, and the same number at 25 yards.

I.

BRERETON	15 yds	25 yds	Total	COURTENAY.	15 yds	25 yds	Total
E.A. Adams	25	21	46	L.K.V. Job	28	18	46
A.E. Preston	25	20	45	A.O. Parker	21	18	39
A.J.E. Helps	23	21	44	W. Saunders	24	18	42
W.L. Armstrong	20	17	37	J.B. Harris	26	19	45
	93	79	172		99	73	172

Silver Spoon: E.A. Adams.

II.

V.J. Loram	18	29	47	W. Saunders	22	21	43
E.A. Adams	24	22	46	G.H. Dawe	15	24	39
R.W. Seldon	18	17	35	J.B. Harris	31	20	51
A.J.E. Helps	26	18	44	C.G. Harris	21	20	41
	86	86	172		89	85	173

Courtenay won by 2 points.
[It's 174, actually.]
Silver Spoon: J.B. Harris.

III.

E.A. Adams	18	21	39		C.G. Harris	15	15	30
A.E. Preston	19	20	39		W. Saunders	28	22	50
A.J.E. Helps	20	20	40		J.B. Harris	22	26	48
R.W. Seldon	16	23	39		L.K.V. Job	24	21	45
	73	84	157			89	84	173

Courtenay won by 16 points.
Silver Spoon: W. Saunders.

[In the evening] an excellent concert was given

Wednesday, 31st July.

G.E.L. Carter (1896-1904) obtained a Second Class in the Final Honour School of Modern History at Oxford. W. Stradling (1890-8), 11th Senior Optime, 1901, has taken his M.A. degree.

[The second day of the match between the School (with Masters) and the Old Boys.]

2nd INNINGS.
SCHOOL. OLD BOYS.

A Taylor, b Wheadon	77	J.F. Orchard not out		0
R.W. Seldon, c Orchard, b Wheadon	21	J.C. Johnson, c Harries,		
		b Taylor		11
Revd. E.C. Harries, b Wheadon	12	R.P. Wheadon, not out		16
J.B. Harries, b Wheadon	0			
S. Bendall, b Wheadon	2			
W.L. Giffard, b Orchard	51			
L.K.V. Job, b Saunders	18			
P.J. Were, c Britton, b Saunders	0			
A.O. Parker, run out	15			
A. Pearce, b Orchard	2			
A.E. Preston, not out	1			
Extras	12	Extras		0
Total	211	Total for 1 wicket		27

The Cricket Season, 1907.

The Cricket Season of 1907 was not begun with any great hopes of success. There was not a single colour left, nor did there seem to be any talent to be unearthed; but, by the end of the season, we were almost inclined to be somewhat pleased with ourselves.

In School matches Dame Fortune evidently had not marked us out as her especial favourites, for we had the worst of the light and the wicket against King's, while her confederate, Time – or rather want of him – deprived us of a victory over Somerset County School. In addition to these misfortunes, the School started badly by losing the first match, indeed, towards the end of June only one game had been won.

Every man in the team, however, was a genuine "trier", and the improvement, which was hoped for, had been slowly materialising, so that, from July 3rd onwards,

not a single match was lost, till the Old Boys came down in their might, and inflicted a crushing defeat.

In the Masters' matches Mr. Taylor has proved himself the mainstay of the team, and heads both the batting and bowling averages, which are better than they may seem to be on paper, considering the apology for a summer which was enjoyed for the greater part of the term.

Turning to the boys, Seldon has shown quite exceptional form for his size, and was, by a long way, the best bat in the team. He has plenty of strokes, and, with a little more strength, should develop into a really first-class bat.

The writer will conclude by offering just a few words of advice. We can never win our School matches as long as we take the field convinced that failure is to be our portion. Too much confidence, as is well known, is a bad thing, *but* too little is far worse. Confidence begets success, and enables us to throw off those attacks of "nerves" which were far too prevalent … Above all, let us remember that keen fielding gives half the battle, gives the bowler encouragement, upsets the opposing batsmen, and just turns in our favour that tide, which bears on its crest the word Success.

W.L.G. [Walter Giffard, the master, member of the team, and, it seems, wicket-keeper too. He was still short of his twenty-first birthday when he penned this sage advice.]

MATCHES PLAYED.

	Won	Lost	Drawn
Masters' XI	4	3	2
Boys' XI	2	4	1
Total	6	7	3

AVERAGES.
BATTING.

	Innings	Times not out	Total Runs	Highest Score	Average
A. Taylor	10	1	257	77	28.5
R.W. Seldon	18	1	285	53	16.8
W.L. Giffard	10	0	166	51	16.6
Rev. E.C. Harries	7	0	111	32	15.8
A. Pearce	15	3	86	10	7.2
J.B. Harris	18	1	116	27	6.8
A.E. Preston	18	6	82	19	6.8
A.O. Parker	14	4	64	15	6.4
P.J. Were	11	2	57	20★	6.3
S. Bendall	15	1	66	17★	4.7
L.K.V. Job	15	1	65	18	4.7

★ Not Out.

BOWLING.

	Overs	Maidens	Runs	Wickets	Average
A. Taylor	153	25	446	38	11.7
A. Pearce	89	9	285	23	12.4
J.B. Harris	94	25	257	18	14.3
A.E. Preston	143	25	413	25	16.5

Rev. E.C. Harries took 5 wickets for 87 runs; W. Elworthy, 12 for 105; P.J. Were, 3 for 46; L.K.V. Job, 6 for 109.

Cricket Colours were awarded to – J.B. Harris (Capt), S. Bendall, R.W. Seldon, A.E. Preston, P.J. Were, L.K.V. Job, A.O. Parker, A. Pearce.

The Library.

During the Summer Term 233 books were issued from the Library – almost exactly half the number issued during the corresponding term of 1906. We have no theory to account for the great decrease, which, we hope, was only temporary.

We acknowledge with thanks the following gifts to the Library:-

[In the following lists – before someone writes and tells me I am wrong - the editor's use of commas and full stops in conjunction with inverted commas and brackets does not follow contemporary usage. I give it as he wrote it.]

From Mr. H.R. Hopper:
"Both Sides the Border," by G.A. Henty.
"At the Point of the Sword," by H. Hayens.
"Frank Fairleigh," by F.E. Smedley.
"The One Before," by Barry Pain.
"Two Little Travellers," by R. Cunningham.

Our hearty thanks are [also] due to Mr. Hopper, the father of one of the present boys [in Form III], for his gift … of the Encyclopaedia Britannica, in 25 volumes, sumptuously bound. We hope that boys in the upper forms will frequently find occasion to consult the pages of this valuable acquisition.

From A. Small (1863–70):
"The Young Cricketer's Tutor," by John Nyren.

From R.P. Chope (1874–81): [whose generosity was almost as inexorable as his industry]
"Flowers of the Field," by C.A. Johns. (With 92 coloured plates and 245 other illustratons).

"Stag Hunting on Exmoor," by P. Evered. (With 74 photographic illustrations).
"Crystallography," by J.B. Jordan. (With a set of 40 models of crystals).
"Memoirs of Benvenuto Cellini." [I bet that was in hot demand.]
A second set of Stereoscopic Slides: "The Natural History Museum."
"Puck of Pook's Hill," by Rudyard Kipling.
"Drake and the Dons," by R. Lovett.
"Famous Discoveries by Land and Sea."
"Captain Singleton," by Daniel Defoe.
"Typee," by Herman Melville.
"Tom Brown's Schooldays," by Thomas Hughes.
"The Wreck of the Grosvenor," by W. Clark Russell.

From C. Bendall (1900–4):
"Barnaby Rudge," by Chas. Dickens.
"The House of the Wolf," by Stanley Weyman.
"The Prince and the Pauper," by Mark Twain.
"Adventures of Tom Sawyer," by Mark Twain.

From R.J. Buckingham (1900–6):
"All Astray," by Ascott R. Hope.

From H.J. Harris (1903–7):   [He left at Easter.]
"Rupert of Hentzau," by Anthony Hope.   (Sequel to "The Prisoner of Zenda.")

From W.G. Jewell (1906–7):   [He too left at Easter.]
"Three Midshipmen," by W.H.G. Kingston.

End of July entries.

Devon County School.
Balance Sheet.
Made up approximately to July 31st 1907.

Liabilities		£	s	d	£	s	d	Assets	£	s	d	£	s	d
Debenture Stock (Old)					80	.	.	Land	607	9	7			
Debenture Debt. (New)	Earl Fortescue	1000	.	.				Buildings	10813	8	.	11420	17	7
	M. B. Snell	1350	.	.				Furniture and Effects	381	8	1			
	W. H. Adams	500	.	.				Less 3% written off for depreciation	11	8	6			
	R. P. Chope	150	.	.	3000	.	.		369	19	7			
Mortgage Debt.	Earl Fortescue				2000	.	.	Stock and Plant	437	5	1	807	4	8
Scholarship Funds.	"Shephard Jew"	64	15	11				River Plate & Gen. Invest. Trust Co. 4% Pref. Stock				1000	.	.
	"Old Boys"	72	2	.	136	17	11	Amount due from Parents	209	.	10			
School Library					20	1	2	Less 10% reserved	20	18	.	188	2	10
Games Fund					50	13	7	Bank – Balance on Current a/c				116	4	8
Tradesmen – due on accounts					205	12	2	Officers – Secretary, Headmaster & Matron						
								Petty Cash in hands of	48	5	11			
Balance					8091	15	4	W. A. Knight – due on Headmaster Book	4	4	6	52	10	5
				£	13585	.	2					£ 13585	.	2

Dr.			Profit and Loss Account.				Cr.		

1907			£	s	d	1907		£	s	d
Jan 1	To Balance		1033	18	3	Jan 1	By 10% reserved for Parents – reversed	24	.	.
July 31	Guarantee Fund (closed)		36	11	1		Sir T. Acland – written off	231	18	9
	10% reserve on Book Debts		20	18	.		Viscount Clifden do	231	13	2
	3% depreciation on Furniture		11	8	6		Earl Fortescue – release of part of Mortgage	892	15	.
							Capital a/c – closed	240	.	.
	Balance		8091	15	4		Debenture Stock – surrendered	7568	.	.
							Profit on 2 Terms working	6	4	3

Statement of Receipts & Expenditure Jan. 1st to July 31st 1907.

Expenditure		£	s	d	£	s	d	£	s	d	Receipts	£	s	d	£	s	d
Tuition	Salaries				492	11	2										
	Advertisement	53	.	.							Fees from Parents for Board, Tuition, Music						
	Chemicals	11	1	10							and all extras	1177	11	7	1177	11	7
	Prizes	7	12	3													
	Stationery	19	16	6	91	10	7	584	1	9	Balance of Board of Education grant for 1906	60	15	.			
Board	General	5	13	6							Less amount granted to Masters	34	1	3	26	13	9
	Bread, Cake & Flour	54	6	8													
	Meat	208	18	10							Balance of Interest Charges account				22	7	.
	Dairy – Butter, Milk & Eggs	56	13	11													
	Groceries	63	16	4							County Council Grant for Science Master				93	6	.
	Vegetables	32	17	.													
	Ale & Mineral waters	11	15	.													
	Coal & Coke	66	1	3													
	Oil, Lamps & Glasses	15	14	11													
	Wages	183	15	5	699	12	10										
	Less Repayments by Masters & Boys	63	4	9													
	Allowance for Masters Board – charged in Tuition	83	6	8													
	Sundry Small receipts	1	11	.													
	Balance of Garden account	31	12	6													
	do Poultry do	1	4	3	180	19	2	518	13	8							
Rent, Rates & Taxes					40	1	10										
House Repairs and Renewals					27	13	7										
Furniture Repairs & Household Requisites					18	4	.										
Legal Charges – Messrs Ford, Harris & Ford					38	8	5										
Sundries – Scholarships, Insurances, Licences,																	
Cheque Book, Sick Room Requisites,																	
Annual Lists, Secretary Salary,																	
Hire of Piano & Sundries					86	11	10	210	19	8							
Balance – Profit								6	4	3							
						£ 1319	19	4					£ 1319		

The six-monthly July balance sheet. In Judy Taylor's impeccable handwriting.

August

Thursday, 1st August.

The number of School Challenge Cups is gradually increasing. For the latest addition we are indebted to Dr. Wiliam [sic] Hill (1870—1874), whose Dormitory Sports Cup was won by Courtenay this year ... [see 20th May] To future benefactors we might perhaps suggest cups for cross-country running and for shooting.

Weather.

> "When that chill June with sleet and icy shoures
> Hath frozen all the sap in summer's floures,
> And cuckoo, waxing wroth, with irous din
> Cries out that winter is icumen in ... "

The following table shows the temperatures and rainfall during the three months of the Summer Term, 1907 – a term which, we hope, will long hold the record for cold and rain. The year 1907 has so far presented the extraordinary phenomena of April being colder than March, and June as cold as May. [An autumn editorial later complained that 'all the cricket weather has somehow got into the Christmas Term', when the football was 'in full swing'.]

	May.	June.	July.
Highest Temperature	68°	66°	79°
Lowest	40°	48·5°	51°
Average	54·9°	55°	61·9°
Rainy Days	20	24	12
Total Rainfall	3·14	4·59	2·50

The total rainfall for the term was 10.23 inches, compared with 7.76 in the previous summer, and 5.34 in 1905.

[These figures are punctuated strictly according to the text of the *Register*. That is, the decimals in the three columns have the decimal point midway; the decimals in the summary sentence underneath have the decimal point on the line. Heaven knows why – though, with such precision of punctuation, as indicated a hundred times elsewhere in the *Register's* pages, it is quite likely that there was a good reason.

[Finally, the word 'irous' in the third line of the verse. It is Middle English - Chaucerian. Comes from the Latin root meaning 'anger' – think of our old word 'ire'.]

Friday, 2nd August.

At the 75th annual meeting of the British Medical Association, held at Exeter from 27th July to [today] ... Dr. William Hill (1870-4) opened the special discussion in the Laryngology, Otology, and Rhinology Section, on "The Treatment of Chronic Suppuration of the Middle Ear without resort to the Radical (Complete) Mastoid Operation." [sic]

[This looks like the Dr. 'Wiliam' Hill who presented the Dormitory Sports Cup recorded yesterday. From celebration to suppuration – a big leap.]

Saturday, 3rd August.

Old Boys' News.

[A school would not normally have many entries for August, because of the summer holidays. This gives the editor the chance to put in some of the many titbits which the *Register* published about its old pupils. News about them would have come in anyway in dribs and drabs, so few of the items would have been tied to a particular date – except, as luck would have it, for the piece under 2nd August above. All the following notes, and others entered under later dates, come from the *Registers* – three of them from February, June, and October, 1907, and one from February, 1908, which of course would look back to the previous Christmas Term.]

M.B. Snell, J.P. (1866-70) has been appointed Deputy-Chairman of the International Financial Society, Ltd. [An ex-head boy, later a stockbroker, and clearly 'doing very well', he was one of the team who had put together a recent rescue package for the School's finances – see 15th May, 2nd October, and 2nd November.]

Bullen Spicer (1871-3), the well-known Army and Civil Service tutor, has been successful in getting one of his pupils the second place in the recent competitive examination for Commissions in the Indian Police. There were nearly 200 candidates, and Mr. Spicer's pupil passed at the first trial, after only six month's [sic] special coaching. [See also 1st March.]

F.B. Ollis (1870-3), chief constructor of Pembroke Dockyard, has been appointed constructive manager of Chatham Dockyard. [Would he have been involved in the building or maintenance of the new Dreadnought battleships? The first was completed in 1907.]

A.E. Barrington (1870-2), Bailiff of Dartmoor, was the recipient, on the occasion of his recent marriage, of a handsome silver bowl, silver candlesticks, and an illuminated address, from the Dartmoor tenants of the Prince of Wales and other residents of the Princetown district. [The prisoners too?]

S. Algar (1903-4) has just left England to take an appointment as civil engineer under the Hudson Company of New York. The Company is boring a tunnel under the Hudson River between New York and New Jersey. It is estimated that the tunnel will take about eight years to complete.

Saturday, 10th August.

More Old Boys' News.

Ernest J. Stroud (1884) has been elected first Captain of the recently formed "Plymouth (Sir Francis Drake) Bowling Club." [sic] The Club has been granted a suitable site for a bowling green on the Hoe, "upon which," the Secretary alleges, "the game has not been played since the ever-memorable time when Sir Francis Drake first sighted the Spanish Armada." Everybody is familiar with the tradition of Drake's sublime bravado on that occasion through the graphic description in Kingsley's famous novel, *Westward Ho!* and the picturesque representation in Seymour Lucas's no less famous picture, but Henry Newbolt's fine poem, *Admirals All*, is not so well known as it should be:-

> He was playing at Plymouth a rubber of bowls
>   When the great Armada came;
> But he said, "They must wait their turn, good souls,"
>   And he stooped and finished the game.

Other Old Boys noted as bowlers are Charles Newland (1875-9), who has won many trophies in New Zealand, and C.R. Doe (1877), who is one of the best players in the Torrington Club – the champion club in the county, and the only one with a continuous history from the days of Drake himself.

N. Dyer Hurdon (1860-1) of Exeter, Ontario, is described in the papers as the organizer of the ceremony of "Raising the Flag" which was presented to the school of that town by the schools of Exeter, England. He is said to be "a most enthusiastic loyalist, who is known far and wide as one who delights in doing honour to all that is British." [I can't go on putting 'sic' at these points, merely to indicate that the inverted commas in this sort of situation should be inside the full stop, not outside it, or I shall be in line for the label of 'pedant' just as much as the late Mr. Chope was. Clearly the editors did not regard the point as important, if indeed they regarded it at all. They did it all the time.] Two of his sons, dressed as sailors, took part in the ceremony, the flag being raised amid the cheers of the people, the band playing "God Save the King", and the volleys of the soldiers. Mr. Hurdon's song, "We'll keep the old flag flying," was also sung.

Friday, 16th August.

[A second glimpse of the brave and resourceful Westcott Stile Abell – see 8th February. A third appears on 21st September.]

W.S. Abell (1890-2) has been appointed Instructor in Naval Architecture at the Royal Naval College, Greenwich, to date 16th August. He has recently been granted a patent for an ingenious invention for automatically controlling the cooling or heating of buildings or ships by the circulation of a constant volume of a gas or liquid. The thermostatic device comprises electrical resistance thermometers arranged in a Wheatstone bridge circuit, and this controls the operation of an electromotor for working a single valve which divides the current of gas or liquid into two portions, one of which is heated or cooled while the other is kept at the same temperature until the two portions are again mixed together for further circulation. The temperature of the space affected is thus automatically kept between two given temperatures. [So now you know.]

Another Old Boy, H.R. Hearson, (1874-7), of Shanghai [whose activities were also recorded on 8th February], has also obtained a patent for an instrument for centering and gauging iron bars in preparation for the operation of turning

or boring in a lathe. It works on the principle of the iris diaphragm employed in photographic cameras. [Ah!]

Saturday, 17th August.

More than one inch of rain fell today.

Tuesday, 20th August.

G.E. Mortimer (1891-6) who, while at School, won the Fives Competitions for two or three years in succession, has continued his successes in Huddersfield, where he is now living. He won the Huddersfield Five Club Singles Cup in three consecutive years, and with his partner won the Doubles no less than four times.

Harold H. Hilton (1877-8) has expanded the article on his early golfing days, quoted in the last *Register*, into a book entitled "My Golfing Reminiscences," which has recently been published by Nisbet and Co.

[Hilton, who did not learn his golf at school, was however lionised as the School's 'most distinguished athlete' – *Register* CXXXIII, June, 1907, p. 251 – almost certainly written by the tireless R.P. Chope, in one of his exhaustive articles for that magazine's weary editors. He – Hilton – was the only amateur to have won the Open Championship twice - up to 1907, that is. He also won the Amateur Championship of England twice, and that of Ireland four times.]

Monday & Tuesday, 26th & 27th August.

W. Stradling (1890-8) has been playing cricket for the Somerset Stragglers during the vacation. In the match against North Devon at Instow [today and yesterday] he compiled 65 runs in the second innings, including eight 4's and four 3's.

[For information on Stradling, see 8th February.]

Saturday, 31st August.

W. Stradling [still playing for Somerset Stragglers], in the match against Sidmouth … played another good innings of 63.

A gifted Old Boy – William Stradling. He was the son of a milk roundsman from Chittlehampton. He won every cup, prize, medal, and honour in the School's gift, went on to read Maths at Cambridge, and became a teacher.

End of August entries.

September

Monday, 2nd September.

The following boys [have] entered the School. Names in italics are those of day boys:-

FORM III.
L.A. Murless, Exmouth
S.H. Oatway, Barnstaple
J. Pow, Combemartin
[elsewhere we have had 'Combmartin', but not, so far, 'Combe Martin'}

FORM II.

G. Anstey, Filleigh	J.E. Pidsley, Sidmouth
*G.L. Blight, Port Isaac, Cornwall	*J. Wells, Winchester
A.E. Brooks, East Buckland	W.J.B. Wood, Bristol

* Sons of Old Boys.

The Entrance Examination for Old Boys' Entrance Scholarships was announced: 'Full particulars can be obtained from the Head Master, and we hope that readers of the *Register* will make these Scholarships known among their friends.'

Wednesday, 4th September.

W. ANDREW (1896-8) died at Dicty, Wyoming ... of typhoid fever ... aged 24. Familiarly known as "Polar," he was very popular at School. His death was very sad, as he had been away from home for nearly five years, and died without any of his friends knowing of his illness.

Tuesday, 10th September.

Engineer Commander Wallace Wright, R.N. (1875-80), was appointed to the "Isis" on recommissioning.

Monday, 16th September.

The appointment of Mr. Walter Longueville Giffard to the staff was made definitive. [See 5th May.]
Mr. Ernest Murray Bagshawe has joined the staff in succession to Mr. Duke, who left in July [after only one term]. Mr. Bagshawe was a student at Gloucester Theological College, and has since been a master on the training-ship "Worcester," and at St. Anne's, Redhill.

A School Choral Society has been formed ... and [plans to meet] on Thursday evenings after Preparation.

The Choir.

The following boys [form] the School Choir. . . :-
A.L.J. Youings (12), R.W. Seldon (11), H.G. Hopper (7), A.J.E. Helps (5), L.G.H. Major (5), A.H. Austin (4), E.A. Adams (4), C.G. Harris (4), H.J. Richard (4), G.H. Dawe (2), E.B. Driver (2), A.P. Moor (3), E.W. Oakey (2), M.R. Roberts (2).
The figures in brackets denote the number of Terms in the Choir.

Tuesday, 17th September.

The enlargement of the heating apparatus in the east wing is to be carried out this winter ... . The last instalment of the debt on the Cricket Pavilion has been paid [the old one had blown down in a storm in 1903]; ... a room has at last been set apart solely for Art work, thereby relieving the pressure on the ordinary class-rooms; and finally the desks in Big School [see 29th July] have been rearranged, so that the principal light falls from the left. [So presumably no pupils were left-handed? Or were *allowed* to be left-handed?]

Saturday, 21st September.

The Training of Engineers.

'The development of engineering science, with the attendant increased application of its principles to the uses of everyday life, is one of the striking features of modern civilization. It seems likely that at no distant date some form of instruction in elementary engineering science will be included in the curriculum of secondary schools.'

[This is how W.S. Abell began his article for the *Register*. An Old Boy of the School (1890-92), Abell by this time had a distinguished record behind him in naval engineering. On 16th August (q.v.) he had been appointed Instructor in Naval Architecture at the Royal Naval College, Greenwich. His brother (1892-95) pursued a closely similar career. See 8th February.

His article is included here – or rather the barest of references to it – because it indicates one or two features of interest, and even possibly of relevance to today.

First, he was clearly right about about the increasing importance of a science like engineering to modern society. Sadly, he was over-optimistic in his prediction that 'some form of elementary engineering science will be included in the curriculum of secondary schools'. We are still waiting for this.

And finally, it offers a fertile idea to harassed editors of school magazines who may be short of ideas: why not include in each number a similar article, written by an current expert and a practitioner, on a profession, trade, or calling, to give student readers an insight into life at the sharp end of various jobs and careers?

In keeping with the thoroughness of writing in those days, Mr. Abell's remarks on 'the training of engineers', which he referred to as 'this brief note', ran nevertheless to nearly six pages.]

The School Choir, with its choirmaster, Mr. Taylor (who was also the local church organist). On the back is written 'Xmas 1907' in Mr. Taylor's careful handwriting. By dint of comparing the faces with those of a play cast of 1908 (in which the actors were identified) – see p.159 – I solved several problems. Three more faces belonged to known sportsmen, which took me further. Finally, the Register *printed the number of terms each boy had served. It seemed logical to suppose that those with the longest service might be in the front row, and those with 'middling' service might be in the middle, and so on. And that did the trick. I can feel fairly confident in naming them all. See the Boys' Biographies.*

Saturday, 28th September.

Football.

FIRST XI. (WITH MASTERS) *v.* BARNSTAPLE TOWN.
Won, 6-3.

This match was played at home … Both the ground and the weather were just right for a good fast game. The School started playing uphill, and some ten minutes from the kick-off Mr. Taylor scored. The Town were not long before they equalised, but then Bendall raced away to the top corner and put in a good centre, which Mr. Giffard turned into the net. Once more ahead, the school settled down to good Footer [sic], Seldon being the next to score, while Mr. Giffard added a fourth. The Town then got going again, and scored twice – one a rather lucky shot from long range – but the School were not to be denied, and, putting on two more goals, ran out easy winners by 6 goals to 3.

A portrait and biographical sketch of Professor Hearson appeared today in the *Western Weekly News.* [See also 8th February.]

[Today marks the end of] the longest rainless period of the year so far – twenty-two days. [Predictably, with autumn coming, it proved to be the longest rainless period of the whole year.]

Monday, 30th September.

[This has proved to be] the driest month (·90 inch) [of the year to date].

End of September entries.

October

Tuesday, 1st October.

Old Boys' News.

The article on "Old Boys as Athletes" in the last *Register* [written by that distinguished Old Boy, R.P. Chope – who else? – but not included in this book] should have included the name of J. Arnold Hill, A.C.A. (1887-8), as a distinguished oarsman. He rowed from 1892 to 1900, first for the Anglian Club, and afterwards for the Thames Rowing Club, of which he is now Honorary Auditor. During this time he won about twenty "pots". He rowed in either an eight or a four at most of the Thames Regattas, including the Metropolitan, Kingston, Molesey, Walton, Reading, and Henley, and he rowed at Henley in 1895 against the Dutch crew that came over and made a record for the Thames Cup, which they succeeded in taking out of the country for the first time in its history.

[Mr. Chope's article does deserve quoting, however, for this titbit. There has been much uncertainty about the winter game played at the Devon County School – was it football or rugby? Mr. Chope records that the School played football according to its own rules till about 1876, when it switched to rugby. Then came three headmasters (1888 to 1906), each with sympathy for the Association version, allied to high skill and distinction in the game. So the return switch was made. The School did not revert to rugby again until the mid-1920's.]

J. Pearce (1900-5) has been gazetted Second-Lieutenant in the 4th V.B.D.R. ['V.B.D.R'? See 1st February.]

Cricket in the Past.

[Guess who wrote this. Mr. Chope was a compulsive contributor to the *Register*. There is something unstoppable about an energetic and determined benefactor, and the editors were only human. It is to their credit that they inflicted, and actually confessed to having inflicted, 'severe condensation' upon his articles (see 4th May), and worried about braving his wrath once the magazine was in print. I have had to do the same, or Mr. Chope would have been threatening to take over this book as well. When it is pointed out that the original ran to nearly seven pages, the reader may well begin to sympathise with the editors. I am luckier than they were; I do not have to face Mr. Chope's displeasure. This effort appeared in the October, 1907 number. Here it is, with necessary gaps, in Chope's own words.]

'My note [note – three and a half pages!] on "Football in the Past" ... was received with so much favour that I am encouraged to give a corresponding note on cricket. However, I must explain at the outset that the D.C.S. never had its own rules for cricket, as it had for football. Cricket was always cricket, unless one has to except the popular "tip and run" in the "dimmit," when the light was failing, and an occasional single-wicket match. It may be, too, that such matches as the First Eleven v. the Next Twenty-two, and the First Eleven with Broomsticks v. the Second Eleven with Bats, would nowadays be considered rather as curiosities suitable for a country fête than as serious cricket ...

'I must confess, not without some fear and trembling, that cricket was never a favourite game of mine ... However, long before I played for the School, I occupied the important post of scorer – and only those who have acted in the capacity know how important it is – and thus saw more cricket than falls to the lot of most boys who were better players than myself.

'After this lapse of time I cannot enumerate all the grounds we visited, but I have distinct recollections of ... the best "foreign" ground, and the one on which we played most frequently ... Instow, the ground of the Gentlemen of North Devon. Beautifully situated on a sandy soil, the pitch was good in all weathers. When I first went to the School, the line from Taunton to Barnstaple was not opened, so the boys drove in a break [an open, four-wheeled, horse-drawn carriage] to Barnstaple and then took train, and the railway officials were so obliging as to stop immediately opposite to the cricket ground, which ... is a considerable distance from the station. After a time this concession was withdrawn, and the boys then began the practice of throwing out their bags and other things to save themselves the trouble of carrying them back to the field. This, of course, took some time, and on one occasion J.A. Potbury delayed so long that his bag struck against the hut by the side of the line and bounded back beneath the wheels of the carriage. Fortunately, the bag and its contents suffered more than the train, but from that time the practice was prohibited ...

'A still more romantic, but much less suitable, situation for a cricket ground was that at Winsford, in the heart of Exmoor. This was reached by a lovely drive of seven or eight miles from Dulverton up the valley of the Exe. The cricket field was the only bit of level ground in the place, and was situated by the side of the river, into which it was easy to hit the ball, and it was so wet and swampy that it is said Mr. Llewellin once pitched a ball rather short and it stuck in the mud between the wickets. The only parallel case I remember took place at the School after I left – a swallow on the wing was killed by the ball between the wickets in the ordinary course of bowling. The quaint thatched inn at Winsford – "The Royal Oak" – once witnessed a sensational finish to a stag-hunt. Being hard pressed, the stag made his way into the back entrance of the inn, and in the passage met a waitress carrying a tray of glasses, which, strange to say, was not dropped. The stag, seeing an open doorway, passed into the best sitting-room, which was prepared for guests, while the ready-witted waitress shut the door. Thus trapped, the stag was easily secured, the field watching the proceedings through the narrow window panes. ...

'The School match against Brushford ... was marked by a curious incident. Mr. Sydenham and Baker (of Winsford) were batting, and in taking a short run they were watching the ball so closely that they came into violent collision in the middle of the pitch, like a pair of rams. Baker's mouth was badly cut … Sydenham lay stunned on the ground for some minutes … his first action on recovering consciousness was to get up and continue his run … oblivious of the fact that the wicket had been put down long before.' [Could this have been the inspiration for the incident at the end of the famous cricket match described by A.G. Macdonnell in his book *England Their England*?]

Wednesday, 2nd October.

FIRST XI. *v.* SOUTH MOLTON Y.M.C.A.
Won, 5 – 0

[The Register offers no date for this match, but it is placed on the page between the dated matches of Saturday, 28th September and Saturday, 5th October, and the normal alternative day for matches was Wednesday. Nor, unusually, does the report say where the match took place. But, since the next report, from 5th October, refers to their 'first away match', we know that this one was played at home.]

For their second match the school had as opponents the South Molton Y.M.C.A., and gained an easy victory by 5 goals to *nil*. Though possessing several good men, the Y.M. did not work together well enough to cause much anxiety to Preston and Were, while Lewis had an easy time between the sticks.

The result was that our forwards, given plenty of chances, showed some really effective combination. Seldon was the first to score, after some nice passing by the whole of the front rank, while Bendall put in some good centres from the left corner-flag, most of which were turned to account, Seldon doing the hat-trick, while Petherick obtained the other two.

The Reading and Debating Society.

The 111th meeting. There were 26 members and 3 visitors present.

S. Bendall was in the chair. [He was the newly-chosen President – see 25th March. It seems that the master in charge, Mr. Fry, had decided that the Society was now, after four years, sufficiently established, and its members sufficiently experienced in debating protocol, to allow the pupil president to take the chair. Bendall presided, with one exception, at all the other debates, till he left at the end of the Christmas term. Full stops present or absent by courtesy of the Hon. Sec..]

The minutes of the previous meeting having been read and confirmed, J.B. Harris, before the ordinary proceedings had commenced, moved, "That at the next meeting the rules be revised, and afterwards printed. R T H Hooper second the motion.

The president, having welcomed the members, then called upon Mr. Britton [an Old Boy, now a visitor or a student teacher - see 25th March, 3rd June, and 13th December] to propose his motion which was in favour of Socialism." [Where did these inverted commas come from? And there is another pair missing seven lines up. Indeed the Secretary's punctuation generally was a mite random, as will be seen.]

The hon. member commenced by saying, that it was a great mistake to class socialism with anarchism. A socialist did all in his power to help his fellow creatures, but an anarchist was just the opposite.

The great aim of Socialism was to make all men as equal as possible, and to do this they had at first to do away with the land lord principle. Already people had formed colonies with this object in view, and these were the people who were building up Socialism

He then went on to say that under Socialistic management the question of the "Unemployed" would be successfully dealt with. An organisation would be formed for the purpose of dividing them up into skilled and unskilled workmen.

The skilled unemployed workmen would be given "work" that would suit his [sic] knowledge, whilst the unskilled man would be taught some useful occupation.

Each person would be compelled to work for about 8 hours per. day. In this way it was hoped that incomes would become more equal.

Of late years machinery had been introduced into some kinds of work. The hon member thought it would be a fine thing when the dangerous work of the miner was done by machinery.

All these changes would however take place very gradually indeed.

W.L. Giffard in opposing commenced by saying that at present Socialism was only a theory. The theory was that all classes should be made equal. It was impossible to put this in practice as superior beings would always go ahead of inferior.

The hon member thought it impossible to solve the question of the unemployed. There would always be men who would rather sponge upon other people than work for themselves. At the present time socialists were advocating equality of sexes and women suffrage.

If these were obtained the whole system of domestic life would be altered. Another drawback to Socialism was the way they treated religion. With them religion is put aside. Without religion a state soon becomes degenerate and decays, for example Rome.

G.C. Fry. Esq explained that he was not a Socialist. On the other hand he had been gradually drawn further and further away from Socialism. He thought that in England, it would be very hard to form a community for the purpose of paying people who worked under Socialistic principles. Even now it was hard enough to obtain an honest County Council.

He thought that millionaires did not deserve their money. They did not obtain their money honestly, but simply by good fortune. The income tax should be so regulated as to fall heavily on such people.

W.L. Miles Esq said that he had no particular theory on the subject of Socialism, but he thought it impossible to work it practically. He explained that machinery did not at present stop men in a coal mine from inhaling nauseous gases.

Rev E C Harries thought that Socialism would stamp out all individualism. The fame of inventors and discoverers would be forgotten.

W L. Giffard Esq. Summing up disagreed with Mr Fry on the question of machinery. Without machinery civilisation would recede. He thought it would not be an encouragement to a man to work if he had to always share his income with other people.

J Britton. Esq. In conclusion explained that with Social-ism every man would have a share in the profits of the work he is doing.

He thought that Socialism would be the perfection of lawmaking.

The House then divided & the motion was lost by 3 votes to 22 [One wonders, in a school like this, whether the majority were Liberals or Conservatives.]

The House adjourned at 8.- 30 pm.

Old Boys' Gathering.

The monthly social gatherings of the London section proved so enjoyable last winter that it was unanimously decided to hold another series during the present winter. The place of meeting has been changed to Anderton's Hotel, Fleet Street, and the day to the first Wednesday in each month, with the one exception of January, when the Annual Dinner took the place of a "Social". The October … gathering … [was] presided over … by Prof. T.A. Hearson, M. Inst. C.E., M.I.N.A., F.I.P.A.,Vice-President of the Old Boys' Association, and Chairman of the London Committee.

The *Western Weekly News* reported:-

"A goodly number of the London section of the Devon County School Old Boys' Association gathered at Anderton's Hotel … at the first social of the session. Prof. T.A. Hearson, who presided, was supported on his right by Mr. M.B. Snell [see also 15th May, 3rd August, and 2nd November], and on his left by his son, Mr. H.F.P. Hearson, last year's captain of Cambridge University Rugby XV, and now captain of the Richmond team.

"A supper preceded the smoker. The latter was under the capable management of Mr. G.M. Chard. After a pianoforte sole by Mr. Hooper, came Mr. Eastman with 'The Yeoman's Wedding.' A very humorous recitiation by Mr. Hearson, jun., followed, entitled 'The Jubilee Cup,' by Quiller Couch. Later he gave 'Etiquette.' Following Mr. Harding, who sang 'The Wood,' came Mr. R.P. Chope, with a reading from Jan Stewer's collection – 'A Love Affair.' ['Jan Stewer' was the pen name of Arthur Coles, who for years wrote articles and stories in the Devon accent for the *Devon and Exeter Gazette*. R.P. Chope, besides being a fearsome polymath and a ruthless contributor to the School magazine, was also an expert on the Devon accent, and gave frequent recitations up and down the county.] Jan Stewer was again requisitioned when Mr. Small gave 'Squire Thorne's Fire Escape.' 'Drinking,' a song by Mr. Smith, was followed by Mr. Eastman, who sang 'The Sailor's Grave.' Mr. A.J. Pride sang 'The Song of the School,' the chorus of which was taken up with great heartiness."

FIRST XI. (WITH MASTERS) *v.* BARNSTAPLE Y.M.C.A. Won, 4 – 2

Our first away match was played in Rock Park… under conditions not exactly conducive to good football, for the grass was too long, and rain fell throughout the game, and rendered accurate kicking impossible.

The School lost the toss, and Mr. Taylor kicked off towards the Pavilion end, but the Y.M. were responsible for most of the attacking. A miskick by one of our backs led to a scramble in front of goal, from which they scored, and before the game was ten minutes older they had scored again. Just before half-time, however, a faulty clearance by the home goal-keeper enabled Mr. Giffard to score our first goal. After change of ends the school showed much better form, and Mr. Taylor put us level with a real hot drive, while soon afterwards Seldon shot hard for goal and the ball glanced off one of their backs into the net. The next goal came from a good centre by Bendall, and five minutes later the whistle blew for time, leaving us victorious by four goals to two.

Monday, 7th October.

University Local Examinations.
HONOURS LISTS.

[The Oxford Local Examinations, and the Cambridge ones, were set up in 1858, to provide a national system for measuring the progress of secondary pupils right across the country. They each had a Junior and a Senior section, and national lists were published, not only of schools' joint successes, but also of pupils' individual achievements. So a school could come top of the national league, and the Devon County School did so in the 1860's – three times. A boy could also come 'top' in the whole country, and some pupils of the Devon County School did just that too. The 'Locals', as they became known, were the ancestor of School Certificate till 1950, 'O' and 'A' Levels till 1988, and GCSE thereafter.]

Mr. R.P. Chope [who else?] published, in the October number of the *Register*, an exhaustive list of all the leading exam successes gained by the School since 1862, right up to 1906 [including his own - he scored triumphs in 'Class I' in both senior and junior sections of both universities - of course.]

Wednesday, 9th October.

FIRST XI. *v.* SOMERSET COUNTY SCHOOL. Lost, 1 – 4.

Played at Wellington … and resulted in a win for the home team by four goals to one. The first half was very evenly contested, the game being very fast. After half-time, however, superior combination gradually wore down our defence, with the result stated above.

SECOND XI. *v.* SOMERSET COUNTY SCHOOL 2nd XI.
Lost, 0 – 1.

While the 1st XI. were away at Wellington, the 2nd team received a visit from Somerset County School 2nd XI., and a most enjoyable game ensued. The School kicked off with the sun at their backs, and for some time neither side got going, but our opponents soon forced two corners, both of which proved fruitless. Half-time arrived with the score sheet blank. From the restart Wellington pressed, but Squire and Parker played a sterling game at back, and managed to keep them out till about fifteen minutes from the end, when, from a scrum in front of goal, they scored the only goal of the match. Both sides missed several chances of scoring, but Wellington deserved to win, for they were much superior forward.

Saturday, 12th October.

FIRST XI. *v.* NORTH MOLTON.
Won, 4 – 0.

… We were at home to North Molton, and a good game resulted, for we had to fight harder to win than the final score might indicate. Molton chose to play uphill, with the wind at their backs, but could make little headway against a strong defence. Bendall opened our account with a characteristic rush, while Seldon shortly afterwards added the finishing touch to an effective piece of combination. Our opponents fought hard to prevent further score, but, by the time the whistle went, we had added two more goals, thus winning by four goals to *nil.*

Entertainment.

… Mr. H. Stafford Webber paid us a second visit [the first was in March, 1906], and gave a Dramatic Recital which was intensely enjoyed both by the School and by a considerable number of visitors. The following was his programme:-

PART I.

Scenes from "As You Like It."

1. The Quarrel
2. Rosalind is banished.
3. Adam implores Orlando to flee from his brother's vengeance.
4. The Forest. Rosalind meets Orlando, who takes her for "a pretty youth."
5. Touchstone and his rival.

PART II.

1. Fuzzy-Wuzzy … … … … … … … Kipling
2. The Young Idea … … … … … … … MS.
3. Scandal … … … … … … … … Anon.
4. A Pastoral Play … … … … … … … Anstey
5. Dialogue from a London Dinner Party … Anthony Hope
6. Admirals All … … … … … … … Newbolt
7. The Enthusiast's Proposal.
8. Reminiscences of a Dramatic Sketch.

Sunday, 13th October.

Mr. Webber – [see above – 12th October] who [is] staying with the Head Master for the week-end, kindly gave the boys some readings, including the speeches of the Chorus in *Henry V*, Tennyson's *Voyage of Maeldune*, and several shorter pieces.

Monday, 14th October.

… An Ordinary Meeting of the Governors, duly convened by the Secretary, [was] held at The George Hotel, South Molton.
<u>Present</u> The Rev J.H. Copleston (in the Chair). Messrs. G.C. Smyth-Richards, C.
Pearce, G.A.W. Thorold, W.P. Hiern & J. Sanders (Governors), also R.P. Chope & The Rev J.H. Thompson (prospective Governors), the Head Master (The Rev E.C. Harries) and the Secretary.

1. The minutes of the last meeting were read and confirmed.
2. A letter was read from the Rt. Hon. Earl Fortescue, resigning the Chairmanship of the Governing Body, and another one respecting the stand the County Council have taken with regard to the School.
3. The Report of the Inspectors of the Board of Education on the School was received and discussed.
4. Resulting from the Governors' application to the County Council for a grant towards the cost of new heating apparatus for the east wing of the School buildings, a letter from the Education Committee, dated 19th September, enquiring what steps the Governors were taking in order to earn the highest grant payable under the new Regulations of the Board of Education for Secondary Schools was read, and this together with the stand that the County Council had more recently taken with regard to the School (as was understood from the newspaper reports – no official communication having been received) were fully discussed. The main points considered were the denominational character of the School, the percentage of the free places to be offered to boys from Elementary Schools, and the constitution of the Governing Body under the new Scheme. It was resolved that a letter, which had been drafted and which was read at the Meeting, should be sent to the Chairman of the County Education Committee, giving a detailed explanation of the Governors' position with reference to the new "Regulations for Secondary Schools" issued by the Board of Education. The Secretary was instructed to send a copy of this letter to the Board of Education.
5. A letter was read from the Board of Education, dated August 23rd, asking for confirmation of the Governors' resolution of June 29th, whereby the Governors resolved not to comply with the provisions of the New Regulations, entitling the School to Grant at the higher rate, but in view of the action taken by the County Council, such confirmation was not given.
6. Cheques to the value of £280 " 5 " 8 were presented and signed.

[Even after reading the minutes of the previous meeting as well, on 29th July, one is left somewhat in the dark as to exactly what the 'stand' was that the County had taken, and what the 'action' was that it had decided upon.]

Wednesday, 16th October.

First XI. (With Masters) *v.* South Molton.
Lost, 0 – 3.

Played at South Molton ... The players that took part in this game will probably remember it for many years to come. There was a terrific wind, while a blinding, stinging storm of sleet added not a little to our discomfort. The School started downhill, but soon found it impossible either to give or take a pass with any degree of accuracy, while, time after time, the wind drove the ball clean out of the field of play. Our opponents, who were the heavier team, scored three times in the first half, but in the second we made a better fight of it, for at any rate, we prevented their scoring again, while we had rather bad luck in not scoring at least once ourselves.

Thursday, 17th October.

Deceased, at Detroit, Michigan, U.S.A. – James Ley Waldon, eldest son of the later John and Mary Waldon, of Fisherton, Bishopstawton, aged 66. [He] was one of the first three scholars of the Devon County School.

[*The North Devon Journal* printed news of this on 24th October. Waldon was a cousin of one of the other two – Henry Dendle, who died only two months later – see 16th December.]

Saturday, 19th October.

[The Auditor, Joseph Kingdon, reported,] 'I have examined the School accounts from the 31st December 1906 to the 31st July 1907 with the Vouchers relating thereto and do hereby certify the ... Balance Sheet to be correct.' [See 28th January.]

Runs.

THE NORTH-WEST RUN.
... held in glorious weather ... a very even contest.

BRERETON				COURTENAY			
R.W. Seldon	...	...	19	A. Pearce	...	...	20
S.A. Loram	...	...	18	L.K.V. Job	...	...	17
N.K. Pearce	...	...	16	T.H. Richards	...	...	14
A.E. Preston	...	...	13	J.B. Harris	...	...	12
T. Williams	...	...	10	C.G. Harris	...	...	11
W.L. Armstrong	...	...	8	H.H. Hicks	...	...	9
W. Elworthy	...	...	6	W. Saunders	...	...	7
V.J. Loram	...	...	5	L.W.E. Grant	...	...	4
J.E. Pidsley	...	...	2	W.W. Owbridge	...	...	1
P.J. Were	...	...	0	G.H. Dawe	...	...	0
			——				——
			97				95

Day Boys: H.G. Woolaway, 15; S.D.S. Craddock, 3.

[The efforts of day boys were often recorded separately like this, as if they were some kind of unorthodox species. Harries, the HM, had very set views about the huge value of the boarding principle.]

Brereton won by two points.

The Reading and Debating Society.

112th Meeting. S. Bendall was in the chair. There were 23 members present. [The number of boys on roll in September stood at 72, so this attendance represents nearly a third of the whole school. Which meant either that there were was a vigorous interest in debate, or that the debating room was a temptingly warm place to go to on a bleak autumn evening when nothing else was happening. Remember, no computer games, no videos or film projectors, no television, no radio. Come and join the Society, and enjoy both its knowledge, and its spelling and punctuation.]

The minutes of the previous meeting having been read and confirmed, the President called upon the Secretary to read the rules as revised. He then proposed that these rules should be adopted by the society and should be printed. J.B. Harris seconded the motion. On being put before the House the motion was carried unanimously.

J.B. Harris then read a most interesting paper on "Hindus and their Religions.

The Hon. member commenced his paper by giving a brief account of how Hindus are supposed to have come into India.

The Religion of the Hindu's, he said, was one of the few pagan faiths which have possessed sacred books in which sound maxims of morality were written. [One of the common curses of recent writing - namely the compulsion to put in apostrophes to indicate plurals - is, as can be seen here, nothing new. The writer had indeed been guilty more times than the text indicates, because somebody – presumably Mr. Fry, the master in charge of the Society – had been through these minutes and had put in pencil corrections. Some renegade apostrophes, however, escaped his eagle eye, and have survived to be recorded here. Elsewhere in these minutes too, and in others for other debates, I have left what the hard-working Secretary wrote – punctuation, spelling, and all. It is a pity that I cannot show how hard he really did work; his handwriting would put most people to shame now - pupils *and* masters. Poor lad – he also got ticked off at the next meeting for not providing a sufficiently detailed record of the speeches. – see 23rd October.]

The Hindoos at first worshipped a Trinity of which Brahma was the creator. Brahma worship however soon decayed and Vishnoo and Siva in their turn took his place. Water-worship comes largely into their religion and to the Ganges, Jumna and other sacred rivers thousands of worshippers come all the year round. As the Greeks adored – Athor – so the Hindus worship Bhavini in the form of a bull.

He next gave a short account of the castes of India.

The Fakirs he went on to say, were the most fanatical sect in India, & would go to any end in order to obtain favour as they thought, with their particular deities

India was the birthplace of Bhuddism, but now it practically only exists in Cashmere and Nepaul.

112th October 19th. S. Bendall was in the chair. There were 23 members present. The minutes of the previous meeting had been read and confirmed. The Presindent called upon the Secretary to read the rules as revised. He then proposed that these rules should be adopted by the society and should be printed. J. B. Harris seconded the motion. On being put before the House the motion was carried unanimously

J. B. Harris then read a most interesting paper on "Hindus and their Religion.

The Hon. member commenced his paper by giving a brief account of How Hindus are supposed to have come into India

The Religion of the Hindus, he said, was one of the few pagan faiths which have possessed sacred books in which sound maxims of morality were written

The Hindoos at first worshipped a Trinity of which Brahma was the creator. Brahma worship however soon decayed and Vishnoo and Siva in their turn took his place.

A page from the Minutes of the Reading and Debating Society. It seems that the insertion of apostrophes to indicate the plural is by no means a recent bad habit.

Benares is the holiest of Hindoo cities. In their belief it is not a part of this world, but is built on the end of Siva's trident. By breathing its sacred air the Hindoo think they have cleansed themselves of their former sins, and then commit suicide, thus gaining a direct route to heaven.

In conclusion the hon. member gave a description of the Juggernaut festival in which the idol used to be dragged round the town by thousands of devotees, who would throw themselves under the wheels to die in the service of their God – The paper was illustrated with lantern slides –

S. Bendall after congratulating the hon member on his paper, said that the Thugs always reminded him of the Jesuits, for both seemed to have a particular liking for strangling. [That's what it says.]

G.C. Fry Esq stated that Buddism which started in India had now practically deserted it for China and Ceylon.

He remarked that the Hindu's held their lives very cheaply. It was like this in China where if a man is condemned to death he often persuades some one else to die for him.

Later on in the evening the hon member explained that on account of religion and caste it was very difficult to deal with plague and famine.

Rev E C Harries thought that it must be very difficult to govern a country, which has castes, without insulting them on their religious views

If one offends them on a religious point there is no knowing what they will do, in fact "Religion" was the real cause of the Indian Mutiny.

W. Saunders related two anecdotes dealing with the religion of the Hindu's.

The House adjourned at 8 - 25 p.m.

Monday, 21st October.

The Athletic News [on this date] said that "the Crouch End Vampires have discovered a capital centre forward in T.C.A. Julyan, who on Saturday scored three fine goals out of the four by which the 3rd Kent R.G.A. were beaten." [R.G.A? I welcome suggestions.] Julyan, it will be remembered, played centre forward in the unbeaten School Eleven of 1903-4. [A photograph of this triumphant team was published in the April number of the magazine *Health and Strength* in 1907. See 8th April.]

Wednesday, 23rd October.

The Reading and Debating Society.

[The Secretary has given the punctuation and spelling his personal attention.]

113th Meeting. S. Bendall was in the chair. The minutes of the previous meeting having been read the Rev. E.C. Harries objected to the brief way in which certain speeches had been recorded. The minutes were then confirmed, the Sec. having stated that he would rewrite more fully the said speeches.

L.K.V. Job then proposed "That the Society should make a donation of 10/- [50p.] towards the deficit incurred on the entertainment given by Mr Stafford Webber." R.W. Seldon seconded the motion.

On being put before the House the motion was carried unanimously.

The President then called upon Mr Fry to proposed his motion *"That this House is in favour of women having the right to vote on the same conditions as men."*

The Hon. member commenced by pointing out that the old patriarchal theory of society had rapidly given place to the modern society of individuals. In the old theory woman was but a mere slave of man.

Turning to the question of voting the Hon. member reminded the House that 70 years ago, only a very small section of the populace had a right to vote; but since then it had increased until now nearly every male has the right.

By this means some men of a very low intellectual standing are given a privilege, which is kept from women who may be of greater intellectual power.

The Hon member went on to say that in New Zealand and New South Wales women had had the right of voting for some time and still the countries seemed to prosper.

At the present time women were getting into all sorts of responsible positions in this country, and it seemed unjust that intellectual women should not have something to do with the government of the country even if it was only to vote.

E.W. Bagshawe opposing commenced by giving a list of some of the more important positions that a woman could hold nowadays. She could be a Queen, Regent, Peeress; she could sit in the House of Lords, but not speak, and enjoyed many other privileges.

The hon member thought that if females had anything to do with the politics of the country, their tongues would bring them into trouble and cause civil strife.

He then gave some examples of women who had attempted to govern this country. Q. Elizabeth had become vane [sic] and audacious, and combined coarseness with meanness; on the other hand Queen Victoria guided by an excellent husband had been all that could be desired. In conclusion the hon. member pointed out that "The hand which rocked the cradle did not rule the world.

He thought it would be foolish to give a women the right to vote because if given a little she would want a lot – she would not be satisfied with the thin end of the wedge –

S. Bendall said that he would rather see a woman behave as they did in the past age, when they fainted at the least thing than see her in the streets discussing politics. He thought that if a woman had a vote she would vote for the woman's man. As a matter of fact educated women did not wish for a vote.

J.B. Harris thought that only women with certain qualifications should have the right of voting.
On being called upon by the President A.J.E. Helps explained, amid great applause that he had nothing to say.

W. Saunders said that in former times when new ideas had been started, they had generally been laughed at by people in general & all kinds of prophesies [that's what he wrote] made as to what would happen if these ideas were put in practice. Most of these problems have since been proved to be wrong. Why then should not the forecasts made at the present time with regard to what women would do if they had a vote, prove false. He did not say why as the country belonged as much to women as to men, they should not have something to do with the government of it.

L.K.V. Job thought that Elizabeths [the Secretary, besides putting in unnecessary apostrophes, was capable of leaving out necessary ones] reign was a very successful one, & that it was an example of what a women [he obviously had trouble with singulars and plurals too] could do when at the head of affairs

A.H. Austin thought that if the women had a vote, the man in future would rock the cradle.

Rev. E C Harries said that if men and women held seats in Parliament at one time they might disagree on some great question.

This might cause a deadldock between the two sexes – a mass of men against a mass of women.

On the other hand he thought that women saw the evils of drink; and might do a good deal towards solving the drink problem. One great reason why women would not be a success in Parliament is that on the whole they are fickle and are apt to change their opinion to easily.

W.L. Giffard Esq. thought that since many women are intellectually superior to men, they ought to use their cleverness in bringing up their children, thus sowing good seed.

E W Bagshawe Esq in summing up, replied to Mr Job that Queen Elizabeths reign was a success with regard to naval affairs; but her constitution was a failure

He pointed out that it was her private character which he had attacked especially.

G.C. Fry Esq. in conclusion did not see why women should pay taxes and yet not be represented in Parliament, or why if a woman had the right of voting it would make her leave her domestic affairs. At the present time voting takes place about once in six years [he was pretty well right; it was the Parliament Act of 1911 which reduced the maximum life of a parliament from seven years to five].

He advised certain members of the society to argue on principals [sic] and not on single individuals and not to judge a theory by its lowest advocate.
L.G.H. Major also gave his opinion.
The House then divided and the motion was lost by by [sic] 11 votes to 13.
The House adjourned at 8 – 30.

[This was not the first time that the Society had debated women's suffrage. In February, 1906, the minutes recorded one member's suggestion for dealing with interruptions by women at political meetings: 'at every hall a mouse should be kept, which could be let loose as necessary'.]

Thursday, 24th October.

FIRST XI. (WITH MASTERS) *v.* SOUTH MOLTON.
Lost, 3 – 4 .

Played at Taunton. The ground was dry, though the long grass rather spoilt our short-passing game. Taunton pressed straight from the kick off, and before the game was five minutes old their inside left scored, while the same player added a second. Things looked none too bright for us, for they continued to press, but just before the interval Mr. Taylor got through and reduced their lead.

The second half began in much the same way, for Cloud got through and scored a beautiful goal, but then the School began to find their feet. Seldon scored from a centre by Bendall, who was also responsible for the pass from which Mr. Giffard scored. Then came a great struggle for the lead, but Cloud, amid great excitement, finished up a fine individual effort with a shot which gave Lewis no chance, and left Taunton winners of a splendid game by 4 goals to 3.

Obituary.

The *North Devon Journal* today printed an obituary of Frederick Henry White, a pupil from 1876 to 1881, who had died of "malarial fever" at Berbera, East Africa, on 9th June, 1901 [!] … "He was on a five months' special mission as accountant from the Foreign Office, and had nearly completed his work when he fell a victim to the disease and died after only two days' illness. Evidence of the high esteem in which he was held was afforded by letters of appreciation and condolence sent to his widow by the Marquis of Landsdowne (then Foreign Minister) and by White's colleagues at the Foreign Office."

The obituary continued:

"White had a long and distinguished career at the D.C.S., and, although he took little part in athletic sports and games, he was beloved and respected by everybody, and was second to none in popularity … He obtained First Class Junior Honours at the Cambridge Local Examinations in 1877 and 1878, and at the Oxford Examination in 1878. He obtained First Class Senior Honours at both the Oxford and Cambridge Examinations in 1880, on both of which occasions he stood 2nd in England in Drawing. In 1881 he won one of the Royal Agricultural Society's Junior Scholarships, and on the Prize Day, 1882, he was awarded one of the much-coveted Fortescue Silver Medals … In this year he competed at the examination for Clerkships in the Civil Service, and stood 9th in order of merit among about 600 candidates. He was selected for service at the Foreign Office, and he remained in that office until his death."

[On the face of it, high merit at 'Drawing' and a junior scholarship from the Royal Agricultural Society do not seem to fit a young man for a career in accountancy. But he seems clearly to have been a high flyer – natural material for recruitment by the Foreign Office – witness their regular trawling through the first-class degree-holders in Oxford and Cambridge. Again, on the face of it, it seems unlikely that the slender F.O. staff at Berbera, an obscure seaport on the southern coast of the Gulf of Aden, would be in dire need of an accountant. Berbera was in what was then British Somaliland, which was noted for the pitiable state of its economy.

Now take a look at the disturbed politics of the region at the end of the nineteenth century – rivalry between England, France, and Italy in Egypt, the Sudan, Somaliland, and Abyssinia; the warlike activities and Muslim fundamentalism of the Mahdi and the Mad Mullah; the West's natural suspicion of the motives of the infidel Turkish Empire, which reigned supreme on the other side of the Red Sea; the vulnerability of trade routes *through* the Red Sea, now that the Suez Canal had been opened, and so on and so on. Is it altogether too fanciful to suggest that 'accountancy' for our man in Berbera was just a cover? The obituary comments cryptically that he was on a 'special mission'. And, curiously, the death of an obscure 'accountant' in the back of beyond prompted a personal letter of sympathy from no less a personage than the Foreign Secretary. Even more curiously, it took six years for the local paper to catch up with news of his death. Or at any rate to (be allowed to?) publish it.

So – was our Frederick Henry White a spy? And did he really die of 'malarial fever'?]

Saturday, 26th October.

FIRST XI. *v.* TAUNTON SCHOOL 1ST XI.
Lost, 3 – 4.

Taunton School journeyed down to play us, and, while congratulating them on their victory – the second obtained on our ground – we may at once say that we were unlucky to lose, for an injury to Were, early on in the game, practically deprived us of his services.

The game started very auspiciously for us, for Bendall raced away and scored within ten minutes of the start, while Seldon with a high shot put us two up within a few minutes. The enthusiasm of the spectators knew no bounds. Then came the accident referred to, which seriously weakened our defence, while Taunton School fought desperately hard to reduce our lead. A miskick by one of our backs led to their first goal, and a minute later their inside left, who was unmarked, sent the ball past Lewis. Soon after half-time our hopes were again raised, for Bendall got away by himself and scored with a beauty; but Taunton School gradually, by superior pace, wore us down, and, scoring twice more, ran out winners by 4 goals to 3.

[There is no shortage of evidence from the School's early days about pupil support of sports teams and touchline fervour. For most of them, on a Saturday afternoon, it was about all there was to do.]

Monday, 28th October.

The editors of the *Register* apologised for the late publication of the new edition, which was caused 'partly by the fact that the Cabot Press has recently changed hands'.

It was announced that the next *Register* would be published early in February. [Which it was, if the date at the top of the title page is to be trusted.]

Extra copies of the *Register* could be obtained from the Editor at 6d. each [2½ p.]

Tuesday, 29th October.

[The merciless Mr. Chope produced yet another lengthy article for the *Register*, with his characteristic unstoppable self-justification and attention to remorseless detail. Here his six and a half pages, which were almost certainly the residue left after brave cuts by the editor, have been filleted further.]

Old Boys in the Medical Profession.

As it is one of the objects of the *Register* to place on record all distinctions gained by Old Boys, it seems fitting to follow up the lists previously given for the Army and the Navy by similar lists for what are generally termed "the learned professions." In no sphere of life have Old Boys distinguished themselves more than in the medical profession. Two of them are Fellows of the Royal College of Surgeons and University Professors, viz., Leonard Rogers, Professor of Pathology at the Medical College, Calcutta, and Hadley Williams, Professor of Clinical Surgery at the Western University, Canada ... Two have obtained the distinction of notice in "Who's Who?", viz., Rogers and Scanes Spicer, Head of the Throat Department at St. Mary's Hospital, London. So far as is known, the only other Old Boys recorded in this publication are L. Raven Hill, the famous *Punch* artist, and Harold H. Hilton, the equally famous golf champion.

[There followed twenty-five entries about Old Boy medics, from which just a few scraps are included here.]

ANDREW, WILLIAM ... M.D.,. C.M., (Edinburgh) ... Mayor of Launceston ... J.P. ...

DYER, SIDNEY REGINALD., M.D., L.R.C.P., M.R.C.S ... Barrister-at-Law, Middle Temple ... Member of the Devonshire Association for Advancement of Science, Literature, and Art ... late Medical Officer, H.M. Prison, Dartmoor ...

HENWOOD, JOHN DAVEY ... retired with rank of Deputy Inspector-General of Hospitals and Fleets ...

HILL, GEORGE WILLIAM ... Surgeon for Diseases of Ear, Nose, and Throat, Ealing Hospital for Deaf, and to Association for Welfare of Feeble-Minded ...

ROGERS, LEONARD ... Major, Indian Medical Service ... Honorary Member of the American Society for Tropical Medicine ... numerous scientific papers in medical journals ... on Fevers, Snake Poisons, Liver Abscess, etc.

SPICER, ROBERT HARRY SCANES ... Honorary Physician to the Royal Society of Musicians of Great Britain ... Fellow of the Royal Medical and Chirurgical Society ...

TARR WILLIAM ... Indian Medical Service ... certificated for Equitation, and for Persian, Pushtu, and Urdu languages. ...

[And so on and so on. Extracts are selected not so much to show great distinction as to indicate the diversity of contribution – although distinction there certainly was. This was from a school which had fewer than 70 pupils in 1907, and which had never had more than about 150, and was at one time down to 31, indeed close to closure twice in its near-fifty years of history. It is difficult to see how the average number of leavers per year during that time could have been much over 10. That's about 500 altogether. So this contribution to the medical life of the nation – and Chope freely admits that the list is 'probably far from complete' (he can't resist the 'probably') – is, for a small, obscure school back of beyond, pretty good going. The more so when you also take in their contribution to the Admiralty Service – see 8th February.]

Wednesday, 30th October.

FIRST XI. *v.* H.S. YOUINGS' XI.
Won, 3 – 0.

H.S. Youings [almost certainly a relative of A.L.J. Youings in the Fifth Form. There were Youings' in the School right through the 20th century, and the Youings businesses (undertakers and tobacconists) still operate in Barnstaple] kindly brought out a team to play the School, and a most enjoyable game resulted, despite the fact that it was raining the whole time. School seemed rather stale; probably they still felt the effects of the game with Taunton, while Parker took the place of Were, still on the injured list. In the first half play ruled even, nor was there any scoring, though both goals had narrow escapes, but in the second the visitors were handicapped by an injury to one of their men, which necessitated his going into goal. From a well-placed corner Bendall scored our first goal, and he also added a second some ten minutes later, while we were somewhat lucky in gaining a third point, for the ball was put through by an opponent.

The Reading and Debating Society.

114th meeting. S. Bendall was in the chair. The minutes of the previous meeting having been read and sundry alterations made [see 23rd October], were confirmed. The President then called upon W. Saunders to read his paper on "Some Inventions of the Nineteenth Century".

[Again, remember that the Secretary did not hold a doctorate in punctuation.]

The hon. member commenced by giving a description of the Steam Hammer.

This machine he explained was very simple in principle. To raise the hammer steam is admitted below the piston. When the communication with the boiler is shut off and the steam below the piston allowed to escape, the piston with the mass of iron, which formed the hammer, falls.

Some Hydraulic Machines were next described the Hydraulic Press being one. In this apparatus water is forced through a small tube into a large, and very strong cylinder inside of which is a piston. To this piston a strong iron table is attached. The goods to be pressed are placed on this table, and when the ram rises are squeezed against another fixed table.

The Hydraulic crane was also described. Short descriptions of a Rock Boring machine, and of a Prospecting Machine followed. The hon member in his description of these explained the advantages of the diamond drill over the old fashioned steel drill.

He next described Edison's original Phonograph. Edison obtained his ideas from the Phonautograph invented by Scott some years before. The Phonautograph would record sounds but would not reproduce them. The device which converted the phonautograph into a phonograph was the substitution of tin foil, in the place of the blackened paper used in Scotts apparatus.

The hon member concluded his paper by giving descriptions of some of the first attempts at inventing an instrument for transmitting speech, and a description of Bell's telephone. In his form of telephone the transmitter and receiver are identical, each consisting externally of a small cylindrical ebonite box, with a handle about 4 inches long.

The instrument consists of a long steel magnet, on one end of which is wound a small coil of insulated wire, the ends of which pass through the handle, and are connected with wires which link them up with the batteries. Close to the coil covered end of the magnet is a very thin iron diaphragm which, when thrown into vibration by the voices, produces certain currents in the coil of wire, the disc being magnetised by the magnet. The currents passing through the coil of the receiving instrument raise or lower the intensity of the magnetic force in it, so that the distant disc reproduces the vibrations of the transmitter.

The paper was illustrated by handmade lantern slides. [I bet that was a help.]

S. Bendall congratulated the hon. member on his paper, and expressed a wish that some of the new members would speak. He then described a modern apparatus which will dig up earth mechanically. The apparatus is fixed to a crane for the purpose of swinging it round. On pulling a lever the appliance drops its contents.

G.C. Fry Esq. congratulated Mr Armstrong & Mr Saunders on their attempt at slide making and expressed a wish that other members would do the same.

From his own experience he did not think the telephone was a perfect instrument. Great mistakes are often made owing to the indistinct way messages are transmitted by this apparatus. The hon. member thought it wonderful that people had been content with slow travelling for such a long time. There had been no improvement in rate and means of travelling from the time of Caesar until the year 1800.

A.H. Austin thought that although the telephone is rather an imperfect instrument yet it is, inspite of this, a very useful convience [sic] at times.

E.M. Bagshawe Esq was of opinion that people, on the whole at the present time are very slow to realise what great benefits they obtain from the numerous modern inventions now in use.

E.A. Adams described briefly Brunels block machine. Brunel distinguished himself in other lines for he invented machines for winding cotton and for making shoes.

W.L. Armstrong considered the Safety Lamp to be one of the most useful inventions, & the one which had saved more lives than any other invention brought out in the past century. He explained that although the lamp was called the "Davy Lamp" yet it was invented by George Stephenson. Davy, a Cornishman stole the invention & and patented the lamp, thus depriving Stephenson of the honour due to him.

The House adjourned at 8 – 15.

There were 24 members present.

The Shooting Range. Mr. Fry was in charge of shooting, though it would take a very good detective to prove that he is the one with the binoculars.

Thursday, 31st October.

This has been the wettest month of the year so far (6.16 inches).

End of October entries.

November

Saturday, 2nd November.

An article - a portrait and a biographical sketch - appeared today in the *Western Morning News* on M.B. Snell, J.P. [He was an ex-Head Boy, stockbroker, J.P., rescuer of the School's finances, and general benefactor. (See 15th May, 3rd August, 2nd October, and 18th November.) The Old School Library still bears his name over the door.]

Sunday, 3rd November.

John F.R. Morris died, aged 55 years, at Marwood, North Devon. [It is today a 'suburb' of Barnstaple.] He was at the School in the early sixties. His business as a silk merchant took him to Paris, where he was living during the siege of 1871. [In the Franco-Prussian War of 1870-71 the Prussian army invaded France and reached Paris, where the Germans in the end dictated peace terms.] About twenty years ago he settled at Marwood, and has been most successful as a breeder of Devon Cattle, one year gaining all the big prizes for Devons at the Royal Agricultural Show, while his bulls have been exported to all parts of the world.

Tuesday, 5th November.

Rifle Shooting.

[This is an arbitrary choice of date, as the *Register* did not supply one. However, as the report referred to 'weekly practice' and 'bad weather', and the *Register* weather report for 1907 said that October was the wettest month, it would therefore be reasonable to place the event round about now rather than earlier.]

Owing partly to bad weather and partly to the necessity for repairing some of the rifles ... [the] shooting was somewhat inferior, both in quality and quantity, to that of the summer term. [The first] Dormitory Competition [was] held between teams selected on the results of the weekly practice. [For the second, see 10th December.]

Brereton won by the narrowest possible margin – one point.

BRERETON				COURTENAY.			
A.E. Preston	22	18	40	L.K.V. Job	15	22	37
A.J.E. Helps	22	22	44	J.B. Harris	25	18	43
P.J. Were	18	18	36	W. Saunders	19	12	31
A.L.J. Youings	16	13	29	A.O. Parker	22	15	37
	78	71	149		81	67	148

Brereton won by one point.
Silver spoon: A.J.E. Helps.

Wednesday, 6th November.

SCHOOL HOUSE MATCH.
Courtenay 1, Brereton 0.

The first of the House Matches was played, Courtenay winning a great game by 1 goal. It was unfortunate for Brereton that they were still without Were, but it had the advantage of making the game more open. The pace all through was great, and in a game where everybody worked his hardest it would be invidious to mention any names, but special praise may perhaps be meted out to the smaller members of each team, who were not the least bit overawed by their larger and heavier opponents.

Old Boys' Monthly Social Gatherings.

The November meeting was held [once again] at Anderton's Hotel, Fleet Street. The *Western Weekly News* reported:

"The musical arrangements were in the hands of Mr. A.J. Pride, who is to be heartily congratulated on the programme he submitted. Mr. Collings proved himself an efficient accompanist. Mr. Hunter gave an acceptable rendering of 'May Morning', as did Mr. Will Jacobs, of 'Laugh, and the World laughs with You.' ['Acceptable' – the reporter was not exactly over-committing himself.] Mr. Leonard Lyall's 'Thora' was warmly applauded, but his 'Glorious Devon' met with still greater favour, and as an encore he gave 'Because.' Mr. Walker, the possessor of a very fine falsetto voice, sang 'The Arrow and the Song.' Songs of a humorous character largely preponderated, those contributing including Mr. Church, 'I Didn't Like To' and 'I didn't know what to Say'; Mr. Holmes, 'The Hydropathic Treatment'; Mr. Noble, 'Not a Bad Sort, am I?' and 'I'm going to Sing you a Song this Evening'; and Mr. Wilkins, 'The Salvage Man.' Mr. Sanderson sang 'The Jolly Sailor Boy,' and Mr. Messenger 'The Little Irish Girl.'"

Saturday, 9th November.

FIRST XI. (WITH MASTERS) *v.* HOLY TRINITY.
Lost, 2 – 4.

[The date of this match is not given explicitly, but in the magazine its report comes between the House Match of Wednesday, 6th, and the following School match of Wednesday, 13th. As the vast majority of matches were played either on a Wednesday or a Saturday, this date seems a fair guess.]

... The School, unfortunately, were without the services of Mr. Taylor, and his absence handicapped our playing powers considerably. Trinity attacked right from the start and proved a rare handful for our defence to deal with, for their front line was fast, to a man. By a bit of fine combination they broke away, and Brisley scored with a hard ground shot. The School were not long in drawing level,

Mr. Giffard giving Bendall a pass in front of goal for the latter to score, but, though we scored once more, our visitors added no less than three goals, chiefly by the aid of superior pace, and a good understanding among the forwards.

The Reading and Debating Society.

[The spelling and punctuation belong, as usual, to the Secretary.]

115th Meeting. The Minutes of the previous meeting having been read, G.C. Fry Esq proposed that the word "trivial" should be erased. The proposal was seconded by A H Austin. On being put to the House the proposal was carried unanimously. The minutes were then confirmed. S Bendall then called upon J B Harris to take the chair. S Bendall was then called upon to read his paper on Robespierre, illustrated by lantern slides.
Robespierre was born at Arras on May 6th 1758. His family were of Irish descent, and lived at a little village called Carvin near Arras. He was the eldest son of a family of four and was educated at the Collège Louis – le Grand at Paris. On completing his law studies he returned to his native village. He was appointed criminal judge of Arras in 1782; which he however resigned to avoid passing a sentence of death. In 1783 he was elected member of the Academy of Arras. In 1784 he obtained a medal for an essay on the question whether the relatives of a condemned criminal should be punished or not.

He first came into public notice when the states-general met on May 5th 1789, and spoke freely in the constituent assembly, soon becoming one of the leaders. After a short period he left the assembly and joined the Jacobin Club, where he gathered a large number of admirers around him, fanatics like himself.

His greatest triumph came on Sept 30th 1791, when he was crowned with Pétion, by the people of Paris, as one of the two incorruptible patriots.

He was now one of the chief leaders in France, but he soon found that he had many enemies. The chief of these were the Girondin party who unlike Robespierre wished for war with Austria. He was accused by them of aiming at the Dictatorship but he had no difficulty in rebutting this attack

After this, there was one long struggle between Robespierre and the Giroddin [sic] Party, which continued until the latter were crushed by the execution of their leaders on Apr 5th 1794. After the crushing of the Girondin party Robespierre began to develop a policy distinct from that of his colleagues, and this policy ended in his downfall. He increased the pressure of the Terror, so that no one should accuse him of moderantism [sic again]. The result was that between June 12th and July 28th the day of his death, 1285 victims perished on the guillotine.

Now however the majority of the great committee began to feel that he was growing too powerful, whilst the Dantonists were burning to avenge Danton's death.

The result was that his popularity speedily decreased, until on July 27th when he stood up in the assembly to speak, he was attacked with cries of "Down with the tyrant" The excitement increased and at five o'clock in the afternoon he was arrested with his remaining supporters

He was soon released by the troops however, only to be taken to the Hotel de Ville where he was detained. The mob then attacked the Hotel and Robespierre was shot in the lower jaw.

The next day, after a night of agony, Robespierre was taken before the tribunal, where his identity as an outlaw was proved, and without further trial he was executed with 19 of his adherents on the Place de la Revolution on the 10th Thermidor 1794.

J.B. Harris after congratulating the hon member on his paper expressed his opinion of Robespierre. He thought that Robespierre's character was not so bad as it was pictured. The fact that he had resigned his position as a judge rather than give a death sentence proved this to a certain extent.

G.C. Fry Esq. was of opinion that the period, dealt with by the hon. member in his paper was the most important of European history. He thought that in Paris at that time people were put to death for very trivial causes for example, - a girl was found in the neighbourhood of Robespierre's house with a knife in her possession Although she had committed no crime yet she was executed.
The House adjourned at 8 – 5
There were 22 members present.

Saturday, 9th November, contd.

Old Boys.

The *South Wales Argus* printed this article today:
"Alderman T. Parry, J.P., the new Mayor of Newport, was born in 1852 at Llandegveth, Caerleon, and was educated at West Buckland, but in 1866 he entered the audit office of the old Monmouthshire Railway at Newport. In 1873 he decided to abandon railway work, and commenced business as an auctioneer. He has been a Fellow of the Institute of Auctioneers since 1897, and in 1902 was Chairman of the South Wales and Monmouthshire Branch of the Institute. Mr. Parry has been a member of the Monmouthshire County Council since its creation in 1889, and has been unopposed since the first election. He has been a member of the Newport Borough Council since 1893. He was nominated as a county magistrate by the late Duke of Beaufort in 1894; was made a J.P. for the Borough in 1903; and was Chairman of the Newport Chamber of Commerce in 1899. He has been for ten years Chairman of the Asylum Committee of the County Council."

[You can't get much more worthy than that.]

Engineer-Lieutenant T.W. Cleave, R.N. (1883-6), was appointed to H.M.S. *Eden*, a torpedo-boat destroyer at The Nore.

Wednesday, 13th November.

SECOND XI. *v.* CHALONER'S SCHOOL,
BRAUNTON, 1ST XI.
Won, 3 – 0.

… The 2nd XI. paid their annual visit to Chaloner's, and returned victorious by 3 goals to *nil.* For the greater part of the first half, it must be admitted, the School never got going, chiefly because the high wind, in conjunction with a small, light ball, completely upset all notions of combination; but they improved as time went on and fared better when playing against the wind. Saunders scored with a long drive, soon after changing ends, and Pearce obtained our second, while we were indebted to one of our opponents for our third and last goal.

Saturday, 16th November.

FIRST XI. *v.* KING'S COLLEGE 1ST XI.
Won, 1 – 0.

Played at home … The School won the toss and elected to play uphill. King's College were the first to be dangerous, but their final shot went wide. Each side then attacked in turn, Parker sending in a couple of hot centres, one of which struck the crossbar. The defence on both sides was good, and it looked as though there would be no score in the first half, when one of their backs, in trying to ward off an attack on the left, miskicked straight to Seldon, who made no mistake with his shot. On crossing over, King's attacked for some time, but Preston and Were played a great game, the former bringing off some well-timed tackling, while the latter kicked a beautiful length. [This boy Were, remember, was only in the Third Form – year 9 today. It is possible, of course, that he was in fact older than the average for the year, but was backward academically. However, he did finish the year by being promoted to the Fifth Form – see 20th December.] The School now set up such a hot attack that one of their backs fisted the ball in front of the goal. Seldon failed with the ensuing penalty. No further scoring took place and the school won a very hard game by one goal to *nil.*

Monday, 18th November.

Governors' Meeting.

At an Ordinary Meeting of the Governors, duly convened by the Secretary, and held at The George Hotel, South Molton …

Present. Prebendary R. Martin (in the chair), Rev. J.H. Copleston, Messrs. G.C. Smyth-Richards, G.A.W. Thorold, M.B. Snell – Governors: The Rev. J.H. Thompson, Rev. J. Newman, Messrs. R.P. Chope, D.J.C. Bush – prospective Governors: Mr. R.B. Wyatt (Liquidator) and The Rev. E.C. Harries (Head Master). [Mr. Wyatt is here again, witnessing some of the haggling over the small print of the change in the School's status.]

1. The minutes of the last Meeting were read and confirmed.
2. A letter from Mr. Young – the County Education Secretary – dated 29th October was read making a suggestion as to how the Conscience Clause for Boarders might be met. Also another letter dated November 11th from the County Education Committee pointing out that "The Committee are not prepared to rescind the resolution passed by them on the 3rd October," and that "The Committee think it essential to the success of the School that the highest possible grant should be obtained from the Board of Education."
3. The following resolutions were put forward and carried nem. con.
   a) That this Meeting is willing to accept the principle of Public Control
      (Proposed by the Rev. Copleston & seconded by Mr. Smyth-Richards)
   b) That the Governors will make regulation in accordance with Article 5 of the Regulations for Secondary Schools. [Full-stoppery is a mite inconsistent. Not like Mr. Taylor.]
      (Proposed by Mr. Thorold & seconded by Mr. Smyth-Richards)
   c) That Clause 49 of the published draft Scheme stand as it is, subject to the approval of the Board of Education.
      (Proposed by Mr. Smyth-Richards & seconded by Rev. Copleston).
   d) That the percentage of 25 of free places for boys from Elementary Schools, as laid down by the Board of Education, be accepted.
      (Proposed by Mr Smyth-Richards & seconded by Mr. Thorold)
   d) That the Governors agree to the suggested constitution of the Governing Body, Subject to the condition that persons selected from those named in Clause 4 of the Scheme should be regarded as the first representatives of the County Council and other Local Bodies.
      (Proposed by Mr Smyth-Richards & seconded by Mr Thorold). . . .
   [Mr. Smyth-Richards seems to have had a busy meeting.]
4. The Governors decided to carry out the work of heating the east wing of the School Buildings by means of a hot-water low-pressure system, and Messrs Wippell Bros. and Row's tender was accepted. Also, to meet the recommendation of the Government Inspection, it was decided to erect partitions in the Big School and in the 3rd Form Class Room. All details of the work were left in the hands of the Secretary and the Head Master.
5. The Secretary was instructed to write to Mr. J. Carter of Exmouth, who had removed one of his sons from the School without the required Term's notice, and had refused to pay the Term's Fees in lieu of such notice, that the Term's Fees would be remitted on condition he paid the cost of the writ which had been issued against him, and the other costs of the School Solicitor. [This was the penultimate episode in a saga which had been running in the Minutes since 12th December, 1906, when Mr. Carter's

'indebtedness to the School (already) amounted to £126 " 2 " 4'. The Minutes of 23rd February recorded that the Secretary had been told to threaten legal action from 'Messrs Crosse Day & Wyatt'. This has to be our Mr. Wyatt the 'Liquidator'. A margin note in the Minutes said that £75 had been paid, but 'about £40' was 'still owing'. It was the 'penultimate' episode because we do not know whether Mr. Carter finally settled. The threat of legal action in the case of a previous tight-fisted parent had worked only a year or so before, when a Mr. J.E. Richards, of Longsight, Manchester, had finally disgorged all of £10.50 for a whole term's fees for his son – Minute No. 2., 30th July, 1906. The School had got as far as briefing a barrister, Mr. A.F. Seldon, to represent them in court – see Seldon biography. Perhaps Mr. Carter was made of sterner stuff, because I can find no record in the Minutes of his paying, right up to July, 1908. If the fees were only £10.50 a term, it looks as if Mr. Carter had been getting away with murder for years. He had put four sons through the School!]

Cheques to the value of £75 " 3s. " 9d were presented and signed and payment thereof ordered.

Wednesday, 20th November.

FIRST XI. *v.* NORTH DEVON SCHOOL 1ST XI.
Won, 7 - 0.

… The School gained the biggest victory of the term against North Devon School. The latter, taken as a whole, were much lighter, and though they stuck to their work pluckily right to the bitter end, were unable to prevent our scoring seven goals, of which Seldon got four, Elworthy two, and Bendall one.

[It has proved impossible to find out, or deduce, whether it was played at home or away. Nor, frankly, do I know where or what 'North Devon School' were. They were not Barnstaple Grammar School, obviously. It is possible that they were a new creation of the Balfour Education of 1902, which led to many new secondary schools all over the country, as Forster's Act of 1870 did for primaries. It is quite possible then that they might not yet have acquired their own sports field; it may also explain why their prowess had not had time to establish itself. Or perhaps no suitable teacher had been appointed to bring them on. With all those new secondary schools, qualified teachers would not have been very thick on the ground.]

The Reading and Debating Society.

116th Meeting. There were 26 members present. The minutes of the previous meeting having been read and confirmed the president called upon A.E. Helps to state his motion "That in the opinion of this House the present age is superior to all past ages"

[As usual, the punctuation of the proceedings was at the discretion, or indiscretion, of the Secretary.]

The hon member then commenced a very systematic speech first pointing out how very much better travelling is now a days than it was in the past, and then discussing the Religions of the past and present. He thought it rather unpleasant to have the knowledge that one may be taken, at any moment, for the purpose of providing a human sacrifice.

There was a time too in history when justice was exercised in a very unfair way. Judges were easily bribed to give any particular decision that was needed and punishments of a barbarous nature were inflicted

In the past too when a person became ill instead of being carefully nursed back to his normal state of health, as is done now, he was left to look after himself as best he could and in most cases died.

When compared with the past the hon member thought no one should have any hesitation in voting for the present Age.

A.H. Austin opposing pointed out to the honourable mover that in past ages there was no great need of doctors as there were not so many diseases.

He thought that sport and games had deteriorated. In the past our ancestors indulged in manly exercises but now we were content with ping pong and diabolo [an old playground game involving tops and string].

As regards dress, at the present time people dress for show, but in the past the first consideration was comfort and usefulness.

Talking of inventions the hon member owned that many very useful inventions were now in use which we could not do without but on the other hand in the past they had never known what it was to be helped by patent machines and so did not miss them.

Rev E C Harries speaking against the motion thought that although human sacrificing appeared to us a fearful thing yet in those days people valued their lives less.

The hon member was of opinion that the invention of printing has not benefited people at all. The Daily papers keep us in a whirl of excitement, which is not beneficial to our health; with the result that in past ages when everybody passed their life in a careless fashion, they lived many years longer.

S. Bendall [who was presiding – see the reference by the following speaker] gave a few points for both sides of the question. He thought that a rich man would be in favour of the present age, whilst a man of scanty means & poor intellect would probably think that men of his class had a better time in the past than he does now.

W.L. Giffard Esq. differed with the pres. With regard to the question whether the rich man had a better time now than in the past. In the past they had everything their own way and had everything done for them by slaves. Almost all poor men were slaves. He thought the poor man had a much better time now than then. In the past the poor man was hanged for the most trivial offences without even having a trial.

L. Major thought that some of the food we eat at the present time is not above suspicion. The ancients seemed to thrive on their plain fare

E.W. Elworthy [normally listed as plain 'W. Elworthy'] discussed the merits of the steam plough and afterwards joined in a heated argument with A. Pearce & N.K. Pearce as to whether the brown and black bread eaten so much in the past was more wholesome than white.

E M Bagshawe Esq. pointed out the many benefits we obtain now from modern implements. He thought that people were not so polite now as they have been in past centuries.

J.B. Harris, A.O. Parker, R. Seldon E. Adams also spoke. The president then called upon A H Austin to sum up who having repeated some of the fact already mentioned about food, went on to discuss the clothes of the ancients

He thought that furs were much more comfortable and practical than those we wear today.

He explained that the hardy nature of the human race in the past probably enabled them to recover from illnesses to which we might now succumb.

A.E. Helps in conclusion explained that he could not see much in the dress of the ancients. He thought they must have felt the cold. In his opinion school masters have a better time now than in the past. His argument being that the students used sometimes to get out of the control of their masters and gave them a very bad time.

The house then divided and the motion was won by 12 votes to 10.

The House adjourned at 8 − 34.

Thursday, 21st November.

Football.

SCHOOL HOUSE MATCH.
Brereton 2, *Courtenay* 1.

Brereton had Were back again [see 26th October], but Courtenay were unfortunately without their captain, Harris, still nursing a "crocked" knee. The game was as keen and fast as the first one. Brereton scored first, but Courtenay stuck to their guns till they drew level, and then both sides went at it "hammer and tongs." Neither side could score again until, hardly a minute from time, Bendall got away and put in a good centre, which led to Brereton's second goal. With the whistle going for time immediately afterwards, a memorable game thus ended in favour of Brereton by two goals to one.

Saturday, 23rd November.

Football.

FIRST XI. *v.* FILLEIGH.
Won, 3 − 2.

Played at Filleigh in pouring rain. [No date given, but the report is printed between the House Match of 21st and the game against Barnstaple Town on the 27th. So Saturday seems far and away the most likely date, given the evidence of the rest of the term.]

The School played down the slight slope first and did the greater part of the attacking, Bendall scoring twice. Soon after change of ends Filleigh improved and attacked continuously, scoring twice; but Seldon scored again for the School, who just managed to prevent the home team scoring again, though they had desperately hard work to retain their lead of the odd goal in five.

Wednesday, 27th November.

Football.

FIRST XI. (WITH MASTERS) *v.* BARNSTAPLE TOWN.
Won, 4 − 2.

Played at home. Barnstaple brought out a strong team, including Turner and Thomas, of Parish Church fame, but they had to go away defeated by 4 goals to 2. Rain was falling when Turner kicked off for the town, who, for a quarter of an hour, kept up a terrific bombardment of the School goal. Mainly owing to poor shooting, they could only score once, while the School backs gradually forced them back and set our forwards going, only to see them pulled up for off-side. Still the School pressed, and just before the interval Seldon scored, while just after it Mr. Taylor scored a lovely goal from an awkward angle. The Town outside right was next responsible for a good dribble and centre, the ball going off one of our players into the net. From a scrum in front of the Town goal Mr. Giffard headed through, and, just before time, the same player added our fourth and last goal.

Friday, 29th November.

Old Boys.

At the annual dinner of "Devonians in London" at the Hotel Cecil … the Chair was taken by Earl Fortescue, and a separate table was reserved for Old Boys of the D.C.S. and their friends. For this occasion, all Old Boys were considered "Devonians," whether natives of the county or not. [As the notice of the dinner freely admitted, so that a 'large number' would attend.]

Saturday, 30th November.

The Runs.

THE BRAY RUN.

BRERETON.		COURTENAY.	
S. Bendall	19	A. Pearce	20
W.L. Armstrong	12	R.T.H. Hooper	17
E.A. Adams	9	E.W. Oakey	16
J. Wells	8	W. Saunders	15
S.A. Loram	6	H.C. Batting	14
E.H. Southcombe	5	C.G. Harris	13
N.K. Pearce	4	A.P. Moor	11
L.A. Murless	3	W.W. Owbridge	10
W.H. Pugsley	2	S.H. Oatway	7
T. Williams	0	W.E. Ayre	1
	68		124

Day Boys: H.G. Woolaway, 18.
Courtenay won by 56 points.

End of November entries.

December

Tuesday, 3rd December.

An examination was held for the Old Boys' Entrance Scholarship. [See the announcement of 2nd September.]

Wednesday, 4th December.

Reading and Debating Society.

117th Meeting. J.B. Harris was in the chair. There were twenty six members present. [Errors and inconsistencies at the whim of the Secretary. Perhaps the observant reader might like to spot them.]

The minutes of the previous meeting having been read and confirmed, W.L. Armstrong read a very interesting and instructive paper on Locomotives.

The hon member in opening stated that it was at Newcastle that the railway might be said to have begun. Coal was first carried in panniers but later on carts were used; and first wood, then stone, and lastly iron plates were laid down on the cart tracks.

Thus the railway originated. The flange was first cast on the rails, but in 1789 it was cast on the wheel.

The first locomotive steam carriage was built by a Frenchman named Cugnol, who constructed one which ran on three wheels, but it was only able to travel at 2½ miles an hour.

The first really successful steam carriage was built by Richard Trethwick [sic] at Redruth. He took it to London, where it performed successfully for one day, but it was removed during the second day.

Trethwick built his locomotive at Pen-y-darran in S. Wales in 1803. This engine could draw 10 tons weight at 10 miles an hour.

Several methods of securing adhesion between the rails and wheels were then described by the hon. member.

He then related the various attempts of Mr Blacket of Wylam, who had an engine built from the same plans as Trethwick's, but it was thought [sic] light to be used on the plate way. His second locomotive blew up at the first trial. His third engine could only go at 1 mile an hour with 10 waggons, and was so heavy that it was constantly breaking the iron plates.

George Stephenson now took up the question of locomotive traction. He constructed his first engine at Killingworth. It was however unsuccessful. Soon afterwards Stephenson invented the steam blast, which was one of the greatest steps in this subject ever made.

A prize of £300 was offered by the directors of the Liverpool & Manchester railway for the best Locomotive produced on the first of Oct. 1828 to satisfy certain conditions.

Four engines were entered for this competition viz, "The Rocket", the "Novelty", the "Sanspareil" & the "Perseverance". When tried all the engines broke down except the Rocket, which thus won the prize.

The hon member concluded by saying that every engine was now built with the same principle more or less as the Rocket, and thus it may be regarded as the pattern of every locomotive.

The paper was illustrated by lantern slides some of which were handmade by W.L. Armstrong which were afterwards presented to the society.

J.B. Harris congratulating the hon member on his paper, and on the slides he had made thought the interest which has been taken in railways is shown by the enormous mileage of the present day, over 500,000 mls. which has been made in less than a century. He remarked how much more comfortable travelling was nowadays than in the past. As regards guage [sic] the GWR have tried a 7ft guage but the government interfered.

Rev. E.C. Harries stated that the broader guage was used in England to within 15 years ago. He remember [sic] how Cornwall consisted at one time entirely of the broader guage, and how the G.W.R. changed the entire length of the permanent way in that county during a Sunday.

Taylor Esq. explained the principle of fixing the metals to the sleepers and explained that the broad guage was stopped because it was too expensive. The strain on the train was much greater & breakdowns were frequent

The railroad is more important than the rolling stock. At the present time the GWR have the best line, they having increased the weight of the metals to a wt of 100 lb per yard

G C Fry Esq. welcomed Mr Taylor on his re appearance, and went on to discuss French lines. From his own experience he found them slower than the English lines although the fares were less. He pointed out that the reason why the English guage is 4ft 8½in is because the lines were first laid for carts to run on and it has remained the same ever since.

W. Saunders thought that since railways had made such great strides in such short time, perhaps we might see a perfect flying machine within the next 30 yrs or so.

E.M. Bagshawe related a short anecdote and on Mr Fry stating that he had ridden 4th class in Germany, explained that there were 5 classes in Norway, the 5th being reserved for Railway officials & Government officers.

A.H. Austin gave his vues [sic] on French railways.

The House adjourned at 8 – 20 p.m.

Old Boys' Socials.

The *Western Weekly News* reported:

"On this occasion a new departure was made – ladies were invited to the supper, and, judging by the result, the innovation was appreciated." The Chair was taken by T.R. Potbury, Esq., B.A., Master at University College School, and he was supported by Alderman E.W. Sloper,

J.P., Mayor of Hornsey, who wore his badge of office. [See 14th December.] "Among the ladies present were Mrs. Potbury, Mrs. Hearson, Mrs. Small, Miss Greenyer, Mrs. Stokes, Mrs. Grills, Mrs. Collings, Mrs. Congdon, Mrs. Lambert, Mrs. Harris, Mrs. Shawyer, Miss Nancy Ellison, and Mrs. Lister Lewis. Mr. A. Small was responsible for the programme, and the fare provided by him did him great credit. Following a pianoforte solo by Mr. Aethel Collings − who proved himself an efficient accompanist throughout the evening − Mr. Eastman sang 'The Jolly Sailor.' High praise, indeed, must be accorded to Miss Greenyer for her recitation, 'A Skipper's Story', in the vernacular. In 'In the Twilight,' Mr. Holmes proved himself capable of rendering a humorous song in a pleasing manner. Mr. R.P. Chope kept the audience intensely amused with Jan Stewer's account of 'The Electric Light Scheme.' [For Jan Stewer, see 2nd October.] We have heard many renderings of Jan's stories, and Mr. Chope's was certainly one of the best. This remark applies equally to Mr. Small, who gave several 'Yarns' in the vernacular. Mr. R.D. Grant sang 'The Mill Wheel' in a pleasing manner, and Mr. Rudd caused much merriment while he was singing 'Jan's Courtship.' Later, Mr. Rudd sang 'Widdecombe Fair,' the company joining in the chorus. Mrs. Lewis was loudly applauded for her rendering of 'For All Eternity.' Conjuring exhibitions were given by Signor Corelli and Mr. Maurice Garland.

Responding to the toast of 'The Ladies,' Mr. H. Lambert, secretary to His Majesty's Theatre, made an amusing and appropriate reply. Alderman Sloper … , in a reminiscent speech, proposed the health of the chairman. This was enthusiastically received, and a brief reply by Mr. Potbury brought an enjoyable evening to a close." [Mr. and Mrs. Potbury had been married earlier in the year − see 7th January.]

The following Old Boys answered to the "roll call" at one or more of the gatherings [2nd October, 6th November, 4th December]:−

W.S. Abell (1890-2), G.M. Chard (1883-6), R.P. Chope (1874-81), W.W. Clarke (1876-9), A.R. Congdon (1873), F.J. Couch (1884-7), A.C. Cramb (1889-91), T.H. Gale (1883-6), W.E. Grills (1883-4), G.W. Harris (1883-8), T.A. Hearson (1859-63), J.L. Hooper (1892-5), J.C. Johnson (1896-1901), W.H. Lee (1870-1), E.O. Lisle (1891-3), R.A. Mountjoy (1862-3), W. Perrin (1895-7), H.S. Potbury, Sidmouth (1883-7), T.R. Potbury (1880-4), A.E. Pride (1894-6), A.J. Pride (1893-5), T.P. Puddicombe (1891-6), J. Rickard (1876-8), J.W. Shawyer (1885-8), E.W. Sloper (1881-4), A. Small (1863-70), M.B. Snell (1866-70), H.B. Squire (1868), J.J. Turner (1870-2), R.P. Wheadon, Ilminster (1896-7).

[Interesting that 14 out of the 30 in the above list were pupils at the School for only two years or less. And still the School was able to develop a grip on them which brought them back to these reunions, it would appear, time and again. *Registers* for other years record similar levels of attendance at similar gatherings.

Note the presence of 'E.O. Lisle', listed in other numbers as 'E.Orchard Lisle'. At least four more Orchard Lisles attended during the 20th century, and were noted benefactors; and, from the following generation, another Orchard Lisle recently retired as Chairman of Governors.]

Weather.

More than one inch of rain fell today. [See also 20th April and 17th August.]

Saturday, 7th December.

Football.

Matches	Played	Won	Lost	Drawn	Goals	
					For	Against
Masters' X	6	3	3	0	19	18
1st XI.	8	6	2	0	27	10
2nd XI.	2	1	1	0	3	1
	—	—	—	—	—	—
Total	16	10	6	0	49	29
	—	—	—	—	—	—

The First XI … was as follows:−
 Goal. − C. Lewis.
 Backs. − A.E. Preston, P.J. Were.
 Half-Backs. − L.K.V. Job, J.B. Harris, W. Saunders.
 Forwards. − A.O. Parker, R.W. Seldon, S. Bendall (captain), W. Elworthy, W.F. Kingdon.
 The Head Master, Mr. Taylor, and Mr. Giffard played in Masters' Matches. The following also played on one or more occasions: T.H. Richards, D.T. Squire, H.G. Woolaway, C.H. Petherick, A. Pearce, W.L. Armstrong, A.L.J. Youings.
 Football Colours were awarded to P.J. Were, C. Lewis, W. Elworthy, L.K.V. Job, W. Saunders.

Tuesday, 10th December.

Shooting.

The second Dormitory Competition, between teams selected on the results of the weekly practice. [See 5th November.] Brereton was hopelessly beaten.

BRERETON.				COURTENAY.			
A.J.E. Helps	22	15	37	J.B. Harris	20	20	40
E.A. Adams	14	18	32	L.K.V. Job	22	22	44
A.E. Preston	15	21	36	W. Saunders	20	20	40
R.W. Seldon	9	11	20	G.H. Dawe	16	26	42
	—	—	—		—	—	—
	60	65	125		78	88	166
	—	—	—		—	—	—

Courtenay won by 41 points.
Silver Spoon: L.K.V. Job.

Friday, 13th December.

Reading and Debating Society.

118th Meeting. S. Bendall was in the chair. There were 25 members present.

The Devon County School Football team (with Masters).   Back row, L. to R. – Preston, Lewis, Harris, Job. Middle row, L. to R. – Bendall, Taylor, Harries, Giffard, Seldon. Front row, L. to R. – Elworthy, Were.

The minutes having been read and confirmed the Treasurer was called upon to read the statement of accounts.

Statement of Accounts (Christmas Term 1907)

	£ s. d.			£ s. d.
To cash in hand	2 19 5	By donations to		
" Subscriptions	1 8 0	Entertainment fund	10 0	
		By slides on India		
		and Mantles	8 0	
		" Slides on Robespierre	3 8	
		" " " Railways	3 11	
		" Postage	2½	
		" Balance	3 1 7½	
	£4 7 5		£4 7 5	

[For pre-decimal coinage, see note in Prospectus – Fees.]

The meeting was then given up to "Impromptu speeches"
The following is a list of the subjects spoken on by the various members selected to speak.

J. Britton Esq.   That Limericks and diabolo [see Minutes for 20th November] have made the nation what it is.

[This young man had left the School in 1905, and went to read Maths at Cambridge, graduating in 1908. His name pops up from time to time in the Minutes, and he figures in a Staff photograph for this year – 1907. See also 14th December – the Concert. So presumably he came back to do some work as a student teacher during college vacations. He had already, in 1905, between leaving school and entering university, taken up a temporary post at Wesley College, Sheffield. (*Register*, May, 1905, p. 37.) See also 25th March, 3rd June, 10th July, 2nd October.]

W.L. Armstrong   Is it right to do a little evil for a great good?

S. Bendall   Who was the greatest general who ever lived?

Rev. E.C. Harries.   Do newspapers do more harm than good?

W.L. Giffard, Esq.   Which will be the most powerful nations in 1950?

R.T.H. Hooper   Should the House of Lords be abolished?

G.C. Fry, Esq.   Music hath charms to sooth [sic] the savage breast. Is it true?

L.K.V. Job   Which is the better Town or Country life?

A.E. Helps   Are there such things as Ghosts?

W. Saunders   Is it better to be a bigger fool than one looks, or to look a bigger fool than one is?

C. Lewis   Should the sale of alcoholic drink be prohibited?

T.H. Richards — Where ignorance is bliss; is it folly to be wise?

J. Britton Esq. — by special request. "Ghosts."

The House adjourned at 8 o'clock.

Saturday, 14th December.

The *Western Weekly News* printed this article on another Old Boy, T.R. Potbury. [See 7th January and 4th December.]

"Mr. Thomas R. Potbury was born in 1866, and is the sixth son of the late Mr. John Potbury, of Sidmouth. He entered the Devon County School in January, 1880 [one of three sons to do so], and in less than two years was head boy. [So was one of his brothers a few years before.] In 1881 he had the unique distinction of being the first junior in all England in both the Oxford and Cambridge local examinations. [These – both universities set two exams, the 'junior locals' and the 'senior' locals - were the founding ancestors of the present GCSE and A Level exams. Tables of individual performances were regularly published. So schools could not only boast of coming top in overall school performances; they could trumpet the fact that one of their boys had beaten everybody else in that particular subject – in the country.]

"In subsequent years he obtained first-class honours as a senior in both examinations. For three years he was awarded the Brereton Scholarship, the highest tenable at the school – twice he obtained a junior scholarship of the Royal Agricultural Society – and for two years he was head monitor, besides being a prominent member of both the cricket eleven and the football fifteen. [Note 'fifteen'. Controversy still continues about the exact nature of the 'football' which was played at the School during this period.] On leaving he was awarded the Fortescue silver medal for special merit, the highest honour the school could give. In 1884 he was offered an open Mathematical Scholarship at Queen's College, Cambridge, which he did not accept, but in the following year he obtained one of higher value at Christ's College, in the same University, where he went into residence in October of that year. [Which shows either arrogance, supreme confidence, or a large slice of luck.] He graduated in the Mathematical Tripos of 1889, but failed to do himself justice, for he was placed at the head of the second class – the 'Senior Optimes', as they are generally called – instead of among the 'Wranglers.'

"Since leaving Cambridge Mr. Potbury has been engaged in the teaching profession. He was for some time mathematical master at Beaumaris Grammar School; then he became Principal of Brondesbury College, Kilburn; and he is now mathematical master at University College School ... [An odd progression, from 'Principal' back to 'mathematical master', especially with a man of his gifts and record.] At the beginning of this year he married the eldest daughter of the late Mr. John Drew, of Sidmouth. [So, for all his travels and his distinctions, he married a local girl. See above. Perhaps, as he was 41 years old by this time, she was about all there was left, or he was getting desperate.]

"Mr. Potbury's eldest brother (J.A.) was the Principal of Queen's College, Demerara, where he died in May, 1903. Another brother is Captain F.J. Potbury, 3rd V.B. Devon Rifles, and a well-known shot. ['V.B.' – 'Volunteer Battalion?'

See 1st February.] A third brother is a prominent member of the Sidmouth cricket eleven, and captain of the School Old Boys' Eleven."

[One is tempted to comment, 'Phew!']

In the same issue, the editor turned his attention to another Old Boy:

"Alderman E. Sloper, J.P., [see also 4th December] Mayor of Hornsey, was born at Wiveliscombe, Somersetshire, in 1865. He received his early education at Taunton, at what was then known as Church College, and from here he went to the Devon County School, West Buckland. He commenced commercial life with Stuckey's Bank, at Bristol, remaining there eight years, during part of which time he played Rugby Football for Bristol. He came to London in 1890, having secured an appointment with the British Bank of South America. His present position is that of sub-accountant. Soon after his arrival at Harringay, Mr. Sloper became identified with the local Conservative Association, and also with the Literary Society. In 1894 he was elected a member of the District Council, a position which he held until the Borough Councils came into existence. He became a member of the Hornsey Borough Council, and when the School Board passed away he was elected on the Education Committee. He was one of the first aldermen of the borough, and last month was elected Mayor. Alderman Sloper was for two years and a half a member of the Middlesex County Council, and has rendered considerable public service as one of the Alexandra Park trustees."

Saturday, 14th December, contd.

The Breaking-up Concert was given, which was also attended by numerous visitors. The banjo selections and accompaniments were extremely popular. The following was the programme:-

PART I.

1. PIANO DUET	"Une Fête de Trianon"	A.H. AUSTIN & A. TAYLOR.
2. CHORUS	"Jack Frost"	CHORAL SOCIETY.
3. SONG	"The Admiral's Broom"	REV. E.C. HARRIES.
4. BANJO SELECTION	"Queen of the Burlesque"	MRS. LUTLEY, R.W. LUTLEY, REV. E.C. HARRIES.
5. SONG	"Extras"	E.M. BAGSHAWE.
6. OCTETTE	"Sweet and Low"	
7. RECITATION	"The Revenge"	G.C. FRY.
8. PLANTATION SONG	"De ole Banjo"	CHORAL SOCIETY.

PART II.

1. PART SONG	"The Hardy Norseman"	CHORAL SOCIETY.
2. SONG	"The Two Grenadiers"	A. TAYLOR.
3. PART SONG	"O, By Rivers, To whose Falls"	CHORAL SOC.
4. BANJO SELECTION	"Black Bess"	MRS. LUTLEY, R.W. LUTLEY, REV. E.C. HARRIES.
5. OCTETTE	"See our Oars with feather'd Spray"	
6. SONG	"O, ain't yer coming out, my Juliet?"	J. BRITTON.
7. CHORUS	"Breaking up for the Christmas Holidays"	CHORAL SOC.
8. PLANTATION SONG	"Goodnight"	CHORAL SOCIETY.

GOD SAVE THE KING.

Monday, 16th December.

Breaking-up Supper.

... the last evening of the Christmas Term ... After the usual Special Prayers and Lesson in Big School [see Prize Distribution, 29th July.], the Head Master read the Form Order for the term, and the lists of promotions and prizes.

He afterwards entertained the School to supper in the Dining Hall. Mrs. Harries [the Headmaster's mother, not his wife; he did not marry till 1918], Miss Hickman, Mrs. Lutley [she of the banjo at the concert – see 14th December], Miss Denny [the Matron], Miss Haywood, and Mr. W.L. Miles [he of the silver spoons – see 8th January] were present, besides the masters and boys. The School Cups and other trophies adorned the scene, all of them, by the fortune of war, being placed this year on the Courtenay tables.

After supper, Mr. G.C. Fry proposed the health of the Brereton Dormitory, which was enthusiastically drunk by their rivals at the other side of the room. S. Bendall responded in a very felicitous valedictory speech, this occasion being his last appearance as Head of the School.

Mr. A. Taylor then proposed the toast of the Courtenay Dormitory, which was also enthusiastically received. J.B. Harris made an able speech in response.

The Head Master then proposed "The Visitors," for whom Mr. W.L. Miles, our one "official spectator" at football and cricket matches, responded with a very effective speech, both serious and humorous.

The whole evening was, on every side, voted a great success.

Old Boys.

Henry Dendle, of Mooracre, Sandford, died, aged 63, after a short and unexpectedly serious illness. He was one of the first three pupils at the D.C.S.; and only survived his cousin, James Waldon, another of the first three, a couple of months. [See 17th October.] He was well-known in a large farming circle, and was held in the highest respect by all who knew him, as a capable, straightforward, and reliable business man and friend. His knowledge of parochial business and his sound judgment made him an excellent chairman of the Sandord Parish Meeting from its beginning.

Tuesday, 17th December.

The following boys left the School. "C" indicates the Courtenay, and "B" the Brereton Dormitory. The figures immediately after the names indicate the year and term of entering the School. [This use of the definite article in front of the names of the dormitories may explain why even today it is customary on formal occasions to refer to the present four houses in the same way – 'the Brereton', 'the Courtenay', and so on.]

FORM VI.

S. Bendall (B.), 1902 (2): Prefect, 1906 (2); Head of School, 1906 (3). Examinations: Preliminary Cambridge Local, 1903; Junior Local, 1904 and 1905; Senior Local, 1906; Institute of Chartered Accountants Preliminary Exam., 1907. Michael Snell English Prize, 1907. President of the Debating Society, 1907 (3). Football Colours, 1906; Captain, 1907. Cricket and Running Colours, 1907. Silver Medal for Swimming, 1907.

L. K.V. Job (C.), 1905 (1): Cricket, Football, and Running Colours, 1907. Silver Spoons for Rifle Shooting, February, March, and December, 1907. [Listed as 'Form V' in January, he had presumably been promoted at Easter or in September.]

FORM V.

E.A. Adams (B.), 1906 (2): Junior Cambridge Local, 1907; Silver Spoon for Rifle Shooting, May, 1907. [Form IV in January – like Job above, promoted during the year.]

FORM IV.

Preston (B.), 1904 (3): Football and Cricket Colours, 1907. Silver Spoon for Rifle Shooting, November, 1906. F. Chave (B.), 1906 (2): Form Prize, III. B., 1907. W.E. Ayre (C.), 1907 (1). T. Williams (B.), 1906 (3). [Chave, Ayre, and Williams had all gone up from Form III during the year.]

Friday, 20th December.

An Examination of Forms IV., III., and II. was held by the Staff ... The upper forms took the Cambridge Local Examinations instead. [For results see 29th December.]

Prizes were awarded to the following boys:-

FORM IV. - M. R. Roberts. "Great Englishmen," by Sidney Lee.
FORM III. - S.H. Oatway. "Don Quixote."
FORM II. - J. Wells. "Robinson Crusoe."

The following promotions were made after the Examination:-

To FORM VI. - H.G. Woolaway. *
To FORM V. - C.H. Petherick *, P.J. Were * [he began the year in Form III], M.R. Roberts, S.J. Widgery, S.A. Loram.
To FORM IV. - S.H. Oatway, L.A. Murless, F.S. Lee, W.E. Ayre, G.W. Anstey, T.P. Isaac, T. Williams.
To FORM III. - J. Wells, G.L. Blight, G.B. Anstey.

* Not Examined. Other names are in order of merit.

Thanks to the continued generosity of various Old Boys, it became possible last term to offer for competition three more Old Boys' Scholarships, of the value of £10 a year, tenable for three years. An Examination was held at the School [on 3rd December] and on the results of it the following boys were elected to Scholarships:-

R.L. Brokenshire, Barnstaple.
W.M.M. Hutchings, Exeter.
C.T.C. Lake, Exeter.

Saturday, 21st December.

Henry Dendle [see 16th December] was buried in Sandford Churchyard, amid general regret ... the Rev. G.T. Llewellin [a former teacher at the School, 1868-79] officiating.

Sunday, 22nd December.

W.N. Manning was ordained Deacon by the Bishop of Salisbury ... and was licensed to the curacy of Potterne, Wilts.

Saturday, 28th December.

The *Register* published the

School List. – Lent Term, 1908.

[Compare it with the List for the start of the Lent Term, 1907, 7th January.]

Head of the School	★ J.B. Harris, South Molton.
Prefects	W. Saunders, Kingston-on-Thames.
	W.L. Armstrong, Shipley, Yorks.
	W. Elworthy, Swimbridge.

FORM VI.

The three senior Prefects, and –	§ L.G.H. Major, Oakhill.
§ R.T.H. Hooper, Teignmouth [see 29th Dec.]	A.O. Parker, Winchcomb, Glos.
¶ C. Lewis, Chittlehampton	R.W. Seldon, Lincoln.
§ T.H. Richards, Ilfracombe	*H.G. Woolaway*, Chittlehampton.

FORM V.

§ H. Matthews, Hayle	A.L.J. Youings, Barnstaple.
¶ H.J. Richards, Chulmleigh	*D.T. Squire*, Filleigh.
§ H.F. Lovell, Chulmleigh	C.H. Petherick, Bude.
N.K. Pearce, Kingsbridge	P.J. Were, London.
§ A.H. Austin, Verwood, Dorset	M.R. Roberts, Ilfracombe.
W.F. Kingdon, South Molton	S.J. Widgery, South Molton .
H.E. Hicks, Berrynarbor	S.A. Loram, Exeter.
W. Elworthy, Swimbridge	C.V. Brook, Totnes.
A. Pearce, Barnstaple	W.J. Paddison, Barnstaple.
A.J.E. Helps, Bridgwater.	

FORM IV.

H.G. Hopper, Lee, Kent	*F.J. Pike*, East Buckland.
§ C.G. Harris, South Molton	¶ S.H. Oatway, Barnstaple.
A.P. Moor, South Molton	L.A. Murless, Exmouth.
V.J. Loram, Exeter.	F.S. Lee, Thorverton.
G.H. Dawe, Barnstaple	*G.W. Anstey*, Filleigh.
W.H. Pugsley, Barnstaple.	T.P. Isaac, Barnstaple.
E.B. Driver, Montserrat.	S. Paddison, Barnstaple.
J.L. Buckingham, North Molton.	S. Trull, Bristol.

FORM III.

J.L. Carter, Exmouth	L.W.E. Grant, Exmouth.
H.J. Dixon, Filleigh.	*W.J. Yeo*, West Buckland.
E.H. Southcombe, Cheltenham.	J. Wells, Winchester.
J. Pow, Combmartin.	G.L. Blight, Port Isaac, Cornwall.
E.W. Oakey, Bristol.	*G.B. Anstey*, Filleigh.
S.D.S. Craddock, Filleigh.	§ R.L. Brokenshire, Barnstaple.
W.W. Owbridge, Teignmouth.	E.W. B. Hoad, Landkey.
W.J. Squire, Barnstaple.	§ W.M.M. Hutchings, Exeter.
H.C. Batting, Silverton.	§ C.T.C. Lake, Exeter.
G.G. Garland, Filleigh.	W.G. Tarr, Bridgwater.
F. Hooper, Bideford.	N. Webber, Tiverton.

FORM II.

A.E. Brooks, East Buckland.	*L.B. Garland*, Filleigh.
J.E. Pidsley, Sidmouth.	*F.T. Garland*, Filleigh.
W.J.B. Wood, Bristol.	T.E. Hayward, New Milton, Hants.
T. Bendall, Bristol.	*R.J. Miller*, Filleigh.
C.E. Brooks, East Buckland.	

Day-boys' names in italics; ★ Shephard Law Scholar; § Old Boys' Scholars; ¶ County Council Scholars.

Sunday, 29th December.

The Cambridge Local Examinations.

The results of these examinations are given below. We congratulate R.T.H. Hooper (an Old Boys' Scholar) on gaining Second Class Honours in the Junior Examination, with distinction in Geography; and also W.L. Armstrong on his First Class Honours in the Senior Examination. It is quite rare for a boy to take a Senior First Class at the first attempt, and only one year after passing the Junior Examination.

SENIOR LOCAL.

Honours, Class I . : W.L. Armstrong.
Passed : W. Saunders, C. Lewis.

JUNIOR LOCAL.

Honours, Class II . : R.T.H. Hooper.
(Distinction in Geography).

Passed :	E.A. Adams.
L.G.H. Major.	A.H. Austin.
A.O. Parker.	W.F. Kingdon.
T.H. Richards.	H.F. Lovell.
H.G. Woolaway.	H. Matthews.

Monday, 30th December.

The Devon County School Old Boys' Association.

NEW MEMBERS 1907

Those marked with an asterisk are Life Members.

[There were 61 altogether. It would be perhaps wearisome to list all of them, but I have mentioned some of the more exotic addresses, and a sprinkling of the English ones as well, just to give the flavour.]

* Aborn, Rev. T.L., Russell, Ontario, Canada	1868-1869
* Barnecutt, C.M., Park Villa, Edgerton Park, Exeter	1906-1907
Bond, E.W., Box 121, Johannesbsurg, Transvaal	1876-1877
Britton, R., Bratton Fleming, N. Devon	1902-1904
* Couch, E.H., 4, Sunridge Terrace, South Circular Road, Dublin	1884-1888
* Gifford, A., Marikuppam, Mysore State, India	1887-1889
* Harris, R.Q., The Bungalow, Leça de Palmeira, Oporto, Portugal	1875-1878
Lee, F., Raddon Court, Thorverton	1880-1882
* Miller, W., Stoodleigh, West Buckland, South Molton	1893-1895
Pearce, E.R., c/o Mrs. Mears, Church Hill, Hednesford, Staffs	1901-1906
Trickey, T., Downes Farm, Crediton	1875-1876
Watts, A., Hilton Road, Natal	1881-1883
Wheaton, W.H., The Laurels, Worcester Park, Surrey	1877-1878
Whiteway, E.V., 22, Albert Embankment, London, S.E	1897-1899

[Names here echo some of those in the School lists for 1907. And this trend continues today – into the third, even fourth generation.

The Miller family, which provided the very first accommodation for the first three pupils of the School, has continued to send its children there, right up to the end of the 20th century.

One – Barnecutt - had joined within months of leaving.

Of the 61 mentioned in the full list, only 10 had stayed at the School for four years or more. Over half had stayed two years or less. So how did the 'Old Boy' bond get built?]

OFFICERS FOR THE YEAR 1908-1909

President.
PROF. T.A. HEARSON, M.Inst.C.E., M.I.N.A., F.C.I.P.A.

Vice-Presidents.
W. FISHER, J.P.

J.W. SHAWYER.

Committee.
Ex-Officio : REV. E.C. HARRIES, M.A., *Head Master.*

J.F. BOWDEN, F.S.I., H.R. CHAMPION, T.R. POTBURY, B.A.

Hon Treasurer.
R.P. CHOPE, B.A.

Hon. Secretaries.
G.C. FRY, M.Sc., F.I.C.

W.C. WHEELER.

Captains.
Cricket : T.R. POTBURY.

Football : C. SAUNDERS.

[Note the continued presence of Chope and T.R. Potbury, who have figured frequently in these pages. Note too W.C. Wheeler, who was associated with the School for 77 years – as successful pupil, Head Boy, captain of everything, pupil teacher, and – much later - caretaker headmaster. He held every office in the Old Boys' Association, and, just by the way, served on the Board of Governors for 57 years.]

The following Gatherings will be held [during the coming year, 1908] :–

PLACE	DATE	GATHERING	CHAIRMAN	TICKETS
Little Barnfield Hall, Exeter.	Sat., Jan. 4 5.15 for 5.30 p.m.	Informal Social (Devon v. Somerset at Exeter.)	R. PEARSE CHOPE B.A.	2s. 6d.
Anderton's Hotel (Masonic Temple)	Tues., Jan 7 6.30 for 7 p.m.	Annual Dinner	Rev. J.H. THOMPSON Vice-Chairmen : [M.A. R. PEARSE CHOPE, B.A. Rev. R. SEALY GENGE, M.A.	6s.
Anderton's Hotel (St. Dunstan's Room.)	Wed., Feb. 5 7 for 7.30 p.m.	Informal Social	S.R. DYER, M.D.	2s. 6d.
West Buckland	Thurs., Feb. 27	Football Match – Past v. Present.		
Anderton's Hotel (St. Dunstan's Room).	Wed., March 4 7 for 7.30 p.m.	Informal Social	H.B. SQUIRE	2s 6d.
Little Barnfield Hall, Exeter	Fri., March 27 5.15 for 5.30 p.m.	do.	Rev. J.H. THOMPSON M.A.	2s 6d.
West Buckland	July 25-29 July 25 " 26 " 27 " 28 } " 29 } " 28	Jubilee Gathering Old Boys assemble. Old Boys' Sunday. Speech Day Cricket Match – Past v. Present. Annual General Meeting of the Association.	Rev. J.H. THOMPSON M.A.	
Anderton's Hotel, Fleet Street, E.C.	Fri., Oct. 16 7 for 7.30 p.m.	Social	C.W. Sloper, J.P.	2s 6d.
West Buckland	Th. Oct. 22	Football Match – Past v. Present		
Palmer and Edwards', Exeter	Sat. Nov. 7 5 p.m.	Social	Rev. Chancellor Edmonds	2s. 6d.
Anderton's Hotel	Wed., Dec. 2	Smoking Concert	William Hill, M.D., B.Sc.	1s. 0d.

Tuesday, 31st December.

1907.

Devon County School, Ltd.

(IN VOLUNTARY LIQUIDATION)

============================

Statement of Expenditure and Earnings for the Year.

Balance Sheet made up to December 31st.

Profit and Loss Account.

[These accounts still survive, in Mr. Taylor's beautiful handwriting. See the illustrations.]

TAYLOR, Secretary,

F.B. WYATT, Solicitor,

Liquidator.

The Weather of 1907.

A very dry spring and a very wet, cold summer were the dominant climatic features of the year 1907 at West Buckland. The following table shows the great contrast, as regards the first two terms, between 1906 and 1907:-

RAINFALL

	1906	1907
	Inches	Inches
First Term	10·46	6·35
Second Term	7·76	10·23
Third Term	14·67	14·53
School Year	32·89	31·11
Whole Year	46·82	42·40

In 1907 there were three days April 20, August 17, and December 4 on which more than one inch of rain fell; and on seventeen other days the fall exceeded half an inch. Of these twenty very wet days (which together gave us nearly one-third of the total rainfall, four were in December, and three in October. The driest month was September (·90 inch), and the wettest was October (6·16 inches). The longest rainless period was twenty-two days – September 7th to 28th inclusive.

The highest shade temperature of the year was 79° on July 20th. Up to the middle of July the warmest day of the year was April 1st.

Copy of six-monthly December Balance Sheet. Judy Taylor again.

End of December entries.

Staff Biographies

Revd Ernest Charles Harries

Revd. Ernest Charles Harries, B.A. Trinity College, Dublin.

Born 7th June, 1868
Educated Shrewsbury School, 1881-6.
Trinity College, Dublin, 1893-1897. Pass B.A. 1897.
London University (Ext.). Inter. Arts, 1903.
Previous appointments –
Second Master at Wellington (Somerset), Jan: 1897 –
    Dec: 1899.
Devon County School, Jan: 1900 – Aug: 1904 – Second
    Master and Chaplain.
Blundell's School, Tiverton, Jan: 1904 – April, 1907.
Played rugby and cricket for Somerset, regular club
    football.
Appointed Headmaster Devon County School,
    definitive from 5th May, 1907.
Special subjects – History, English, some Maths. Classics,
    French.
Duties, besides that of HM – All History, English V. VI.,
    Maths V. IV., Divinity, School Chaplain. [He coached
    rugby too, and, according to one Old Boy's testimony, could run
    'like a stag' in his sixties, and insisted that the boys should tackle
    him. Understandably, they quite enjoyed 'getting the Old Man'.]
Salary – £100, later raised to £150, and in 1922 to £210.
    – Chaplaincy – £24 – £25. [That's what it says.]
    – Estimated value of board and lodging if given as
       part of emoluments – £140.
    – Capitation Fees – £2 on each boarder, later
       raised to £2.10s. in 1910, and £3 in 1913.
Cricket – School Team with Masters – played against
    South Molton (29th May), 4th Batt. Devon Regiment

(5th June), Dulverton (8th June), South Molton (17th
    July), Dulverton (20th July), the Old Boys – two-day
    match (30th and 31st July).
Spoke regularly at the meetings of the Debating Society
    – 2nd October, 19th October, 23rd October, 20th
    November, 4th December, 13th December.
14th December – performed in the Breaking-up
    Concert.
1915 – he began the series of annual Gilbert and Sullivan
    productions that became a School institution, till
    he retired in 1934. He usually played the leading
    role.
1917 – in the summer, he attended a course at Gosport in
    physical training and bayonet fighting – and
    obtained a 'satisfactory' certificate.
1918 – 6th January – officiated at the wedding of his
    brother, Revd. F.G. Harries, to Ann Bendall, sister
    of the 1907 Head Boy Sidney. [F.G.'s nickname,
    incidentally, was 'Bouncer'.]
In April, Eleanor Bendall, another sister, joined the Staff.
    [By October, Harries had married her. She was 32; he was 50.
    His brother officiated at the wedding. His nickname was,
    predictably, 'Ernie'; his wife's was, equally predictably, 'Ellie'.
    'Ernie' and 'Ellie' – they must have made quite a team.]
Sometime during the year, he presented two books to the
    Library – "Hushed Up at German Headquarters", by
    Wm. Le Queux, and "The Upper Berth", by F. Marion
    Crawford.
1919 – 9th September – his wife gave birth to a son,
    Charles. [Who later attended the School.]
1920 – 9th October – his wife gave birth to twin sons.
    [Who also attended. In the memory of one very Old Boy,
    they were 'little hellers – and you couldn't touch 'em'.]
    – elected President of the South Molton Football
    Club.
1921 – 15th April – his mother, Ellen Priscilla, who lived
    with him, died aged 86. [She is buried in East
    Buckland Churchyard.]

*Harries enjoyed riding, and, from the comfort of the saddle, would
chivvy laggard boys on cross-country runs.*

In his record it states that he played rugby and cricket for Somerset.

He had run a cadet force when he was at Blundell's, and could not wait to set one up at the Devon County School, which he succeeded in doing in 1909. He saw no irony in exchanging his dog collar for a Sam Browne.

He was a keen footballer too. In fact, the perfect exponent of muscular Christianity.

In fact Harries loved dressing up, full stop. For twenty years he inspired annual productions of Gilbert and Sullivan operas, and usually took the starring role. Here he intends to 'make the punishment fit the crime'.

1934 – July – retired. Became a local clergyman at Sandford, near Crediton [where an earlier incumbent was G.T. Llewellin, a previous master at the School].

1938 – 14th January – attended the Old Boys' Dinner. [He must have attended a lot more during his service as Headmaster.]

1946 – on confirmation day, he visited the School as Bishop's Chaplain. 'It was a joy to see him again looking exactly the same as ever.' [He was then 78.] He also served as Rural Dean.

Served on the Board of Governors.

1951 – retired [again] to live at St. Anthony's, 1, Tidewell Road, Budleigh Salterton.

1954 – 10th May – died. 'One pleasant noon in May, his ashes were buried by the side of his mother in the graveyard at East Buckland.' [This was written by Cordy Wheeler, who had been a pupil, a teacher, a governor, a president of the Old Boys' Association, and a caretaker headmaster, and who, when *he* died, was to have been associated w ith the School for 77 years. He also recorded a gentle touch of Harries' humility:] 'A week before he died he told the writer how conscious he was that in some respects he had failed.'

[Ellie lived to be nearly a hundred, and was buried beside him in 1985.]

Adelbert Taylor

Born 6th June, 1873.

Educated at the Choir School, Stratford-on-Avon, 1885-8.

King Edward VIth's Grammar School, Stratford-on-Avon, 1885-1890.

Certificate Trinity College of Music Pianoforte Playing Junior 1889.

Certificate London College of Music Pianoforte Playing Senior 1890.

Certificate Elementary Drawing First Class, 1901.

Teachers' Cert. Woodwork of the Board of Exams. for Educational handwork, 1908.

Teaching posts – Grammar School, Soham. Cambs. April, 1891 – December, 1893.

Grosvenor College, Luton, Beds. January 1894 – July, 1895.

Definitive appointment – Sept., 1895.

Special subjects – Music, Pianoforte and Singing, Drawing, Shorthand, Book-keeping.

Duties – Drawing throughout the School; Singing throughout the School and greater part of Music pupils; all the book-keeping and shorthand; Mathematics in Form II and Form III; Geography in the Lower School (from 1909); Divinity in 1908; Manual Instruction (from 1909); Secretary to the Devon County School Governors; Organist, East Buckland Church.

Salary – As Master £90, raised in 1912 to £105.
– As Secretary £25, raised in 1910 to £60.
– As non-resident, £200, raised in July, 1918 to £220.

Cricket – School Team with Masters – played against South Molton (29th May), 4th Batt. Devon Regiment (5th June), Dulverton (8th June), North Devon (19th

Adelbert Taylor, man of many gifts, all of which he laid at the door of the School for the whole of his working life. Here he is, in his mid-twenties, shortly after his arrival at West Buckland.

This was taken in July, 1907 – a season in which he topped both the battling and bowling averages of the 'Boys with Masters' team.

A keen footballer too, as this 'Boys with Masters' photo of 1906-7 testifies.

In more sombre mood, in a Staff photograph of 1907. A lot of teachers at this time seem to have favoured boots instead of shoes. Perhaps it was the exigencies of the rural conditions.

From a Staff photograph of 1913 – with Harries beside him.

From a Staff photograph of 1919 – look at the toll the War had taken on both Taylor and Harries. And Taylor was only 46 when this was taken.

June), South Molton (17th July), Dulverton (20th July), Barnstaple Banks (25th July), North Devon (for School Past and Present) (27th July), the Old Boys – two-day match (30th and 31st July).

In the season of 1907, he topped both batting and bowling averages.

In both spring and autumn terms, he played regularly for the 'Boys with Masters' football team. Specially mentioned in the report of the game against Taunton Y.M.C.A. (24th October) and Barnstaple Town (27th November).

4th December – spoke at the Reading and Debating Society.

14th December – sang in the Breaking-up Concert, and conducted the Choral Society. [See the photo of him with the Choir.]

1910 – 3rd August – married Miss S.E. Walmsley at St. George's Church, Stockport.

[Adelbert Taylor – 'Judy' Taylor because, so the story goes, he had a voice like that of Mr. Punch – served the School in the above and countless other ways, from 1895 until ill health forced his retirement in April, 1929. He died a few months later, aged only 56, probably of cancer; he was a heavy smoker. He, and his wife and son David ('man of music and mirth'), are all buried in East Buckland churchyard.]

George Cecil Fry

Born 11th October, 1876.

Educated at Boys' High School, Salt Schools, Shipley, Yorks., 1886- 91.

Yorkshire College (now Leeds University – [by 'now' they mean by 1903]), 1891-6.

Cambridge Junior Local Honours 1st Class, 1890.

George Cecil Fry – only the second teacher in the School's history appointed specifically to teach Science.

As his obituary said, he was no athlete, but he chipped in and did his bit – as most staff were expected to do in a small country boarding school. [The complete football team is already printed – p. 45.]

London University Matric. 1st Class, 1893.

Victoria University, B.Sc. ordinary, 1894. B.Sc. 2nd class Chemistry, 1895.

(M. Sc. Leeds, taken without exam 1905).

A.I.C. Exam. 1896 (F.I.C. without exam. 1901).

Teaching posts –

Dronfield Grammar School, Derbyshire 1896-7.

Newbury Grammar School, Berks. 1897-1900.

Archbishop Holgate's School, York, 1900 – 2.

Middlesbrough High School 1902 – 3.

Appointed to Devon County School, December, 1903.

Special subjects –

Physics, Chemistry, Mathematics, Geography. [He was only the second teacher to be appointed specifically to take Science.]

Duties – All Science work – that is, in the whole School; Form VI Maths. and Geography (1908)

- In charge of School Rifle Club, Library, and Reading and Debating Society.
- Editor of School Magazine.

'On wintry afternoons he might be seen leading the runs.'

Autumn term – spoke at every meeting except one of the Reading and Debating Society – 2nd October,

19th October, 23rd October, 30th October, 9th November, 4th December, 13th December.

14th December – performed in the Breaking-up Concert.

1908 – end of Easter term – married. Presents from boys and Old Boys.

Salary – £200, later raised to £220 in Jan. 1911.

Left July, 1911, to enter a Theological Course at Cambridge.

After being ordained, he performed parochial work in Nottingham, Ilfracombe, and in Somerset, where he was vicar of Corfe and later of Fivehead.

1942 – ill health forced his retirement.

1944 – 29th April – died. [His obituary in the *Register* the following November contained these remarks:] 'Though no athlete, [he] always took an interest in School sports. The School *Register* may be said to have gained a new spirit under his editorship: all facts were collected and the events of the Term gracefully arranged, each number ending with wonderful statistics on the weather. [So *he* was the who had stood up to Chope so many times.] He had a profound knowledge of English Literature and, curious enough, much interest in Geography, on which he published several books. His death will be regretted by the writer, who in the early days had a loyal colleague and afterwards through the years a very dear friend.' [This was written by Harries himself.]

G.H. Grimes

B.A. Cambridge. Appointed Lent term, 1907.

J.P.R. Marichal

B.ès L. (Besançon), B.ès. Sc. (Nancy). Appointed Lent term, 1907.

Mr. Duke

Educated at Taplow Grammar School. Age – approx. 20.

16th April – appointed on probation.

5th May – definitive appointment – in charge of all subjects in the Second Form.

– Salary, £45. Value of board and lodging if given as part of emoluments – £40.

1st August – left the School.

Walter Longueville Giffard

[This young man's name goes back to medieval Normandy. There was a well-documented Walter Giffard who came over with the Conqueror. And his manor headquarters in Normandy were a few miles inland from Dieppe, at Longueville. The name – in all its three parts – has survived for over eight hundred years.]

Born 25th November, 1886.

Educated at K.E.S. Louth, Lincolnshire, 1896-1899.

Christ's Hospital, 1899-1903.

Oakham School, 1903-1904.

King's College, 1904. London University. Ext. 1905. London Matriculation, 1905.

Previous post – Durston House School, Ealing W., 1904-1907.

5th May – appointed on probation.

16th September – definitive appointment.

Special subjects – Classics, French, English, Ely. Maths.

Duties – all Latin, Third Form English (1908-09), Divinity and Cricket (1909).

Salary – £70. Raised in Jan., 1909 to £85. Value of board and lodging is given as part of emoluments – £40.

Cricket – School Team with Masters – played against South Molton (29th May), 4th Batt. Devon Regiment (5th June), Dulverton (8th June), North Devon (19th June), South Molton (17th July), Dulverton (20th July), Barnstaple Banks (25th July), North Devon (for School Past and Present) (27th July), the Old Boys – two-day match (30th and 31st July). Wrote the season's cricket report for the *Register*.

Autumn term – spoke at meetings of the Debating Society – 2nd October, 23rd October, 20th November, 13th December.

Autumn term – played for the Boys' and Masters' Football team – specially mentioned in report of the match against Taunton Y.M.C.A. (24th October), Holy Trinity (9th November), and Barnstaple Town (27th November).

17th Dec., 1910 – left to go to a private school at Eastbourne.

[It seems from this that the School got its money's worth out of this young man, who, when he was appointed, was still short of his twenty-first birthday.]

Served in First World War.

1915 – Captain in Oxford and Bucks. Light Infantry.

O.B.E., Greek M.C., Mentioned in despatches.s Later Major.

1968 – 10th August – died, aged 82. [His obituary said that he had been Bursar at Epsom College for many years, before he became Secretary of the G.B.A.(?) 'He was a very good cricketer and soccer player.']

Walter Longueville Giffard – only twenty years old, but full of legs and energy. In the football photos, he dominates the picture by virtue of his flamingo-like legs embracing the shoulders of the boy seated before him. See the DCS Football team – p.104.

Ernest Murray Bagshawe. Interesting that three teachers in such a small staff bore the Christian name Ernest.

Not many teachers boasted such an unusual pair of cricket boots.

One of his ex-pupils, V.J. Loram (Form III), when he wrote to the *Register* to say he had heard of his death, said that the 'Longueville' [see above] in his name 'much intrigued our youthful minds'.

Ernest Murray Bagshawe
16th September – joined the Staff in succession to Mr. Duke.
Formerly a student at Gloucester Theological College, and a master on the training-ship *Worcester* and at St. Anne's, Redhill.
Autumn Term – spoke at the Reading and Debating Society – 23rd October, 30th October, 20th November, 4th December.
14th December – performed in the Breaking-up Concert.
1911 – 25th April – married C.A. Harrison, daughter of R. Harrison, Esq., Marton Hall. [The wedding took place at] St. Peter's Church, Marton-in-Craven.

Ernest Michael Watson
Born 3rd October, 1873.
Educated at an elementary school in Stevenage, Herts.
[No record survives of any college training.]
Trained as an organist at Stevenage, and was employed as organist at South Tawton and South Molton.
Sept., 1896 – appointed to the School, primarily to teach the piano and the violin. [Where did he learn those?] He played the piano for twenty years in rehearsals and performances of the Gilbert and Sullivan operas so dear to Harries' heart, between 1915 and 1934.
In 1918, he joined the Forces – at the age of 44! [Presumably, he could no longer stand being left behind.] The *Register* recorded that he 'spent his spare time tackling the clarinet'. [He returned immediately after the War.]
[I have found no mention of him in the records of 1907, and he does not figure in any staff photograph I have seen before 1913. He figures only spasmodically in staff photos thereafter, despite the fact that he

Ernest Michael Watson – the longest-serving member of the academic staff in the School's history (42 years). But he does not appear in any Staff photograph that I can find before 1913. (See his biographical notes.)

By 1919 he had shed his moustache.

served the School for longer than any other member of the teaching staff in the School's history. One can only conclude that, as a mere musician, he did not really 'count'. Yet for decades he was a well-known figure to generations of boys who bumbled, bawled, and blustered their way through G. and S. He even attracted two nicknames instead of one – 'Watto' (which was predictable) and 'Barch' (which was impenetrable).]

1938 – retired after 42 years' service.

[The Treasurer of the Old Boys' Association wrote to the members, suggesting that a donation of half a crown (12½p.) would be a suitable sum for each to contribute to his leaving present.]

1950 – 5th November – died.

Non-teaching staff –

Miss Denny – Matron.
Served from 1900 to 1909
11th January, 1907 – the Revd. Harries, at the Old Boys' Dinner, spoke of her hospitality and efficiency.
24th February, 1916, she died 'after a very short illness, from heart failure'.
'Old Boys ... will remember her ... for her many kindly acts' ...

George Balment – Gardener and handyman.
Came to work at the School in the year of its foundation, 1858. Served continuously till the infirmities of age forced his retirement in 1916 – after 58 years. He died in his sleep on 16th November, 1921, aged 87, and was buried in East Buckland churchyard. [The *Register* ended its tribute with the words 'one of Nature's gentlemen'.]

W.H. Counter – one of the oldest members of the domestic staff. [Yet he still joined up, because J.B. Harris (*qv*) said in a letter to the HM in the spring of 1916,] 'Counter has joined the Devons at Winchester, and is well but has had to put up with the removal of many teeth.' [Harris wrote this from *Salonika*, so the word had got around – the family grapevine.]

1916 – November – killed near Totnes through falling from the train. The Editor of the *Register* wrote, 'His duties in connection with the boys made him a well-known

George Balment, handyman and gardener, who served the School from the day of its foundation until 1916 – 58 years.

character in our lives; chiefly however he will be remembered as our constant companion in camp. The Commanding Officer of the Corps [Harries himself] will ... feel his loss very much.' [This is yet another good instance of the family feeling that pervaded the School, and, no doubt, many others like it; even though a servant was referred to only by his surname, everybody was known, and everybody mattered.]

William Skinner – Under-gardener.
[Another long-serving School servant. When he died on 6th June, 1918, the *Register* recorded his passing in these gentle terms:] 'A singularly unaffected man, he was always ready to oblige anyone, and he possessed a cheerfulness of manner which will be long remembered ... deeply regretted by a large circle of friends, not least among them being the members of his Sunday-school, where he had laboured ... for forty-two years.'

[I have been unable to discover in School records the names of any of the other domestic staff – cooks, chambermaids, and 'general duties' servants – though we do have a photograph of at least some of them (see illustrations). Most of them would have walked from the nearby villages of West Buckland or East Buckland, because there were no bus services, and no station nearer than three miles; and no teacher, much less a School servant, owned a motor car in 1907. Nowadays, the Bursar must find parking space for senior *pupils*, never mind staff.]

End of Staff biographies.

Boys' biographies – Prefects

[All the information contained in these 'biographies' has come from the records of either the School or the Old Boys. I could have cast the net more widely – War Office records, for example, or local newspaper files, electoral rolls, census returns from the Internet, and so on. But that would have diluted the School's authorship, so to speak. After all, if you publish a diary, you do not include a potted history of the time; you let the diary speak for itself – gaps and all. That is what I have done. What follows is not a set of complete life stories; it is what the School knew, or found out, about its present and past pupils.

If no year is given, the dates refer to the year 1907.

Where I can discover it, I have mentioned which house the boy was in. Only they were not called 'houses' in 1907; they were called 'dormitories'. For obvious reasons. And there were only two – one named after the founder, Revd. J.L. Brereton; the other after an early benefactor and director, the Earl of Devon, whose family name was Courtenay.

Frequently, a pupil is described – it seems, dismissively – as 'Day Boy', and no dormitory title goes against his name. Yet, quite often, later on, a dormitory name does appear. One can only guess that the boy in question transferred from being a day pupil to being a boarder, and so qualified for being included in the human race; the new Headmaster, Harries, had very set views on the value of boarding. And one must remember that the School had been set up as a boarding institution, so Harries was only following tradition.

However, as Harries built up the School, from its modest total of 68 at the beginning of 1907, the number of day boys grew alongside the number of boarders, so it seems that he decided to group them under a new name – and what better name than that of the School's neighbour and benefactor, 'Fortescue' ? I have taken the liberty of reminding you of this at various points in these biographies, so that you don't have to keep turning back to find out what's going on.]

Sidney Bendall, as Head of School, complete with waistcoat and chain (which were sported, incidentally, by many senior boys).

Sidney BENDALL,   Bristol.
Brereton dormitory.
1902 – April – entered the School.
1903 – Preliminary Cambridge Local Examination.
1903 – Junior Cambridge 'Locals' – 1905 too.
1906 – Senior Cambridge 'Locals'.
    – September – appointed Head of School.
The Spring Runs – 24th January – 2nd in the Railway Run.
Football First XI – Forward, Old Colour (1906), Captain.
Reading and Debating Society – 28th Jan. – 102nd meeting – Proposed that 'this House is in favour of a Channel Tunnel'.
– 4th Feb. – 103rd meeting – Congratulated J.B. Harris on his paper about General Gordon.
6th February, special mention in the football game against Barnstaple Town.
7th February – 2nd in the Beeches Run.
12th February – spoke at the Debating Society's 104th meeting in 'Newspapers' debate, the 105th on 18th February, and the 106th meeting on February 25th.
7th March – 7th in the Tuck Run.
11th March – spoke in the debate about professionalism in sport.

25th March – Elected President of the Debating Society for the Christmas Term.
27th March – played in the Scratch Sixes.
Lent term – Shooting – participated in one Dormitory Competition.
5th May – Cambridge Local Examination – Senior Section – passed.
20th May – Athletic Sports – 1st in Open Half-Mile; 2nd in 100 yds., Quarter-Mile, Mile, and Steeplechase; 2nd in Handicap 120 yds.
Cricket First XI – played against Landkey (11th May), King's College, Taunton (1st June), Somerset County School (12th June), Bratton Fleming (22nd June), Taunton School (29th June and 2nd July).
Cricket – School Team with Masters – played against South Molton (29th May), Dulverton (8th June), North Devon (19th June), Summerland Stragglers (10th July), Dulverton (20th July), the Old Boys – two-day match (30th and 31st July).
Cricket – played for School Past and Present against North Devon (27th July).
Awarded his School Colours for Cricket at the end of the season.

From the Past v. Present match of July, 1907.

Cricket House Matches – played v. Courtenay (25th May, 18th June). [Most games were played on a dormitory basis, but the new Headmaster, Harries, soon instituted changes designed to give the School a face-lift, and to bring it more into line with the fashionable public schools. One of these changes was to call the dormitories 'houses' in future. 1907 seems to have been a change-over year, with some competitions – like Shooting – being recorded as between 'dormitories', and others as between 'houses'.]

18th June – Cricket House Matches – played v. Courtenay.

23rd July – House Swimming Competition – won both the Short and Long Races, and member of winning Relay team.

29th July – Prize Day – won the Michael Snell English Prize – *New Land*, by Sverdrup.

– won the Silver Medal for Swimming.

Autumn term – captain of the Football First XI – left wing, mentioned specially in match reports of games against Barnstaple Town (28th September), South Molton Y.M.C.A. (2nd October), North Molton (12th October), Taunton Y.M.C.A. (24th October), Taunton School (26th October), Holy Trinity (9th November), North Devon School (20th November), Filleigh (23rd November), and in the second House Match (21st November). [There are so many mentions in despatches here that the uncharitable thought crosses the mind that perhaps it was the Captain who wrote the match reports.]

2nd October – presided at the Debating Society's debate on Socialism.

Presided also at the 112th meeting of the Reading and Debating Society (19th October), the 113th (23rd October), the 114th (30th October), the 116th (20th November, when he also spoke), as he also did at the 118th meeting (13th December).

9th November – read a paper on Robespierre at the 115th meeting.

The Autumn Runs – 30th November – 2nd in the Bray Run.

- Awarded Running Colours.

Institute of Chartered Accountants Preliminary Exam.

Christmas – left the School.

1913 – passed the final Examination of the Society of Chartered Accountants. [It seems to have taken him a

long time to qualify – six years.]

First World War –

1914 – serving with the South Staffordshire Regiment.

1917 – commissioned in the South Staffordshires.

– –9th August – married Maimie, second daughter of Mr. and Mrs. David Lowden, at Rangemoor Church, Burton-on-Trent. The priest was the Revd. Arthur Lowe. [A relative of Captain Mainwaring?]

He was a regular goal-scorer for the First XI.

1918 – 22nd April – his wife gave birth to a son at Bristol.

[On the 6th January, 1918, his younger sister married Revd. F. G. Harries, the School Chaplain. On the 21st August, 1918, his elder sister married Revd. E.C. Harries, the Headmaster. Each priest officiated at his brother's wedding. Headmaster Harries' wife Eleanor – 'Ellie', or 'Nellie', as she was known to generations of boys – lived to be 99, dying as recently as 1985.

Three of his Sidney Bendall's brothers – Charles (left 1904), William (left 1905), and Tom (left 1913 – *qv*) – also attended the School. All three served in the First World War. Miraculously, all four came home.]

1927 – 14th January – attended the Old Boys' Dinner.

Joseph Bastable HARRIS,
South Molton. b. 1892 Courtenay dormitory.

1902 – May – entered the School. Shephard Law Scholar.

1903 – Form III Prize.

1904 – Form IV Prize.

– Junior Cambridge Local Examinations – Third Class Honours.

1905 – Cambridge Senior Local Examinations, Third Class Honours.

1906 – Form V Prize.

– appointed Prefect.

– awarded the Edmonds Divinity Prize (and in 1905 – *and* in 1907 – see below).

1907 – 24th January – the Spring Runs – 6th in the Railway Run.

28th Jan. – Reading and Debating Society – spoke in the debate about the Channel Tunnel.

4th Feb. – Read a paper on General Gordon to the Debating Society.

Football First XI – Half-back. Awarded Colours.

Joseph Bastable Harris (nickname 'Basil'). One of the longest attenders – eight years. He looked, and, was, so dependable. A schoolmaster all his life.

7th February – 11th in the Beeches Run.

12th February – spoke at the Debating Society meeting in 'Newspapers' debate.

7th March – 4th in the Tuck Run.

11th March – spoke in the debate about professionalism in sport.

27th March – played in the Scratch Sixes.

April – Awarded Football Colours.

Lent term – Shooting – both Dormitory Competitions.

5th May – Cambridge Local Examinations – Senior Section – Class III, Honours.

20th May – Athletic Sports – 1st in Open 100 yds., Quarter-Mile, and Hurdles; 3rd in Handicap 120 yds.

Cricket House Matches – played v. Brereton (25th May, 18th June).

Cricket First XI (captain) – played against Landkey (11th May), King's College, Taunton (1st June), Somerset County School (12th June), Bratton Fleming (22nd June), Taunton School (29th June and 2nd July), Summerland Stragglers (10th July).

Cricket – School Team with Masters – played against South Molton (29th May), 4th Batt. Devon Regiment (5th June), Dulverton (8th June), North Devon (19th June), South Molton (17th July), Dulverton (20th July), Barnstaple Banks (25th July), Old Boys – two-day match (30th and 31st July).

Cricket – played for School Past and Present against North Devon (27th July).

Awarded his School Colours for Cricket at the end of the season.

Summer Term – member of the Rifle Club. Took part in three Dormitory Competitions.

29th July – Prize Day – won the Acland Science Prize – *Starland*, by Sir R.S.Ball.

– won the Head Master's Language Prize – *Shakespeare's Plays*.

– won the Edmonds Divinity Prize – *Helps to the Study of theBible*.

– won a Cambridge Local Honour Prize, Senior, Class III – *Highways and Byeways in Devon and Cornwall*, by Norway.

– won a Silver Spoon for Shooting.

2nd October – participated in the Debating Society's proceedings.

19th October – read a paper on 'Hindus and their Religions' to the Debating Society.

19th October – the Autumn Runs – 9th in the North-West Run. Awarded Running Colours.

23rd October – spoke at the 113th meeting of the Reading and Debating Society.

Autumn Term – Shooting – 5th November, first Dormitory Competition.

10th December, second Dormitory Competition.

– Football – played regularly at half-back for the First XI.

9th November – presided at the 115th meeting of the Reading and Debating Society.

20th November – spoke at the 116th meeting of the Debating Society.

1908 – Jan. to April – President of the Reading and Debating Society.

– Captain of First XI Cricket – and in 1909 and 1910.

– Champion Athlete – also in 1909 and 1910. Set a record in the Mile.

– appointed Head of School.

– Oxford Senior Local Examinations – Second Class Honours, with Distinction in Mathematics – awarded a prize – "The Earth's Beginning", by Sir R.S. Ball.

1909 – March and October – won Silver Spoons for Shooting. Rifleman's Certificate.

– Sergeant in the Officers' Training Corps.

1910 – Math. Scholarship, Selwyn College, Cambridge.

– Awarded the Fortescue Medal [hard to see how they could have withheld it].

– July – left the School.

He played cricket for the School for five years.

His football record was almost as good.

1911 – news reached the School of his being awarded
Football Colours at Selwyn.

1913 – 3rd Class, Math. Tripos, Cambridge.

First World War -

1914 – serving with the Public Schools Corps.

Later – M.C. [So he was promoted, because only officers could
win the M.C.]
– Mentioned in despatches.

1916 – wrote from Salonika – 'Counter [a school servant] has
joined the Devons at Winchester, and is well but
has had to put up with the removal of many teeth.'

1917 – December – torpedoed on his way back to Greece
after his leave. [His nickname appears to be 'Basil'; several
of his friends refer to 'Basil' Harris. There were three Harris
brothers, but, since this Harris' middle name was 'Bastable', it
seems reasonable to attribute the 'Basil' to him.]

1920 – 8th April – married Marjorie Phyllis Dawe, at Barnstaple Parish Church. [Was she related to George Dawe of
Form IV? He came from Barnstaple, and so did Marjorie. In
view of the popularity then of the nursery rhyme 'See-Saw,
Marjery Daw', it seems an odd choice of Christian name.]

1938 – 14th January – attended the Old Boys' Dinner at the
Trocadero Restaurant in London. Referred to as
'Captain'.

1959 – retired from King's School, Canterbury, where he
had been successively Housemaster, Lower Master,
and Second Master in a 'happy and successful career'.

He became a Governor of the School as the nominee of
Cambridge University, until

1964 – when he resigned.

1983 – 24th Feb. – died in his 91st year. [His brother, Cyril
George (qv), lived to be 99.]

W.M. BURRIDGE, Bratton Fleming.

Prefect. Brereton dormitory.

Football First XI – Half-back, Old Colour.

24th January – the Runs – 12th in the Railway Run.

7th February – 12th in the Beeches Run.

11th March – spoke in the debate about professionalism
in sport.

25th March – read a paper on the Crusades to the
Debating Society.

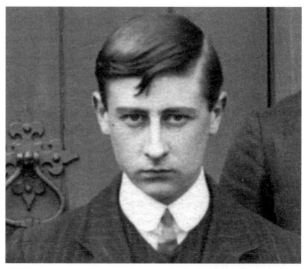

*W.M. Burridge – Prefect – left at Easter. Curiously turned up for
an Old Boys' Dinner 42 years later.*

27th March – played in the Scratch Sixes.

5th May – Cambridge Local Examinations – Senior
Section – passed.

Lent term – Shooting – one Dormitory Competition.

Easter – left the School.

22nd June – played cricket for Bratton Fleming, with his
father, against the School.

1949 – 14th January – attended the Old Boys' Dinner at
the Dorchester.

1952 – attended the Whitsuntide Gathering of Old Boys
at the School.

Wilfrid SAUNDERS, Kingston-on-Thames. [sic – the
purists would have 'Kingston upon Thames'] Entered January,
1904. Courtenay dormitory.

[Incidentally, there was a venerable grammar school in Kingston,
just up the road as it were. One wonders why father sent Wilfrid and
his brother Clement all the way to a boarding school in Devon.]

Sub-Prefect.

January – appointed Prefect.

Reading and Debating Society – 28th Jan. – Opposed the
motion for a Channel Tunnel.

The Spring Runs – 7th February – 3rd in the Beeches
Run.

Football First XI – Half-back.

12th February – spoke at the Debating Society meeting in
'Newspapers' debate.

7th March – 6th in the Tuck Run.

11th March – spoke in the debate about professionalism in
sport.

20th March – 6th in the Long Run.

25th March – Elected Secretary of the Debating Society for
the Christmas Term.

27th March – played in the Scratch Sixes.

Lent term – Shooting – both Dormitory Competitions.

Cricket First XI – played against Landkey (11th May),
King's College, Taunton (1st June), Somerset County
School (12th June) Bratton Fleming (22nd June),
Taunton School (29th June and 2nd July), Summerland
Stragglers (10th July).

Cricket – School Team with Masters – played against

Wilfrid Saunders – made up to Prefect in January. Many boys favoured the three-button, even the four-button, style of jacket – or their mothers did.

Dulverton (8th June).

Cricket House Matches – played v. Brereton (25th May, 18th June).

23rd July – House Swimming Competition – second in both the Short and Long Races. Member of losing Relay team.

Summer Term – member of the Rifle Club. Took part in three Dormitory Competitions.

29th July – Prize Day – won a Silver Spoon for Shooting.

– received the Dormitory Swimming Cup as Courtenay captain.

Exams. – 1904 – passed Preliminary Cambridge Local.

– July – passed the Senior Cambridge Local Examination. [This could be a mistake; the usual local exams taken in the summer were set by Oxford. Cambridge exams took place in December – see Saunders' success below. It is also possible that the School stopped taking the Oxford exams., and stuck solely to Cambridge.]

The Autumn Runs – 19th October – 14th in the North-West Run.

Spoke at the 112th meeting of the Reading and Debating Society.

23rd October – spoke at the 113th meeting of the Reading and Debating Society.

Autumn Term – Shooting – both Dormitory Competitions, 5th November and 10th December.

13th November – 2nd XI football, mentioned in report of match against Chaloner's School of Braunton. [Listed as member of the First XI for the Autumn Term, and was even awarded colours. So either he had gone off form and been dropped – which, as he was a colour, seems unlikely – or, since the School was playing against Chaloner's *First* XI, perhaps the School had been a mite naughty and inserted him into the Second XI to make sure of victory.]

30th November – 6th in the Bray Run.

December – passed the Cambridge Senior Local Examination. [Again? Or at a higher level?]

13th December – spoke at the 118th meeting of the Reading and Debating Society.

1908 – February – awarded Silver Spoon for shooting. Awarded Donegall Bronze Badge.

– July – awarded Cricket Colours.

– July – left the School.

1909 – June – student at University College, London – passed the London Intermediate B.Sc. exam.

First World War –

1915 – has 'recently' obtained Honours in Chemistry.

– sailed to India to take up the post of Professor of Chemistry and Metallurgy in the Sibpur Engineering College, Calcutta University. [In the climate of unthinking patriotism which obtained at the time, it seems odd that he should have gone to India at all, especially as his elder brother Clement – see below – had joined up, like nearly every other able-bodied ex-pupil. Perhaps it was the prestige of the professorship – a rare distinction, one would think, for a newly-qualified graduate – which drew him. But he later changed his mind, and his direction – see below.]

1918 – commissioned in the Indian Army.

[He had an older brother, Clement, who left in 1906, and who played in various cricket matches during 1907, for the combined Masters and School side, and twice against the School, for Landkey and for the Old Boys. He too served in the First World War. **CLEMENT WAS KILLED ON 11TH FEBRUARY, 1917.**]

[Some of these prefects were no doubt confirmed – see biographies from Forms II, III, IV, and V – but the book of confirmation records in the School Archive starts in 1908, when Headmaster Harries was beginning to make his mark. He maintained the records for the next 26 years, in his own hand. I can find no confirmation records dating from before 1908.]

This was taken in 1908, the year he left.

End of Prefects' biographies.

Boys' Biographies – Form V

V.A.

W. Leslie ARMSTRONG, Shipley, Yorks.

Entered May, 1905.   Brereton dormitory.

1905 – Won Form IV prize.

1906 – Won Form V and Latin prizes. Awarded Running colours.

May – appointed Prefect.

Reading and Debating Society – 12th February, spoke in 'Newspapers' debate.

The Spring Runs – 7th March – 3rd in the Tuck Run.

11th March – spoke in the debate about professionalism in sport.

18th March – read a paper at the debating society about James Watt.

25th March – Elected Treasurer of the Debating Society for the Christmas Term.

5th May – Cambridge Local Examinations – Junior Section – Honours, Class I (with distinction in French and Mathematics). [He had taken the exam the previous December.]

20th May – Athletic Sports – 2nd in Open Hurdles, 3rd in Open Steeplechase.

Summer Term – member of the Rifle Club. Took part in one Dormitory Competition.

29th July – Prize Day – won the Chope General Knowledge Prize – *Alexander's Empire*, by Mahaffy; *Chaldaea*, by Ragozin; *Phoenicia*, by Rawlinson.

- won a Cambridge Local Prize, Junior, Class I., distinguished in French and Mathematics – *Wanderings in South America*, by Waterton.

- won the Acland Mathematics Prize – *Pioneers of Science*, by Sir Oliver Lodge.

But a bit of a thespian. At any rate he was recruited for excerpts from As You Like It *on Speech Day, 1908, the year of the School's golden jubilee. As Touchstone the clown he received an honourable mention in the Register.*

The Autumn Runs – 19th October – 13th in the North-West Run.

- 30th November – 9th in the Bray Run.

Autumn Term – played 'on one or more occasions' for the Football First XI.

Reading and Debating Society – 4th December, read a paper on Locomotives.

13th December, spoke at the 118th meeting.

December – Cambridge Senior Local Examination – First Class Honours.

1908 – Won the Acland Science and Head Master's Language prizes.

– July – left the School.

1909 – awarded a Technological Scholarship of £50 by the County Council of the West Riding of Yorkshire, and entered Leeds University to study Engineering.

1920 – appointed Assistant to the Blackpool Borough Engineer. Became associate member of the 'Institution' [sic] of both Civil Engineers and Mechanical Engineers.

W. Leslie Armstrong. No great cricketer or footballer, it appears, judging from his absence from all sporting photographs.

1921 – 21st June – married Miss M. Thornton.

1922 – 8th July – at "Arndale", Poulton-le-Fylde, [Lancashire] "to Mr. and Mrs. W.L. Armstrong, a son".

[Poulton-le-Fylde – so he hadn't moved far from Shipley. He had studied at Leeds, and worked at Blackpool. If the family, as it seems, was so northern-orientated, why was the son sent to North Devon for his education?]

Hinton John HARRIS, South Molton.

Courtenay dormitory.

Member of the School Choir.

Football First XI – Forward, Old Colour.

The Spring Runs – 24th January – 8th in the Railway Run.

Reading and Debating Society – 28th Jan. – Spoke in the Channel Tunnel debate.

7th February – 7th in the Beeches Run.

12th February – spoke at the Debating Society meeting in 'Newspapers' debate.

11th March, spoke in the debate about professionalism in sport.

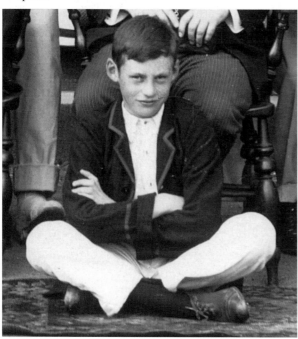

Hinton John Harris – the middle one of the three Harris brothers. He left first, in this year, 1907. A tiny boy, it seems, but he figures in the photos of the Past v. Present Cricket in 1906 and 1905. Probably just making up the numbers.

20th March – 3rd in the Long Run.

1st April – 15th in the *Exmoor*.

5th May – Cambridge Local Examinations – Junior Section – Honours, Class III.

Lent term – Shooting – one Dormitory Competition.

Easter – left the School. Donated a book to the School Library – *Rupert of Hentzau*.

29th July – Prize Day – won a Cambridge Local Prize, Junior, Class III – *Cranford*, by Mrs. Gaskell. [Presumably he returned specially to collect it. South Molton, after all, wasn't far.]

First World War.

1914 – 2nd Lt., 5th Hampshire Regiment.

V. B.

Reginald Thomas Henry HOOPER, Teignmouth.

b. 1893.

Old Boys' Scholar.

Courtenay dormitory.

1906 – Jan. – entered the School.

– July – Form III prize.

25th January – elected member of the Reading and Debating Society.

11th March – proposed the motion in the debate about professionalism in sport.

The Spring Runs – 25th March – 2nd in the Short Run.

29th July – Prize Day – won the Fifth Form Mathematics Prize – *The Life of St. Paul*, by Farrar. – Won the Fifth Form Science Prize – *Life of Cromwell*, by Frith.

2nd October – participated in the Debating Society's proceedings.

Reginald Thomas Henry Hooper – an unrecognisable Corin in As You Like It, *on Speech Day, 1908.*

The Autumn Runs – 30th November – 4th in the Bray Run.

December – Cambridge Junior Locals – Honours, Class II (Distinction in Geography).

13th December – spoke at the 118th meeting of the Reading and Debating Society.

– Confirmed by the Bishop of Crediton at West Buckland Church.

– March – awarded Running colours.

– July – Form V Mathematics prize.

– December – left the School.

1909 – joined the Old Boys' Association.

Served in the First World War.

Leonard Knight Valentine JOB, Ledbury, Hereford.

1905 – Jan. – entered the School. Courtenay dormitory.

The Spring Runs – 24th January – 3rd in the Railway Run.

25th January – elected member of the Reading and Debating Society.

28th January – spoke in the Channel Tunnel debate.

7th February – 8th in the Beeches Run.

12th February – spoke at the Debating Society meeting in 'Newspapers' debate.

11th March – spoke in the debate about professionalism in sport.

20th March – 4th in the Long Run.

Lent term – Shooting – both Dormitory Competitions. Highest individual score in both. Won both silver spoons presented by Mr. W.L. Miles. [See Tuesday, 8th January.]

20th May – Athletic Sports – 2nd in Open Cricket Ball.

Cricket House Matches – played v. Brereton (25th May, 18th June).

1st June – Cricket First XI. – played against King's College, Taunton (1st June), Somerset County School (12th June), Bratton Fleming (22nd June), Taunton School (29th June and 2nd July), Summerland Stragglers (10th July).

Leonard Knight Valentine Job – a first XI cricketer – July, 1907.

Cricket – played for North Devon *against* the School Past and Present (27th July) [presumably as substitute – he went in last and was run out for 1!].

Cricket – School Team with Masters – played against South Molton (29th May), 4th Batt. Devon Regiment (5th June), Dulverton (8th June), North Devon (19th June), South Molton (17th July), Dulverton (20th July), the Old Boys – two-day match (30th and 31st July).

Awarded School Colours for Cricket at the end of the season.

Summer Term – member of the Rifle Club. Took part in two Dormitory Competitions.

19th October – the Runs – 4th in the North-West Run. Awarded Running Colours.

Autumn Term – Football – regular member of the First XI., at half-back. Awarded Colours.

23rd October – spoke at the 113th meeting of the Reading and Debating Society.

Autumn Term – Shooting – 5th November, first Dormitory Competition.

10th December, second Dor. Competition, won Silver Spoon.

13th December – spoke at the 118th meeting of the Reading and Debating Society.

Christmas – left the School.

And a first XI footballer too – December, 1907.

First World War –
1917 – wounded.
1957 – visited the School.
1964 – 13th March – died.

H.H. JONES, Exmouth.

Brereton dormitory.

Member of the School Choir.

Football First XI – Forward.

25th January – elected member of the Reading and Debating Society.

6th February – special mention in the football match against Barnstaple Town.

The Spring Runs – 7th February – 6th in the Beeches Run.

12th February – spoke at the Debating Society meeting in 'Newspapers' debate.

11th March – opposed the motion in the debate on professionalism in sport.

1st April – 8th in the Exmoor.

April – Awarded Football Colours.

Easter – left the School.

Charles LEWIS, Chittlehampton.

Courtenay dormitory.

Sept., 1905 – entered the School, as a County Council Scholar.

Football First XI – Goalkeeper. [He was widely regarded as the best goalkeeper the School had produced. Some even said the best in the region. So presumably he was not playing on 6th March, when 'our defence was weak, particularly the goal-keeper', and the School lost 8 – 4.]

25th January – elected member of the Reading and Debating Society.

Reading and Debating Society – 12th February, spoke in the 'Newspapers' debate.

Charles Lewis – reckoned to be the finest goalkeeper the School ever produced.

Cricket First XI – played against Landkey (11th May), King's College, Taunton (1st June), Somerset County School (12th June), Bratton Fleming (22nd June), Taunton School (29th June and 2nd July), Summerland Stragglers (10th July).

Cricket Second XI – played against the Old Boys Veterans (29th July).

Cricket House Matches – played v. Brereton (25th May, 18th June).

[He made a habit of getting run out – see 10th July.]

29th July – Prize Day – Fifth Form Prize – Tennyson's *Poems.*

Autumn Term – goalkeeper again for the Football First XI. Awarded Colours.

December – Cambridge Senior Local Examinations – passed.

13th December – spoke at the 118th meeting of the Reading and Debating Society.

[He seems to have got through the entire year without taking part in any of the School runs. There were eight of them, and the School authorities were crackers about cross-country. At any rate he is not recorded as having done so. Quite a feat.]

1908 Senior Cambridge Local Exam. Cricket Colours. Michael Snell English Prize, Chope General Knowledge Prize. [These prizes were the *Life of Nelson* by Mahan, and the collected edition of Shakespeare's plays; both are still treasured possessions of Lewis' family.]

Appointed Prefect.

1909 – Lance-Corporal, OTC; Head Master's Language Prize; President of Debating Society; Prefect; Fortescue Medal. [This medal is the highest award in the School's gift. Instituted by the Earl himself, it is given – and by no means every year – for a combination of achievements both indoors and outdoors which have reflected credit on the School.]

1909 – July – left the School.

1910 – Entered St. Catherine's College, Oxford.

1912 – Captained College football team.

1913 – 3rd Class, History Final.

1913-14 – Assistant teacher at Wem Grammar School.

First World War –

1914 – 13th September – volunteered , joined 10th Battalion, Devon Regt.

1915 – Served in Salonika.
 – returned for officer-training.
 – 18th September – gazetted 2/Lt. 16th Battalion, Manchester Regiment.

1918 – served in France and Flanders.
 – 21st March – outside St. Quentin – **KILLED IN ACTION.**

He certainly doesn't look the happiest actor in the School, as, here, a dismal Duke in As You Like It, *performed (well, bits of it) for Speech Day, 1908. His paramour here is Reginald Seldon.*

Lionel George Hart MAJOR, Oakhill. b. 1894.
Brereton dormitory.

January, 1906 – entered the School, as an Old Boys' Scholar.

1906 – Form III Prize.

Lionel George Hart Major – with his soft features, he was a gift for the female parts in plays – as here, in As You Like It *in 1908. The* Register *commented with commendable evenhandedness that he 'looked charming but was too nervous'.*

He looks the typical small, bright, baby-faced boy who mopped up lots of prizes – which he did. A stalwart of the Choir, and he was in Form V! So it seems that his voice broke late – which fits the picture.

Member of the School Choir. By the end of 1907, had served 5 terms.

The Spring Runs – 20th March – 14th in the Long Run.

23rd October – spoke at the 113th meeting of the Reading and Debating Society, and the 116th (20th November).

December – Cambridge Junior Local Examination – passed.

1908 – Confirmed by the Bishop of Crediton at West Buckland Church.
– Rifleman's Certificate. Silver Spoon and Bronze Medal for Shooting (under 15).
– Cambridge Senior Local Examinations – Honours, Class III.

1909 – Cambridge Senior Local Examinations – First Class Honours, distinction in Religious Knowledge and Chemistry. Edmonds Divinity Prize – both 1908 and 1909.

1909 – Appointed Prefect. Acland Science, Acland Mathematics, and Holmes Geography Prizes. Lance-Corporal in O.T.C. Football Colours.

1910 – Fortescue Medal.
– Easter – left the School.

1912 – November – [after] studying Civil Engineering for the last two years, has been appointed Assistant Commissioner in the construction of drainage works for the town of Suva, Fiji Islands, and has just left England.

Served in the First World War.

Arthur Orfeur PARKER, Winchcomb, Glos. b. 1893.
Courtenay dormitory.

May, 1903 – entered the School.

The Spring Runs – 7th March – 9th in the Tuck Run.

Lent term – Shooting – one Dormitory Competition.

20th May – Athletic Sports – 1st in Under 14 220 yds. and Under 15 100 yds., 2nd in Under 15 Quarter-Mile and Cricket Ball.

Cricket House Matches – played v. Brereton (25th May, 18th June).

Cricket First XI – played against Landkey (11th May), King's College, Taunton. (1st June), Somerset County School (12th June), Bratton Fleming (22nd June), Taunton School (29th June and 2nd July), Summerland Stragglers (10th July). Awarded Colours.

Cricket – School Team with Masters – played against South Molton (29th May), Dulverton (8th June), North Devon (19th June), South Molton (17th July), Dulverton (20th July), the Old Boys – two-day match (30th and 31st July).

Awarded School Colours for Cricket at the end of the season.

Summer Term – member of the Rifle Club. Took part in one Dormitory Competition.

Autumn Term – Football 2nd XI – special mention in the game against Somerset County School (9th October).

Autumn Term – Shooting – first Dormitory Competition (5th November).

– Football – First XI. Special mention in report of the match against King's College (16th November). Regular member of the First XI. – at forward.

20th November – spoke at the 116th meeting of the Reading and Debating Society.

December – Cambridge Junior Local Examination – passed.

1908 and 1909 – Senior Cambridge Local Examinations – distinction in Religious Knowledge.

Arthur Orfeur Parker – a most unusual second name. He was a successful cricketer and footballer. Later a very successful doctor.

1908 – Confirmed by the Bishop of Crediton at West Buckland Church.
   – Lent Term – Rifleman's Certificate, Football Colours, Winner of Under 15 Fives Competition, runner-up in Open Competition. Summer Term – Junior Champion Athlete.

Autumn Term – appointed Prefect.
   – Cambridge Senior Local Examinations – Honours, Class III.
   1910 – Lent Term – Silver Spoon and Donegall Badge for Shooting; Winner of Open Fives Competition.
   – Autumn Term – President of Debating Society.
   – Corporal in Officers' Training Corps [formed only in March of that year].
   – Senior Cambridge Local Examinations [again] – distinguished in Religious Knowledge.

Easter, 1910 – left the School.

1911 – February – recently [gone to] the Colonies – Manitoba.

1914 – [reported as] playing football for the Medical College at Manitoba University.

First World War –

1915 – with the R.A.M.C., Canadian Contingent.

1916 – 2nd Lt. – DCLI [Duke of Cornwall's Light Infantry –

this seems very unlikely, in view of his medical experience both before and after this. It could therefore be a simple mistake – though it is also true that wars produced all sorts of unusual postings.]
   – visited the School during the summer.

1923 – now a doctor. In February, his wife gave birth to a son at Swan River, Manitoba.

1924 – appointed Surgeon to the Woodland's [sic]

Whether he became a regular actor is open to doubt; the folded arms pose could easily have come out of a football photograph.

Hospital, Northfield, Birmingham.

1929 – has been consulting surgeon to the Ministry of Pensions (Welsh Area) and to the Llynypia Hospital, as well as Assistant Surgeon to the Shropshire Orthopaedic Hospital and to the Prince of Wales Hospital, Cardiff.

Norman Kingsley PEARCE, Kingsbridge. b. 1893. Brereton dormitory.

1903 – May – entered the School.

1905 – won the *Exmoor* Cup.

The Spring Runs – 24th January – 5th in the Railway Run.

20th March – 5th in the Long Run.

1st April – 7th in the *Exmoor*. Awarded Running Colours.

*Norman Kingsley Pearce – no relation to Arthur Pearce of Form IV.
He finally made it to the First XI in 1909.*

Lent term – Shooting – one Dormitory Competition.
20th May – Athletic Sports – 3rd in Under 15
    Steeplechase.
Cricket Second XI – played against the Old Boys Veterans
    (29th July).
Cricket House Matches – played v. Courtenay (25th May,
    18th June).
The Autumn Runs – 19th October – 5th in the North-
    West Run.
20th November – involved in 'heated argument' at the
    116th meeting of the Reading and Debating Society.
30th November – 17th in the Bray Run.
1908 – Confirmed by the Bishop of Crediton at West
    Buckland Church.
    – Awarded Rifleman's Certificate.
    – Awarded Cricket Colours.
    – December – Cambridge Junior Local Examin-
        ations – 'satisfied the Examiners'.
1909 – won Shooting Prize. Member of Officers'
    Training Corps.
1910 – Won *Exmoor* Cup [for the second time – see above].
    – Awarded Football Colours.
    – May – appointed Prefect.
    – Senior Cambridge Local Examinations.
    – July – left the School.
First World War –
1915 – 2nd Lt. in the Royal Engineers.
    – M.C.
1916 – Served in Egypt with 9th Corps Signal Company.
    In hospital with a crushed foot.
    – 2nd October – wrote from Suez Canal Defences:
        'If the war is over by next Easter and I can possibly

manage it, I shall trip down and take part in the
Exmoor, if I may be allowed to do so.' [In the
middle of the biggest war the world had seen for a hundred
years, he was planning to come all the way from Egypt to
Devon just to run in a nine-mile cross-country race
through one of the last wildernesses in England. The 'pull'
that the School had over its old pupils is at times quite
staggering.]

1918 – 16th January – He wrote from 'an orchard which
    contains olives, almonds, apricots, grapes, and
    oranges … ' [to wish] 'the dear old School a happy
    and prosperous new year'. [The letter covered four
    printed pages of the *Register*, and referred to visits, in
    between fighting, to Jerusalem, Bethlehem, Hebron,
    Ramleh, and Gaza. He spent] 'a jolly good night in
    the Governor's house [at Hebron], with pictures on
    the walls, carpets on the floor, decent furniture,
    easy chairs, a piano in the corner and a delightful
    fire in another'. [He was distressed by the bombardment
    of Gaza, but said that] 'the Turks are wholly to blame,
    because they used the town and sacred buildings
    therein for ammunition stores'. [Are some more
    recent events in Iraq a curious echo of this?]

And he made it to Prefect, as here, in 1910.

He had also been promoted to full Lieutenant, dated back
    to 18th April, 1917.
[His address in 1912 was given, in an Old Boys' List, as '63, Gauden
    Road, Clapham, SW.' So was that of his elder brother, John
    Cyprian, (1901-04), who also served in the War.]
1921 – 27th June – married Margaret Clare Reid, at
    Funchal, Madeira. [When the Old Boys' List of 1924
    was published, Norman's address was indeed 'P.O. 41,
    Funchal, Madeira' – and his brother was living in Calcutta!]
1925 – 22nd May – his wife gave birth to a daughter at
    Cheltenham. [He is now listed as 'N.K. Pearce, M.C.'
    Did she come home simply for the birth?]
1927 – runner-up in the Madeira Open Tennis Champ-
    ionship.
1974 – died.

Thomas Henry RICHARDS, Ilfracombe.
Courtenay dormitory.
Entered Form III., Jan., 1906. Old Boys' Scholar.
The Spring Runs – 7th March – the Runs – 2nd in the Tuck Run.
Cricket Second XI – played against the Old Boys Veterans (29th July).
Cricket House Matches – played v. Brereton (25th May, 18th June).
19th October – the Runs – 7th in the North-West Run.
Autumn Term – Football – played 'on one or more occasions' for the First XI.
December – Cambridge Junior Local Examination – passed.
13th December – spoke at the 118th meeting of the Reading and Debating Society.
1908 – awarded Running Colours, 1908.
      – Easter – left the School.
First World War –
Enlisted in the North Devon Hussars and served with it in Egypt and Palestine. The regiment was transformed into a machine-gun battalion, and moved to France. He went with them, and was wounded on 2nd September, 1918.
1918 – 9th September – **DIED OF WOUNDS.** [Only 7 weeks before the end of the war.]

Reginald William SELDON, Lincoln. b. 1893.
Brereton dormitory.
Son of an Old Boy (1874-77). [His father died aged only 45 (3rd April, 1906) when Reginald was at the School. He, father, had been a popular fellow among his schoolmates, especially because of his fine female impersonations in amateur theatricals (his son, Reginald, had a very young face – see the photographs – and was in the choir). He, father (obituary, in the *Register* for June, 1906, p. 128), was apparently a popular figure too in the public life of Barnstaple, and a captain of the local Fire Brigade, as well as being a fine footballer, which explains his son's precocious talent. Reginald also went on to play cricket to county standard. Odd that the *Register* of February, 1907 lists Reginald as coming from 'Lincoln'. The Governors' Minutes (12th June, 1906, No. 3 ii) mentioned yet another Seldon, 'of Barnstaple', who was instructed to represent the School in legal proceedings against a parent who had neglected to pay fees – see 18th November.]

1904 – May – entered the School.
1906 – awarded Running Colours and Football Colours.
Member of the School Choir. By the end of 1907, had served 11 terms.
Football First XI – Forward, Old Colour.
The Spring Runs – 24th January – 9th in the Railway Run.
7th February – 4th in the Beeches Run.
20th March – 9th in the Long Run.
1st April – 11th in the *Exmoor.*
20th May – Athletic Sports – 1st in Under 15 Long Jump, 2nd in Under 15 Steeplechase; 1st in Under-5ft. High Jump.
Cricket First XI – played against Landkey (11th May), King's College, Taunton (1st June), Somerset County

Reginald William Seldon. A gifted sportsman, despite his tender features. He won the prize for 'best cricketer' four years running.

School (12th June), Bratton Fleming (22nd June), Taunton School (29th June and 2nd July), Summerland Stragglers (10th July).
Cricket – School Team with Masters – played against South Molton (29th May), 4th Batt. Devon Regiment (5th June), Dulverton (8th June), North Devon (19th June), South Molton (17th July), Dulverton (20th July), Barnstaple Banks (25th July), the Old Boys – two-day match (30th and 31st July).

Cricket – played for School Past and Present against North Devon (27th July).

Awarded School Colours for Cricket at the end of the season. Had the highest aggregate of either boys or masters, and his average was second only to Mr. Taylor's. Described in the end-of-term report as 'by a long way the best bat in the team'.

Cricket House Matches – played v. Courtenay (25th May, 18th June).

Summer Term – member of the Rifle Club. Took part in two Dormitory Competitions.

29th July – Prize Day – won the Cricket Bat for the best cricket of the season.

He was captain of football for three years too.

Autumn Term – Football First XI – Old Colour. Forward. Scored a hat-trick of goals against South Molton Y.M.C.A. (2nd October); specially mentioned in the report of the games against North Molton (12th October), Taunton Y.M.C.A. (24th October), Taunton School (26th October), King's College (16th November), North Devon School – four goals (20th November), Filleigh (23rd November), and Barnstaple Town (27th November).

The Autumn Runs – 19th October – 2nd in the North-West Run.

Shooting – 10th December, second Dormitory Competition.

20th November – spoke at the 116th meeting of the Reading and Debating Society.

1908 – Confirmed by the Bishop of Crediton at West Buckland Church.

    – Rifleman's Certificate.

    – May – won Silver Spoon for Shooting. (Also in May, 1909.)

Corporal in the Officers' Training Corps, founded in March, 1909.

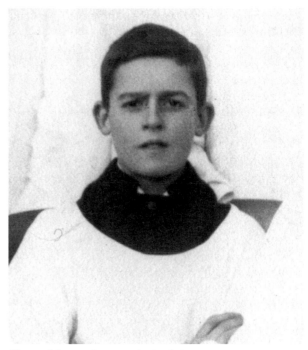

He served for over four years in the choir.

– December – Senior Cambridge Local Examinations.

Won the cricket bat for the best cricketer four years running – 1907-8-9-10.

Captain of Football for three years – 1908-9-10.

1910 – July – left the School.

1912 – November – promoted to the Montevideo Branch of the London and River Plate Bank, has just left England.

First World War –

1915 – was a military landing officer at the Dardanelles. A piece of shrapnel took off the sole of his boot, and a few nights later a shell burst in his tent, killed his companion, but left him uninjured.

Wounded [date not recorded]. Mentioned in Despatches.

1919 – returned to his banking in Monte Video [sic].

14th June, 1921 – married Aileen Ackerley, daughter of Mr. and Mrs. P.C. Towers, at Holy Trinity Church, Monte Video [again, sic].

Later became a Maths teacher at Blundell's School, and taught the son of Arthur Pearce [see Form IV biographies].

1959 – yet recorded in the *Register* as being 'still' at Sao Paolo, Brazil.

Edwin Harold TRUDGIAN, Tregony, Cornwall.

Brereton dormitory.

Football First XI – Full-back.

25th January – elected member of the Reading and Debating Society.

The Spring Runs – 1st April – 9th in the *Exmoor.*

Easter – left the School.

Served in the First World War.

John Ivan WHITE, South Molton.

Entered April, 1902.

Brereton dormitory.

1902 – Summer Term – entered the School.

Member of the School Choir.

The Spring Runs – 7th March – 12th in the Tuck Run.
25th March – 6th in the Short Run.
Cricket Second XI – played against the Old Boys Veterans
(29th July).
Cricket House Matches – played v. Courtenay (25th May,
18th June).
End of Summer Term – left the School.
Served in the First World War.

Arthur Leonard Jack YOUINGS,　　　Barnstaple.
Brereton dormitory.

Arthur Leonard Jack Youings. Member of a prominent Barnstaple family. He served fourteen terms in the Choir, and so deserved his central position in the 1907 group. (See 16ᵗʰ September.)

1904 – Jan. – entered the School.
Member of the School Choir. By the end of 1907, had
served 12 terms.
Cricket First XI – played against Landkey (11th May).
Cricket Second XI – played against the Old Boys Veterans
(29th July).
25th May – Cricket House Matches – played v.
Courtenay.
23rd July – House Swimming Competition – member of
winning Relay team.
Autumn Term – Shooting – 5th November, first
Dormitory Competition.
Autumn Term – Football – played 'on one or more
occasions' for the First XI.
1908 – November – Silver Spoon and Rifleman's
Certificate.
– December – Cambridge Junior Local Examinations – 'satisfied the Examiners'.
– awarded Football Colours.
1909 – Member of newly-formed Officers' Training
Corps.

From As You Like It, *in 1908. A slightly overdressed 'Forester'.*

1910 – awarded Running Colours.
– July – left the School.
1914 – 24th – 27th July – attended the Old Boys'
Gathering.
First World War –
1914 – serving with the Royal North Devon Hussars.
1922 – 2nd October – married Margaret May Hughes.

He made it to the First XI in 1910.

End of Form V biographies.

Boys' Biographies – Form IV

E.A. Adams. From the middle row of the Choir. The Register says he served for four terms, so I am guessing that those with only two to their credit were put in the back row. Schools in Edwardian times were great places for hierarchies.

E.A. ADAMS, Taunton.   Entered April, 1906.
Brereton dormitory.
Member of the School Choir.   By the end of 1907, had
    served 4 terms.
The Spring Runs – 25th March – 7th in the Short
    Run.
23rd July – House Swimming Competition – member
    of winning Relay team.
Summer Term – member of the Rifle Club. Took part
    in three Dormitory Competitions.
29th July – Prize Day – won a Silver Spoon for
    Shooting.
Promoted to Form V.
Autumn Term – 20th November – spoke at the 116th
    meeting of the Debating Society.
The Autumn Runs – 30th November – 12th in the
    Bray Run.
Shooting – 10th December, second Dormitory
    Competition.
December – Cambridge Junior Local Exam – passed.
Christmas – left the School.
1975 – moved to Christchurch, New Zealand.

Albert Henry AUSTIN,   Verwood, Dorset.
1906 – Jan. – entered the School.
    Brereton dormitory.
Old Boys' Scholar.
Member of the School Choir. By the end of 1907, had
    served 4 terms.
The Spring Rurns – 25th March – 15th in the Short
    Run.
23rd October – spoke at the 113th meeting of the
    Reading and Debating Society. Main opposition
    speaker at the 116th meeting (20th November).

Albert Henry Austin. Another 'Forester' in As You Like It *in 1908.*

Austin in the Choir. This is probably my weakest identification; I am going on a faint superciliousness of expression, slightly quizzical eyebrows, and a longish nose.

December – Cambridge Junior Local Examination –
    passed.
4th December – spoke at the 117th meeting of the
    Reading and Debating Society.
14th December – performed in the Breaking-up
    Concert.
1908 – December – Cambridge Junior Locals again –
        (Honours, Class II).
    – left the School.
1909 – joined the Old Boys' Association.
First World War – wounded twice.   M.C.
    Mentioned in Despatches.

1949 – 14th January – attended the Old Boys' Dinner at the Dorchester.

Albert Salter AYRES,   South Molton.
Courtenay dormitory.
The Spring Runs – 7th February – 10th in the Beeches Run.
20th March – 8th in the Long Run.
Easter – left the School.
First World War –
1916 – Gloucester Regiment.
Wounded

F.J. BROOKS,   East Buckland.
Day boy.
1905 – April – entered the School.
1907 – End of Summer Term – left the School.

John Leonard BUCKINGHAM,   North Molton.
Courtenay dormitory.
1904 – May – entered the School.
Easter, 1908 – left the School.
Served in the First World War.

C.E. DRAKE,   Tiverton.
Easter – left the School.

William ELWORTHY,   Swimbridge.
b. 1893.
1902 – May – entered the School.
Brereton dormitory.
1904 – French prize.

William Elworthy. From the First XI photograph of Christmas, 1907.

The Spring Runs – 7th March – 11th in the Tuck Run.
20th May – Athletic Sports – 2nd in Under 15 Hurdles and Long Jump.
 Cricket First XI – played against Landkey (11th May), King's College, Taunton (1st June), Somerset County School (12th June), Bratton Fleming (22nd June), Taunton School (29th June and 2nd July), Summerland Stragglers (10th July).
Cricket Second XI – played against the Old Boys Veterans (29th July).
Cricket – School Team with Masters – played against South Molton (17th July).
Cricket House Matches – played v. Courtenay (25th May, 18th June – when he took 9 wickets in two innings).

Elworthy in more formal mode, taken in 1908.

Autumn Term – the Runs – 15th in the North-West Run (19th October).
  - Football – Played in the First XI forward line. Special mention in the report of the match against North Devon School (20th November). Awarded Colours.
20th November – spoke at the 116th meeting of the Reading and Debating Society.
  1908 - January – appointed Prefect.
  - Confirmed by the Bishop of Crediton at West Buckland Church.
  - March – awarded Running colours.
  - July – awarded Cricket colours.
  - September – President of the Reading and Debating Society.

– December – Cambridge Junior Local Examinations –
'satisfied the Examiners'.

– left the School.

1914 – 24th – 27th July – attended the Old Boys'
Gathering.

1924 – 15th October – married Elizabeth Annie
Sloman, of Hill Farm, South Molton.

1947 – 26th April – died as the result of an accident.

A.J.E. HELPS, Bridgwater. Entered January, 1906.
Brereton dormitory.

Member of the School Choir. By the end of 1907, had
served 5 terms.

Lent term – Shooting – one Dormitory Competition.

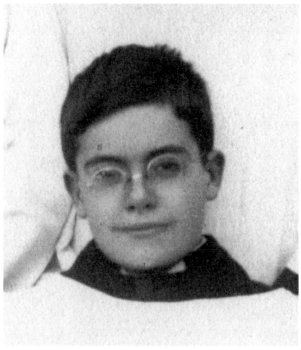

*Helps again, in the Choir. Not much similarity to the previous
picture, thanks to the heavy costume and wig. But Helps is credited
with five terms' service in the Choir, which entitles him to a place on
the front row, and I can name the other four pretty securely. (See 16th
September.) So, this boy, I put it to the court, is called Helps.*

13th December – spoke at the 118th meeting of the
Society.

1908 – Won Silver Medal for Shooting, and Donegall
Bronze Badge.

- He must have been promoted during the year,
because he is listed in the magazine as 'Form V.'

- July – left the School.

Hubert Ernest HICKS, Berrynarbor.
Courtenay dormitory.

1906 – Jan., – entered the School.　　　　Old Boys'
Scholar.

Cricket Second XI – played against the Old Boys
Veterans (29th July).

Cricket House Matches – played v. Brereton (25th May,
18th June).

The Autumn Runs – 19th October – 12th in the
North-West Run.

1908 – Autumn term – won a School Draughts
Tournament.

– November – awarded Football colours.

– December – awarded Running colours.

– Oxford Senior Local Examination.

– Won the *Exmoor* Cup.

– July – left the School.

First World War -

1916 – at the Royal Ordnance Dept.

W.F. KINGDON, South Molton.
Courtenay dormitory.

1906 – January – entered the School.

Autumn Term – Football – played for the First XI. at
forward

A.J.E. Helps. As Audrey in As You Like It *in 1908.*

Summer Term – member of the Rifle Club. Took part
in three Dormitory Competitions.

Autumn Term – Shooting – 5th November, first
Dormitory Competition, won silver spoon.

- 10th December, second Dormitory Competition.

Autumn Term – 20th November – proposed the
motion at the 116th meeting of the Reading and
Debating Society.

December – Cambridge Junior Local Examination –
passed.
1908 – February – awarded Football Colours.
– December – left the School.
[The Kingdon name has popped up many times in the history
of the School. One holder was a long-serving and distinguished
Chairman of Governors. Another gave equally faithful service to the
Old Boys' – later the Old Members' – Association.]

Hubert Frank LOVELL,   Chulmleigh.
Courtenay dormitory.
1906 – January – entered the School.
Old Boys' Scholar.
9th July – Prize Day – awarded Form IV Prize – *The
Life of Christ*, by Farrar.
– awarded Form IV Science Prize – *Stories from
Virgil*, by Church.
– December – Cambridge Junior Local Examination
– passed.
1908 – awarded Form V Science Prize.
– December – Cambridge Junior Local
Examinations – Honours, Class III.
1909 – Senior Cambridge Local Examinations –
Honours, Class II.
1910 – awarded Acland Mathematics and Science Prizes
(in 1911 too).
– awarded Snell English Prize, Chope Essay Prize.
– Senior Cambridge Local Examinations –
Honours, Class III. [What went wrong here? He
won *Second* Class Honours last year. But he put it all right
in 1911 – q.v.]
1911 – Senior Cambridge Local Examinations –
Honours, Class I.
– won Chope General Knowledge Prize.
1912 – awarded Football Second XI Colours.
– awarded the Fortescue Medal. [A rare feat for a boy
who seems to have had very slender sporting credentials in
a sport-mad school – and who, for all his academic prowess,
was never made a prefect. Unless of course there was some
kind of disability. Unlikely, since he was able to join the
Forces – see below.]
– July – left the School.
1913 – after his success in the Civil Service Examination,
was appointed to a Second Division Clerkship in
the Land Values Department of the Inland
Revenue Office.
First World War -
1918 – suffered from a 'bad stomach wound'.
1924 – 22nd March – married Miss E. Warrington.

Harry MATTHEWS,   Hayle, Cornwall.
Courtenay dormitory. Old Boys' Scholar.
1906 – January – entered the School.
– July – Form III prize.
29th July – Prize Day – won the Fourth Form
Mathematics Prize – *The Story of the Iliad*, by
Church.
December – Cambridge Junior Local Examinations –
passed.

– July – Form V Mathematics prize.
– December – Cambridge Senior Local
Examinations – Honours, Class III.
– left the School.
1909 – joined the Old Boys' Association.
First World War -
1916 – 2nd October – married Nora, daughter of Mr.
and Mrs. Lawry, at the parish church of St. Erth.
[St. Erth was a small village in western Cornwall, on the
River Hayle, 4 miles south-east of St. Ives. And where did
Harry Matthews come from? That's it – Hayle, in
Cornwall.]
1918 – joined the Royal Navy. [Why did he wait so long, one
wonders?]

Ralph MAYNARD,   Bude.
Courtenay dormitory.
Football First XI – Forward.
The Spring Runs – 24th January – 4th in the Railway
Run.
16th February, praised for 'fearless' play in the football
match against Chittlehampton.
20th March, 2nd in the Long Run.
1st April – 6th in the *Exmoor*.
April – Awarded Football Colours.
Lent term – Shooting – one Dormitory Competition.
Easter – left the School.
First World War –
– Wounded.

Arthur PEARCE,   Barnstaple.
Courtenay dormitory.
1903 – May – entered the School.
1904 – Form II prize.
Football – played in one or more First XI matches.

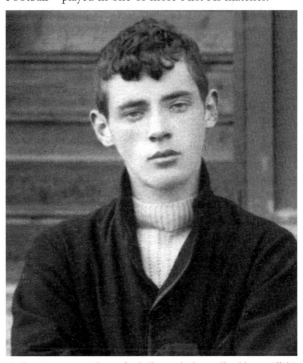

*Arthur Pearce – cricketer, footballer, and above all athlete. All his
photos show him in a slightly challenging attitude. You get the feeling
that it would take quite a lot to impress Arthur Pearce.*

The Spring Runs – 24th January – Winner of the Railway Run.

7th February – Winner of the Beeches Run.

7th March – Winner of the Tuck Run.

20th March – Winner of the Long Run.

20th May – Athletic Sports – 1st in Open Mile, Half-Mile (dead heat), Long Jump, Cricket Ball, and Steeplechase; 2nd in Open High Jump.

Cricket First XI – played against Landkey (11th May), King's College, Taunton (1st June), Somerset County School (12th June), Bratton Fleming (22nd June), Taunton School (29th June and 2nd July), Summerland Stragglers (10th July).

Cricket – School Team with Masters – played against South Molton (29th May), 4th Batt. Devon Regiment (5th June), Dulverton (8th June), North Devon (19th June), South Molton (17th July), Dulverton (20th July), the Old Boys – two-day match (30th and 31st July).

Awarded School Colours for Cricket at the end of the season. He had the best bowling average of the Boys' team.

25th May – Cricket House Matches – played v. Brereton (and clean bowled eight of them). Played again against Brereton (18th June), and took 9 wickets in two innings.

29th Prize Day – received as captain of Courtenay the Dormitory Sports Cup.

The Autumn Runs – 19th October – Winner of the North-West Run.

30th November – Winner of the Bray Run.

Football – played for the Second XI against Chaloner's School, Braunton (13th November), and mentioned in the match report. Also played 'on one or more occasions' for the First XI.

20th November – at the 116th meeting of the Reading and Debating Society, 'joined in a heated argument' with two other members.

1908 – won the *Exmoor* run, and all the other Spring runs as well.

– appointed Prefect.

– Autumn term – came second in a School Draughts Tournament.

– December – left the School.

First World War – served. [No details have survived.]

[Two older brothers attended the School – John, from 1900-1905, and Charles junior, from 1900-1903. Both served in the First World War. Their father, Charles Pearce, was a Governor – a tanner from Barnstaple – see List of Directors for December, 1906. Arthur's son, Richard, went to Blundell's School, where one of his Maths teachers was R.W. Seldon – see Form V biographies. Two of his grandchildren, Tom and Catherine Pearce, attended the School in the 1970's and early 1980's. There were three other Pearces – no relation – who attended the School during the first decade of the nineteenth century – Norman Kingsley (left 1910), from Form V, Edwin Ralph (left 1906), and John Cyprian (left 1904); all three served in the First World War.]

Athelstan Ellis PRESTON, Natal. Entered Sept., 1904. Brereton dormitory.

1906 – November – won Silver Spoon for Shooting.

Athelstan Ellis Preston. Regular cricketer.

Football First XI – Full-back.

The Spring Runs – 7th February – 5th in the Beeches Run.

April – Awarded Football Colours.

Lent term – Shooting – both Dormitory Competitions.

20th May – Athletic Sports – 1st in Open High Jump, 2nd in Long Jump; 1st in Handicap 120 yds.

Cricket House Matches – played v. Courtenay (25th May, 18th June).

Cricket First XI – played against Landkey (11th May), King's College, Taunton (1st June), Somerset County School (12th June), Bratton Fleming (22nd June), Taunton School (29th June and 2nd July), Summerland Stragglers (10th July).

Cricket – School Team with Masters – played against South Molton (29th May), 4th Batt. Devon Regiment (5th June), Dulverton (8th June), North Devon (19th June), South Molton (17th July), Dulverton (20th July), the Old Boys – two-day match (30th and 31st July).

Cricket – played for School Past and Present against North Devon (27th July).

Awarded School Colours for Cricket at the end of the season. He bowled more overs than any other boy in the School team.

23rd July – House Swimming Competition – member of winning Relay team.

Summer Term – member of the Rifle Club. Took part in two Dormitory Competitions.

Autumn Term – played for the First XI. football. Special mention in the report on the game against King's College (16th November).

The Autumn Runs – 19th October – 8th in the North-West Run.

Autumn Term – Football – played regularly at full-back for the First XI.

– Shooting – 5th November, first Dormitory Competition.

Athelstan Ellis Preston. Regular footballer.

Harold John Richards as choirboy in December, 1907.

   – 10th December, second Dormitory Competition.
Christmas – left the School.
First World War –
1917 – served in the South African Forces. [He came from
          Natal, remember.]
1930 – 1st September – died at Durban.

R.M. READ, Exeter.
   Brereton dormitory.
Member of the School Choir
The Spring Runs – 25th March – 12th in the Short Run.
1st April – 5th in the *Exmoor*.
Easter – left the School.

Harold John RICHARDS,   Chulmleigh.   b.
May, 1894.   Courtenay dormitory.
1906 – September – entered the School.   County
Council Scholar.
Member of the School Choir. By the end of 1907, had
served 4 terms.
20th May – Athletic Sports – 2nd equal in Under 5 ft.
High Jump.
1908 – Form V Mathematics Prize.
      – December – Cambridge Junior Local
          Examinations – 'satisfied the Examiners'.
1909 – 25th May – confirmed by the Bishop of Exeter at
          South Molton Church.
      – Senior Cambridge Local Examinations. Also in
          1910.
1910 – appointed Prefect.
      – awarded Chope General Knowledge Prize.
      – September – President of the Reading and
          Debating Society.

Harold John as Prefect in 1910.

      – Rifleman's Certificate.
1911 – January – Head of School.
      – July – awarded 2nd XI Cricket Colours.
      – promoted Lance-Corporal in the O.T.C.
      – left the School.
First World War – invalided home to Toxteth Park Military
    Hospital.
1969 – February – died.

139

F.E. SANDERS, Barnstaple.
Member of the School Choir
Football – played in one or more First XI matches.
Easter – left the School.

David Thomas SQUIRE, Filleigh.
1905 – Sept. – entered the School.   Listed as Day Boy, so was not allocated to a house.
20th May – Athletic Sports – 1st in Under 15 Quarter-Mile, Hurdles, Cricket Ball, and Steeplechase; 2nd in 100 yds.
Autumn Term – Football 2nd XI – special mention in the game against Somerset County School (9th October).   Played 'on one or more occasions' for the First XI.
 1908 – July – left the School.
Served in First World War

Harold George WOOLAWAY, Chittlehampton.
1906 – May – entered the School.
  Day boy.
20th May – Athletic Sports – 2nd in Handicap Half-Mile.
Autumn Term – Football – played 'on one or more occasions' for the First XI.
The Autumn Runs – 19th October – 6th in the North-West Run.

Harold George Woolaway. Died, unromantically, of 'disease' in 1916. A day boy, he would have had to walk six miles to school every day.

30th November – 3rd in the Bray Run.
[In these running results, he was not allocated to a house; instead he was simply listed underneath the other names as 'day boy'.]
December – Cambridge Junior Local Examinations – passed.
December – on the results of the December [internal] exams, he was promoted to Form VI. [So he must have been promoted to Form V at some time during the year.]
1908 – appointed Prefect, won all his colours ('rare for a day boy'). 'The trouble he took in order to assist in games and matches will be understood when we say that he lived six miles from the School.' [Interesting to note how the activities of the day boys were often commented upon as if they were a different species. Day boys were certainly pretty rare; Harries, the HM, was a devotee of the boarding principle. It is quite possible that Woolaway *walked* the six miles to School, did the runs, and then walked six miles home.]
 – December – Cambridge Senior Local Examinations – Honours, Class III.
 – left the School.
1909 – joined the Old Boys' Association – life member.
Played football regularly for South Molton.
First World War – Joined the Naval Flying Corps 'in the first instance', later transferred to the Navy.
DIED OF DISEASE, 27TH DECEMBER, 1916. At Devonport.
[Another *Register* entry for June, 1919 records the date as 1918.]

The following joined the School in May:-

George Henry DAWE, Barnstaple. b. Dec., 1893.
Courtenay dormitory.
Member of the School Choir. By the end of 1907, had served 2 terms.
Summer Term – member of the Rifle Club. Took part in one Dormitory Competition.
The Autumn Runs – 19th October – took part in the North-West Run, but did not win a point, because he was lower than 20th.
Autumn Term Shooting – 10th December, second Dormitory Competition.
1909 – member of the newly-formed Officers' Training Corps. [Harries, for all that he was a clergyman, was mad keen on this. One wonders how voluntary the corps was. Remember that this was the high tide of Edwardian national and imperial pride. Perhaps the boys were all mad keen too.]
 – Junior Cambridge Local Examinations.
1910 – 26th May – confirmed by the Bishop of Crediton at Filleigh Church.
 – July – left the School.
First World War –
1914 – serving with the 7th Hampshire Regiment.
1915 – 2nd Lt. with the 4th Dorsets. [Did he meet William Pugsley (*qv*), who was commissioned in the same regiment in 1918? They had joined the School in the same month and in the same form. And they both came from Barnstaple.]
1918 – 24th August – married Lilian Armstrong, at St. Paul's, Bournemouth.

George Henry Dawe. In the Choir. He arrived in May, 1907, and it said in the Register *of February, 1908 that he had served two terms, and he appears in the back row of four. I'm pretty sure I have two others right by comparison with a play cast, and I think I've got the third, so this identification, I hope, is accurate.*

Stanley Arthur LORAM,   Exeter. b. 1893.
Brereton dormitory.
20th May – Athletic Sports – 1st in Handicap Half-Mile.
Cricket House Matches – played v. Courtenay (25th May, 18th June).
Cricket Second XI – played against the Old Boys Veterans (29th July).
The Autumn Runs – 19th October – 3rd in the North-West Run.
30th November – 15th in the Bray Run.
December – on the results of the December, promoted to Form V.
1908 – Confirmed by the Bishop of Crediton at West Buckland Church.
    – February – awarded Running colours.
    – December – Junior Cambridge Local Examinations – 'satisfied the Examiners'.
    – Left the School.
1909 – joined the Old Boys' Association – life member. Later went to Australia.
First World War –
1915 – returned with the Australian cavalry force.
     Wounded at the Dardanelles [see letter from his brother Victor, 23rd December].
Later obtained a commission in the Royal Air Force.

Stanley Arthur Loram. From a contemporary Register. Sadly, all too many of these photos had to be published, so one assumes that the School had been in touch with the family to secure them. Out of an average roll of just over 130, the School lost 56 members in the Great War to End Wars.

1918 — 15TH JUNE — KILLED.   [Not by enemy action – in a flying accident.]

William Henry PUGSLEY,   Barnstaple.
Entered May, 1907.
Brereton dormitory.
The Autumn Runs – 30th November – 19th in the Bray Run.
1908 – Easter – left the School.
First World War –
1915 – Sergeant in 6th Devons in India. [So was Stanley Oatway, from Form III – and in the same year.]
1918 – won a commission in the Dorset Regiment. [Did he meet George Dawe (*qv*), who had been commissioned in the Dorsets in 1915? Both from Barnstaple, they had joined the School in the same month, and in the same form.]

End of Form IV biographies.

Boys' Biographies — Form III

George William ANSTEY, Filleigh. b. May, 1893. Day boy.

[See also George Bryan Anstey of Form II.]

1906 – May – entered the School.

December – on the results of the December exams, promoted to Form IV.

1909 – 25th May – confirmed by the Bishop of Exeter at South Molton Church.

– July – left the School.

Served in the First World War.

1921 – 11th July – married Lucy Ellen Squire at South Molton.

1946 – 9th November – died. [It was recorded in the July, 1947 number of the *Register*, so one presumes that it refers to the previous November.]

William Elias AYRE, North Molton.

Entered January, 1907.

Courtenay dormitory.

The Spring Runs – 25th March – 9th in the Short Run.

The Autumn Runs – 30th November – 20th in the Bray Run.

December – on the results of the December exams, promoted to Form IV.

Christmas – left the School.

Served in the First World War.

Charles Martin BARNECUTT, Exeter.

Member of the School Choir.

Easter – left the School.

First World War –

1915 – with the 7th Battalion of the Devon Regiment.

Served in the First World War.

1955 – 23rd March – attended an Exeter Branch Reunion Dinner.

1964 – still living at Park Villa, Edgerton Park, Exeter, 'despite a previous report that he had moved'.

V.J. BATTERSHILL, Exeter. Entered September, 1904.

Courtenay dormitory.

The Spring Runs – 25th March, 5th in the Short Run.

End of Summer Term – left the School.

H.C. BATTING, Silverton.

Courtenay dormitory.

1905 – Jan., – entered the School.

The Spring Runs – 25th March, 10th in the Short Run.

1st April – Winner of the *Exmoor*. [It was a handicap race. But he still received a silver medal.]

Cricket House Matches – played v. Brereton (25th May, 18th June).

The Autumn Runs – 30th November – 7th in the Bray Run.

1909 – Easter – left the School.

First World War –

1917 – joined the Inns of Court O.T.C.

Fred CHAVE, Wellington, Somerset.

Entered April, 1906. Brereton dormitory.

29th July – Prize Day – won a Third Form Prize – *Stories from Greek Tragedy.*

Promoted to Form IV.

Christmas – left the School.

First World War –

1918 – served in the Somerset Light Infantry. [Did he put his stories from Euripides and Sophocles in his knapsack when he went on his travels? Light reading in the trenches.]

Seymour David Scotland CRADDOCK, Filleigh. b. Aug., 1893.

Listed as 'Junior Fortescue and day boy'.

Later as Brereton dormitory.

[Perhaps, by switching to boarding status, he had been 'rewarded' by being put in a 'proper' dormitory – or house, as it soon became.]

1906 – September – entered the School.

The Spring Runs – 25th March, 4th in the Short Run.

The Autumn Runs – 19th October – 18th in the North-West Run.

1908 – awarded Running colours.

1909 – joined the newly-formed Officers' Training Corps [or was told to].

– 25th May – confirmed by the Bishop of Exeter at South Molton Church.

1910 – Easter – left the School.

First World War –

1918 – joined the American Field Artillery. [If he had emigrated to the United States, this late admission to the Armed Forces might be explained by the late entry of the US into the War. All the same, the vast majority of young men then would have come home to join up. And he was 25 by this time – quite old to enlist. Why did he wait? Perhaps there is a gap in the record.]

Ernest Bowman DRIVER, Montserrat, Leeward Islands.

b. July, 1895. Courtenay dormitory.

1905 – September – entered the School.

1908 – Rifleman's Certificate.

1909 – won Under-15 Shooting medal and silver spoon.

– Junior Cambridge Local Examinations.

1910 – 26th May – confirmed by the Bishop of Crediton at Filleigh Church.

– won the Donegall Badge.

– awarded Form V Science Prize.

1911 – awarded Second and First XI Cricket Colours. [A rare feat in the same season, I should think, even allowing for the School's passion for awarding colours.]

– December – left the School.

Ernest Bowman Driver – from a cricket photograph of 1910.

The cricket photo made this Choir identification easy – especially the wayward lock of hair.

First World War –
1918 – joined the Royal Air Force. Later – in
    November – he was commissioned.
1921 – 5th July – married Gertrude Ingham, at Beeston,
    Notts.
1922 – 3rd May – his wife gave birth to a son at
    Beeston.
1975 – 6th October – died.

L.W.E. GRANT,   Exmouth.
Listed as 'Junior Fortescue and day boy'.
[When he left, he was listed as belonging to the Courtenay
dormitory – so he too, presumably, had become a boarder.]
January – entered the School.
The Spring Runs – 25th March, 3rd in the Short Run.
Cricket Second XI – played against the Old Boys
    Veterans (29th July).
Cricket House Matches – played v. Brereton (25th May,
    18th June) – for Courtenay!
23rd July – House Swimming Competition – won the
    Junior Short and Long races, member of losing Relay
    team.
The Autumn Runs – 19th October – 17th in the
    North-West Run.   [Now listed as 'Courtenay', perhaps
    because he had switched from 'day' to 'boarding'. When he left,
    he was identified with the Courtenay dormitory.]
1908 – Easter – left the School.

Cyril George HARRIS,   South Molton. b. April,
1895.   Courtenay dormitory.
1906 – September – entered the School.
    Old Boys' Scholar.
Member of the School Choir.
The Spring Runs – 24th January, 7th in the Railway
    Run.
25th March, Winner of the Short Run.
1st April – 3rd in the *Exmoor*.
20th May – Athletic Sports – 1st in Under 13 100 yds;
    2nd in 220 yds. and Hurdles.
Cricket House Matches – played v. Brereton (25th May,
    18th June).

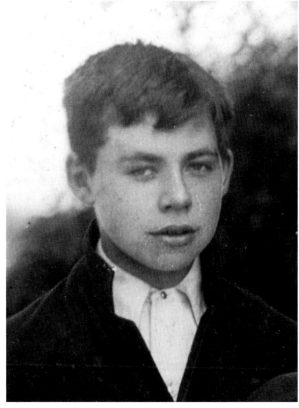

Cyril George Harris . From a named cricket photograph of 1910.

He served ten terms in the Choir.

He came back to play in an Old Boys' Cricket team in 1913, and seems to have matured into a rather good-looking young man – with a strong resemblance to the film actor James Mason. And he lived to be 99.

Cricket Second XI – played against the Old Boys Veterans (29th July).

Summer Term – member of the Rifle Club. Took part in two Dormitory Competitions.

The Autumn Runs – 19th October – 10th in the North-West Run.

30th November – 8th in the Bray Run.

1908 – won *Exmoor* Under-13 medal. [Judging by his date of birth, he only just made it.]

— awarded Running Colours.

1909 – Junior Cambridge Local Examinations – Distinction in Religious Knowledge.

1910 – 26th May – confirmed by the Bishop of Crediton at Filleigh Church.

— awarded Edmond's Divinity Prize (and in 1911 too).

— Rifleman's Certificate. Promoted Corporal in the O.T.C.

1911 – Running Captain.

— awarded Cricket Colours.

— Senior Cambridge Local Examinations.

— December – left the School.

First World War –

1914 – serving in the Public School Corps.

1915 – 2nd Lt. in 10th Devon Regiment.

1916 – 5th January – wrote a long letter to Harries from Salonika. He had met his ex-teacher, Mr. Giffard [qv]. 'I'm sorry to say that in spite of vigorous exercise I seem to be putting on a lot of weight, a common failing, I believe, in the army.'

Mentioned in despatches.

1921 – passed the Final Examination of the Institute of Chartered Accountants.

1925 – 5th November – married Madeleine Chabroz.

1994 – died. [A pretty good age – 99. His brother, J.B., made it to 90.]

Hugh Gordon HOPPER, Lee, Kent. b. June, 1895. Brereton dormitory.

1904 – September – entered the School.

Member of the School Choir.

1906 – Form II Prize.

1908 – December – Cambridge Local Examinations – 'satisfied the Examiners'.

Form IV Science Prize.

1909 – Junior Cambridge Local Examinations – Honours, Class III.

— Form V Science Prize.

1910 – 26th May – confirmed by the Bishop of Crediton at Filleigh Church.

— Senior Cambridge Local Examinations.

1911 – January – appointed Prefect.

— Certificate A. [This was an OTC qualification. It was a sign that the OTC was beginning to gain some status and, to use a modern word, 'image'.] Also promoted Sergeant in the OTC.

— awarded Cricket Colours.

— awarded Football Colours.

— December – left the School.

Hugh Gordon Hopper, from a cricket photograph of 1910.

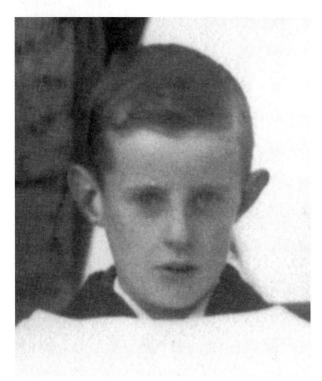

Hence the identification in the 1907 Choir was pretty straightforward.

1914 – Friday, 16th January – attended the Old Boys'
    Dinner at the Restaurant Frascati in London.
First World War –
    – serving with the 12th County of London Brigade.
    – 'an ugly wound in the shoulder'.
    – 2nd Lt. in the Royal Fusiliers.
Later – wounded again.
1922 – 30th October – married Miss D.M. Parry, at St.
    Peter's Church, Liverpool.
1973 – moved to Keswick, Cumberland.

W.G. JEWELL,   Gillingham, Dorset.
Easter – left the School. Donated a book to the School
Library – *Three Midshipmen*.

F.S. LEE,   Thorverton.
    Courtenay dormitory.
1906 – Sept. – entered the School.
December – on the results of the December exams,
    promoted to Form IV.
1909 – July – left the School.

Richard Dennis MEDLAND,   Bude.
Entered September, 1906.
Brereton dormitory.
1906 – Autumn Term – entered the School.
Lent term – Shooting – both Dormitory Competitions.
18th June – Cricket House Matches, played v.
    Courtenay.
End of Summer Term – left the School.
Served in the First World War.

Arthur Percy MOOR,   South Molton.
Courtenay dormitory.
January – entered the School.
The Spring Runs – 7th March, 9th in the Tuck Run.
25th March, 8th in the Short Run.
23rd July – House Swimming Competition – second in
    Junior Short Race, member of losing Relay team.
The Autumn Runs – 30th November – 10th in the
    Bray Run.
1908 – December – Cambridge Local Examinations –
    'satisfied the Examiners'.
    – Form IV Mathematics prize.
1909 – March – member of newly-formed Officers'
    Training Corps.

Arthur Percy Moor. William in As You Like It *in 1908. The
Register commented with rare fulsomeness that he was 'nearly perfect'.*

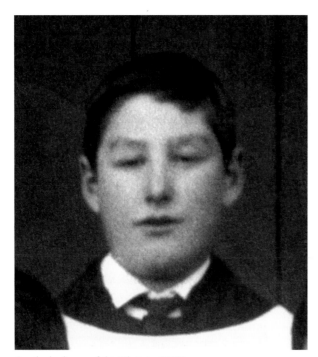

In the back row of the Choir in 1907.

– December – Senior Cambridge Local
Examinations.
– left the School.
First World War -
1914 – serving with the Wessex Artillery.
1915 – Bombardier with the Somerset R.H.A. [Royal
Horse Artillery?]
Later – wounded.
1951 – 25th August – died.

Francis John PIKE, East Buckland. b.
Sept., 1892. Day boy.
1905 – May – entered the School.
– July – Form II Second Prize.
1909 – 25th May – confirmed by the Bishop of Exeter
at South Molton Church.
– Christmas – left the School.

Michael Rookherst ROBERTS, Ilfracombe. b.
Nov., 1894. Brereton dormitory.
1905 – September – entered the School.
1906 – awarded Form II Prize.
The Spring Runs – 24th January, 10th in the Railway
Run.
20th March, 7th in the Long Run.
1st April – 4th in the *Exmoor*.
20th May – Athletic Sports – 1st in Under 13 Hurdles;
3rd in 100 yds.
Cricket Second XI – played against the Old Boys
Veterans (29th July).
Cricket House Matches – played v. Courtenay (25th
May, 18th June).
[At some stage, he must have been put up to Form IV, because
in …]
December – on the results of the December exams, he
was promoted to Form V and awarded a prize – *Great
Englishmen*, by Sidney Lee.

1908 – awarded Running Colours.
1909 – Junior Cambridge Local Examinations –
'satisfied the Examiners'.
– awarded Cricket Colours.
– won the Chope General Knowledge Prize.
– Senior Cambridge Local Examinations – and in
1910.
1910 – 26th May – confirmed by the Bishop of Crediton
at Filleigh Church.
– Rifleman's Certificate.
1911 – awarded the Holmes Geography Prize – and in
1912.
– Captain of Cricket and Football.
– won the *Exmoor* Cup.

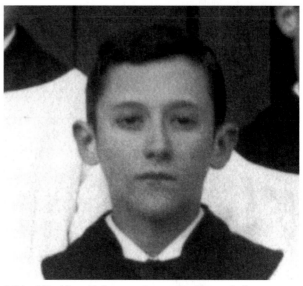

*Michael Rookherst Roberts – a frequently-photographed young man.
Here, first, in the Choir. He can be easily spotted too in the full
School photograph.*

1912 – awarded Shephard Law Scholarship.
– won the Donegall Shooting Badge and Silver
Spoons..
– won the *Exmoor* cup again, and in record time.
[Soon broken – see J .L. Carter, Form II.]
– awarded the Batting and Bowling Average cups.
– Athletics Champion.
– awarded the Edmonds Divinity Prize.
– Sergeant in the O.T.C.
– November – Army Entrance, R.M.C., Sandhurst
(49th on the list).
– December – Senior Cambridge Local Examinations – Honours, Class III [it would seem, at the third
attempt].
– awarded the Fortescue Medal [inevitably].
Left the School.
1914 – 24th – 27th July – attended the Old Boys'
Gathering.
1914 – [reported as] playing football for the R.M.C. – at
outside right.
Passed out 7th in order of merit of Gentlemen Cadets of
the Third Division, and was nominated for appointment to the Indian Army. Temporarily attached to the
Lancashire Fusiliers.

A much-wigged Rosalind in As You Like It *in 1908. The* Register *noted with deadly accuracy that he 'acted well, but did not know his part thoroughly'.*

He was a gifted cricketer, and played for the School for four years.

First World War –
1915 – wrote a letter to the Headmaster, which the HM published in the *Register* for June, about the experience of being gassed.
Wounded later [?].
1919 – serving with the Indian Army.
   – 19th December – married Isabel Fisher at St. Paul's Church, Barrow-in-Furness.
1920 – 30th September – his wife gave birth at Naini Tal, India, to a son. [Didn't waste much time.]

1921 – appointed staff officer (3rd Grade) in the Indian Army.
1926 – qualified for the Staff College, Camberley.
1927 – 14th January – attended the Old Boys' Dinner. Now a captain.
1929 – appointed Assistant Military Secretary to the Western Command of India.
1938 – promoted Lt.-Colonel, to command the 2nd/10th Gurkha Rifles.
Served in the Second World War – reached the rank of Brigadier.
1944 – awarded the D.S.O. for his work in Burma.
1949 – became President of the Old Boys' Association.
   – 25th July – presented the prizes at Speech Day.
1951 – 12th January – attended the Old Boys' Dinner at Simpson's in the Strand.
   – attended the Whitsuntide Gathering of Old Boys. He presented to the School an autographed copy of his book 'Golden Arrow', the story of the 7th Indian Division during the 1939-45 War. It had received 'very favourable reviews'.
1952 – 11th January – attended the Old Boys' Dinner at Simpson's.
1954 – 8th January – attended the Old Boys' Dinner.
1956 – 20th January – attended the Old Boys' Dinner at the House of Commons.
   – also attended the Whitsuntide Gathering.
1957 – 22nd February – attended the Old Boys' Dinner at Simpson's.
   – appointed Colonel of the 10th Princess Mary's Own Gurkha Regiment.

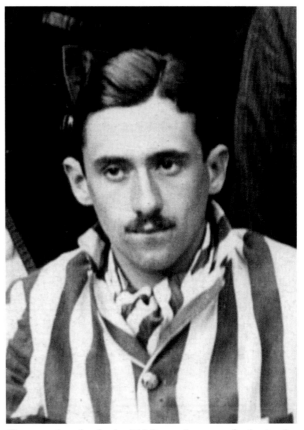

He returned to play for the Old Boys only a year after leaving, but already he was sporting a Sandhurst military moustache.

– attended the Whitsuntide Gathering.

– elected President of the Old Boys' Association for the second time – for the centenary year.

1958 – attended the Whitsuntide Gathering.

– co-opted on to the Committee of the Governing Bodies Association of Public Schools.

1959 – he became Chairman of the newly-formed Friends of West Buckland School [designed to raise funds – it was succeeded, in the 21st century, by the West Buckland Foundation].

1960 – became Chairman of Governors, after several years as a plain governor. He served as Chairman for another eight years.

– elected Fellow of the Royal Historical Society. [His book 'Golden Arrow' is referred to above. He had also edited two volumes of John Connell's biography of Lord Wavell, and had been the author of four volumes of the official history of the war against Japan.]

In 1973, after his resignation from the School's public bodies, he was created Patron of the Old Boys' Association, one of only two in the School's history. [Up to then. The first was Cordy Wheeler, who died in 1972. Cordy had been associated with the School for 77 years. Tom Hitchins, who died in 2004, nearly equalled him – 76 years. Roberts managed a mere 72 years.]

1977 – 28th August – died, aged 82. [A headmaster who had worked with him referred to his 'unseeking willingness to turn his hand to any form of aid to the school he loved so well'.]

[His grandson attended the School in the 1990's.]

He carved out a varied and distinguished Army career, and became a Brigadier in the Gurkhas. He served in both World Wars.

Edward Hamilton SOUTHCOMB,

Cheltenham.   b. June, 1895.

Listed as 'Junior Fortescue and day boy'.

1904 – Entered the School 'at a very early age'. [Nine was 'early', then, at the DCS.]

The Spring Runs – 25th March, 14th in the Short Run.

The Autumn Runs – 30th November – 16th in the Bray Run [now listed as 'Brereton', perhaps because he had changed his status from 'day' to 'boarding'].

1908 – Form III Science Prize.

1909 – member of the O.T.C.

1910 – 26th May – confirmed by the Bishop of Crediton at Filleigh Church.

1910 – left the School, and finished his education at Shrewsbury. [The Headmaster's old school.]

On leaving school, entered a bank, but in 1914 joined the Gloucester Regiment, and obtained a commission in the Manchester Regiment, Nov., 1916

1917 – March – crossed to France.

– June – wounded.

31st July – Killed in action – 'in the early morning'. [He was in the same regiment as Charles Lewis of Form V (*qv.*). Sadly, he too was killed in action the following year.]

Edward Hamilton Southcomb. Although he finished his education at Shrewsbury, he showed his continuing affection for the DCS by leaving ten guineas in his will for a cup for the Games Club. On 31st July, 1917, he was shot by a sniper. Death was instantaneous. His name is commemorated among the 54,000 on the Menin Gate at Ypres.

[He left ten guineas – £10.50 – in his will to provide some trophy for the Games Club. The *Register* remarked that 'the idea of a Champion Shield is favoured by many'. It was also favoured by the Southcomb family, who duly presented a shield to be awarded to the House which wins most aggregate points in the various sporting activities which take place during the School year. Nearly ninety years later, the Southcomb Shield is still so awarded.]

Percy James Were. A big lad for his age, he was playing for the First XI when he was in Form III, as here, in July, 1907.

Percy James WERE, London.

Entered January, 1907.

Brereton dormitory.

Football – played in one or more First XI matches.

[Good going for a third-former. Though he looks pretty large in the team photograph.]

16th February, individual mention in the football match against Chittlehampton.

The Spring Runs – 7th March – 12th in the Tuck Run.

Cricket First XI – played against Landkey (11th May), King's College, Taunton (1st June), Somerset County School (12th June), Bratton Fleming (22nd June – highest score), Taunton School (29th June and 2nd July), Summerland Stragglers (10th July). [Clearly a gifted young cricketer too].

Cricket – played for School Past and Present against North Devon (27th July).

Cricket – School Team with Masters – played against South Molton (17th July), Dulverton (20th July), the Old Boys – two-day match (30th and 31st July).

Awarded School Colours for Cricket at the end of the season.

Cricket House Matches – played v. Courtenay (25th May, 18th June).

29th July – Prize Day – won the Third Form Mathematics Prize. Title not recorded.

The Autumn Runs – 19th October – took part in the North-West Run, but did not score a point. In other words, he came below 20th.

Autumn term – Football – played at full-back for the First XI, but was injured in the game against Taunton School on 26th October, and is not recorded as playing again until 16th November, when he was specially mentioned in the report of the match against King's College. Awarded Colours.

Autumn Term – Shooting – 5th November, first Dormitory Competition.

By the autumn, he was playing football for the School as well. Here he is, enveloped by Walter Giffard's legs. (See p.104.)

In 1913, he returned for an Old Boys' cricket match, along with his old team mates, 'Basil' Harris and Charles Lewis. They have matured into fine-looking young men. Percy was in the School for only 15 months, but the bond created was strong enough to bring him back five years later – further testimony to the extraordinary ability of the DCS to generate affection among its inmates.

December – on the results of the December exams, he was promoted to Form V. [So presumably he had been promoted to Form IV at some time during the year.]

Spring Term, 1908 – continued to play – and well – for the Football First XI.

1908 – Won Fives Open Championship.

Easter, 1908 – left the School.

Served in the First World War.

Samuel John Widgery, as 'Amiens' in As You Like It *in 1908.*

Samuel John WIDGERY, South Molton.
Courtenay dormitory.
January – entered the School.
23rd July – House Swimming Competition – member of losing Relay team.
December – on the results of the December exams, promoted to Form V. [So he must have been promoted to Form IV at some time during the year.]
1908 – December – Cambridge Junior Local Examinations – 'satisfied the Examiners'.
1909 – Rifleman's Certificate.
   – March – Football and Running colours.
   – Member of newly-formed Officers' Training Corps.
   – Christmas – left the School.
First World War –
1914 – Sergeant, Dorset Light Infantry.
1918 – Awarded the Military Cross. [So he must have been commissioned, because only officers could win the Military Cross. Other ranks got the Military Medal.]
1921 – 10th September – married Edna Doreen Waite, at Wolverhampton.
1954 – December – died.

T. WILLIAMS, King's Brompton.
Entered Sept., 1906   Brereton dormitory.
The Spring Runs – 24th January, 11th in the Railway Run.
7th March, 5th in the Tuck Run [a fine effort for a third-former – unless, of course, he was enjoying a big handicap, as was the case in the *Exmoor.*]

The Autumn Runs – 19th October – 11th in the North-West Run.
30th November – Took part in the Bray Run – awarded no points, so below 20th. [Which appears to confirm the conjecture above.]
December – on the results of the December exams, he was promoted to Form IV.
Christmas – left the School.

[The following entered the School in May, and were allocated to two third forms, as follows:-   So there must have been some reconstruction of the whole Third Form since January – evidence of Harries the new broom sweeping clean, or the need to create a new class as a result of the welcome fresh intake – which in turn could have been the result of the early impact of Harries.]

To Form III.B.

Harold John DIXON, Filleigh.   'D'.
[This initial was put beside his name when his departure was recorded –presumably for 'day boy' – so he didn't exactly 'count' as a 'proper' pupil in Harries' eyes].
1908 – Easter – left the School.
First World War –
1916 – Private, Somerset Light Infantry –
   KILLED IN ACTION.

George Garfield GARLAND, Filleigh.
b. March, 1894.   Day boy.
1909 – 25th May – confirmed by the Bishop of Exeter at South Molton Church.
   – July – left the School.
1930's – went to Guernsey as manager for a large established firm.
1940 – he and his wife missed the last boat to England, and were finally interned in a camp at Biberach in Germany. He was appointed camp leader.
1945 – on his return to Guernsey after the War, he received the following letter from Ernest Bevin, the Foreign Secretary: 'The Government desire to convey to you an expression of appreciation and grateful thanks for the unfailing loyalty, untiring energy, and inspiring leadership with which you carried out the exacting and often dangerous task of camp leader at Biberach from 1942 to 1945.'

T.P. ISAAC, Barnstaple.
Courtenay dormitory.
December – on the results of the December exams, he was promoted to Form IV.
1909 – Easter – left the School.

W.J. SQUIRE, Barnstaple.
Courtenay dormitory.
20th May – Athletic Sports – 3rd in Under 13 220 yds.
1910 – Rifleman's Certificate.
   – Member of the Officers' Training Corps.
1911 – Junior Cambridge Local Examinations.
December – left the School.

1914 – 24th – 27th July – attended the Old Boys' Gathering.

1916 – joined the Royal Naval Air Service.

1995 – died. [If he arrived in Form III in May, 1907, this would place him at about thirteen years old. So he would have been born in 1894. This would make him a centenarian – the first one I have been able to discover in the School's records.]

W.J. YEO, West Buckland. Recorded as 'day boy', so not listed as either 'Brereton' or 'Courtenay'.

1908 – December – left the School.

First World War -

1914 – serving with the Royal North Devon Hussars.

To Form III.A.

Victor John LORAM, Exeter. b. 1894.

Brereton dormitory.

20th May – Athletic Sports – 2nd equal in Under 5 ft. High Jump; 3rd in Under 14 220 yds.

Cricket House Matches – played v. Courtenay (25th May, 18th June).

Summer Term – member of the Rifle Club. Took part in one Dormitory Competition.

The Autumn Runs – 19th October – 16th in the North-West Run.

1908 – Confirmed by the Bishop of Crediton at West Buckland Church.

Victor John Loram, as 'Silvius' in As You Like It. *(This photograph has been an absolutely invaluable document.)*

– awarded Rifleman's certificate.

– December – Cambridge Junior Local Examinations – 'satisfied the Examiners'.

– awarded Running Colours.

1909 – member of Officers' Training Corps.

1910 – awarded Football Colours.

– July – left the School.

1909 – joined the Old Boys' Association – life member. [So clearly the sources for the last two pieces of information clash. I have seen nothing definitive to resolve the problem. But it is scarcely a nail-biting matter.]

1915 – 23rd December – wrote from 'the Front' – from the 3/1 Wessex Division Signal Company, Royal Engineers, Bulford Camp, Wilts. He was issued, he said, with a Douglas bicycle. 'The "Douglas" is a jolly good bicycle to take you over rough country, and beats other machines at this work.' He mentioned his brother Stanley, who had been wounded at the Dardanelles. [And who later died in a flying accident – Form IV *(qv.)*.]

1990 – died. [Aged 96 – the fourth ex-pupil to have reached 90 or more. And they are only the ones to have had their achievement recorded.]

Eustace William OAKEY, Bristol. b. Feb., 1894.

Courtenay dormitory.

20th May – Athletic Sports – 2nd in Under 14 220 yds; 3rd in Handicap Half-Mile.

The Autumn Runs – 5th in the Bray Run.

1908 – awarded Running Colours.

1909 – won under-15 Fives Competition.

– awarded Football Colours.

– member of the new Officers' Training Corps.

1910 – 26th May – confirmed by the Bishop of Crediton at Filleigh Church.

Eustace William Oakey. Yet another 'Forester' in As You Like It. *The staff of the Forest of Arden seem almost to have outnumbered Robin Hood and his Merrie Men.*

He served five terms in the Choir.

December – left the School.
First World War -
1914 – listed as serving – no mention of unit.
1915 – 2nd Lt. with 3rd Battalion, Warwickshire
Regiment.
1960 – 1st May – died after a long illness.

Cyril Hambley PETHERICK,   Bude.   b. 1893.
Brereton dormitory.
29th July – Prize Day – won a Third Form Prize – *The
Early Days of Christianity*, by Farrar.
– won the Third Form Science Prize – *Stories of King
Arthur.*
Autumn Term – Football – played 'on one or more
occasions' for the First XI.
[He must have made a good impression, because, after arriving only
in May, he picked up two prizes in July, and must have been
promoted to Form IV in the Autumn Term, because in. . . .]
December – he was not examined, but promoted to
Form V.
  1908 – confirmed by the Bishop of Crediton at West
Buckland Church.
  – awarded Form V Prize.
  – awarded Football Colours.
  – December – Cambridge Junior Local
Examinations – Honours, Class III.
1909 – awarded Snell English Prize.
– appointed Prefect.

– awarded Running Colours.
– Senior Cambridge Local Examinations – Honours,
Class III.
1910 – President of the Reading and Debating Society.
– awarded Holmes Geography Prize.
– Sergeant in O.T.C.
– Head of School.
– December – left the School.
1911 – May – recorded as ' "cramming" in London for a
Civil Service examination'.
1914 – 24th – 27th July – attended the Old Boys'
Gathering.
First World War.
1914 – 2nd Lt. – 6th Battalion, Royal Inniskilling
Fusiliers.
– Gazetted full Lieutenant.
1915 – took part in the landing at Suvla Bay [in the
Dardanelles]. At the end of the first day, he was one
of only four officers surviving in his battalion.
– 9th July – married Irene May, of Rathgar,
Dublin.
1916 – promoted Capt. Inniskilling Fusiliers.
1917 – attached as Instructor to No. 16 Officers' Cadet
Battalion.

Cyril Hambley Petherick. He played for the First XI in 1910.

In the same year he was appointed Head of School. He looks a reliable lad; perhaps it is no coincidence that his nickname was 'Uncle'.

– 5th April – at Rhyl, his wife gave birth to a baby son.

1923 – Principal Clerk to the Ministry of Finance, and recommended for the O.B.E. for his work in connection with Northern Ireland. [This was just after the partitioning of Ireland – between the Irish Free State and Ulster ('Northern Ireland').]

1938 – 14th January – President of the Old Boys' Association. Took the chair at the Old Boys' Dinner at the Trocadero Restaurant, London. He was also a regular attender at the Whitsuntide Gatherings of Old Boys. Now Assistant Secretary to the Ministry of Finance, Government of Northern Ireland. Later became Principal Secretary.

1942 – awarded the C.B.E. in the Birthday Honours List.

1945 – 23rd December – died at Oxford following an operation. His two sons served in the Army during the Second War and his daughter in the Wrens. [The obituary, *en passant,* let slip that his nickname was 'Uncle'.]

[The following entered the School in September:]

Lionel Ambrose MURLESS, Filleigh. b. 1892.
Brereton dormitory.
The Autumn Runs – 30th November – 18th in the Bray Run.
December – on the results of the December exams, promoted to Form IV.
1908 – [he must have been promoted during the year, because the magazine of this year lists him as] 'Form V'. [At 15, he was certainly old for Form III.]

Between January and July, he was confirmed by the Bishop of Crediton at West Buckland Church. [Most confirmations, from the surviving record, seem to have been either in March or in May.]

July – left the School.

1909 – joined the Old Boys' Association.

Stanley Herbert OATWAY, Barnstaple. b. Oct., 1895.
Courtenay dormitory.
County Council Scholar.
The Autumn Runs – 30th November – 14th in the Bray Run.
December – on the results of the December exams, promoted to Form IV, and awarded a prize – *Don Quixote.*
   – won Under-13 Fives Medal.
   – awarded Form IV Prize.
   – December – Cambridge Junior 'Locals' – 'satisfied the Examiners' – plus Distinction in Drawing.

Stanley Herbert Oatway. Despite his small size, he made it to the First XI in 1910, and later became Captain of Football.

1909 – Form V Prize.
  – Junior Cambridge Local Examinations –
    Honours, Class I.
1910 – Senior Cambridge 'Locals' – Honours, Class III.
1911 – ditto.
  – 31st March – confirmed by the Bishop of
    Crediton at East Buckland Church.
  – awarded Football Colours.
  – awarded Second XI Cricket Colours.
1912 – Senior Oxford 'Locals' – Honours, Class I
    (distinction in Latin).
  – Certificate 'A'.   Sergeant in O.T.C.
  – awarded First XI Colours.
  – appointed Prefect.
  – awarded Headmaster's Languages Prize – also in
    1913.
  – Captain of Football.
  – awarded Michael Snell Leaving Scholarship.
1913 – January – elected President of the Reading and
    Debating Society.
  – awarded Running Colours.
  – Senior Oxford 'Locals' – Honours, Class I
    (distinction in Latin and Greek).
  – won both Batting and Bowling Average Cups.
  – awarded Fortescue Medal.
  – July – left the School.
1914 – 24th – 27th July – attended the Old Boys'
    Gathering.
  – autumn – [reported as] playing football for St.
    Catharine's College, Oxford.

First World War –
1914 – serving with the 6th Devon Regiment.
1915 – still with the 6th Devons, in India. [See W. Pugsley,
    Form IV.]
  – 2nd Lt. with the 82nd Punjabis.
Later – wounded twice.
1919 – serving in Syria.
1924 – March – moved to California.
1938 – 14th January – attended the Old Boys' Dinner at
    the Trocadero Restaurant, London. [All the way
    from California? Knowing the great 'pull' the School had
    over its past pupils, it is by no means unlikely.]
1944 – presented some books to the School Library.
1952 – working with the Shell Oil Co. in California – at
    Los Angeles, 17.
1962 – living at 2679, California Street, San Marino,
    California.
  – gave a 'further' year's subscription of an American
    periodical to the Library. [He was thanked again in
    1953 for the same thing.]
1954 – presented a prize for a Geographical Essay
    competition.

J. POW, Combemartin. [You will have seen elsewhere
both 'Comb Martin' and 'Combmartin'.]
Brereton dormitory.
1908 – July – awarded Form III prize.
    December – awarded Form IV prize on the results
    of the Christmas Examination – "Roman Life in
    the Days of Cicero", by A.J. Church. [No, you're
    probably right.]
1909 – July – left the School.

End of Form III biographies.

Boys' Biographies – Form II

F.W. BALMAN,   Chittlehampton.
Easter – left the School.

Tom BENDALL,   Bristol.
Brereton dormitory.
[Brother of the Head Boy. There were also two older brothers, Charles and William, who had left in 1904 and 1905 respectively. See note on Sidney Bendall.]
January – entered the School.
The Spring Runs – 25th March, 20th in the Short Run.
1913 – July – left the School.
First World War –
- joined the Forces.
1916 – visited the School during the summer.
1917 – came home suffering from consumption. [A much more common word then than 'tuberculosis'.]

[It seems odd that, in a School where nearly everyone had exam. successes, prizes, and colours recorded in great detail, and where his older brother was Head of School and had a CV running to whole pages, the only achievement Tom notched up in six years was twentieth place in one cross-country run – and a short run at that. Perhaps he did do other things, but declined to fill in his leaving form as a sort of protest against the celebrity of brother Sidney. Or perhaps he was not very robust, and simply not up to games. Just got into the Forces by sheer determination to be like his elder brothers, but could not sustain the effort – hence the 'consumption'.]

John Lovelace CARTER,   Exmouth   Listed as 'Junior Fortescue and Day Boy'.
1905 – May – entered the School.
The Spring Runs – 25th March, 19th in the Short Run.
20th May – Athletic Sports – 1st in Under 11 100 yds.
29th July – Prize Day – won the Form II Prize – *The Arabian Nights*.
1910 – Junior Cambridge 'Locals' – Honours, Class III.
    – won *Exmoor* Under-15 Medal.
    – awarded Running Colours. Captain in 1914.
    – Junior Athletics Champion.
1912 – awarded Football Colours. Captain in 1913.
    – awarded Second XI Cricket Colours. First XI Colours in 1914.
    – Senior Cambridge 'Locals' – and in 1913.
    – Certificate 'A'.
1913 – January – appointed Prefect.
    – Easter Monday, 24th March – won the *Exmoor* Cup, 56 seconds faster than the record set only the previous year by M.R. Roberts (q.v.).
    – awarded the Fry Geography Prize.
    – September – elected President of the Reading and Debating Society. [His older brother –G.E.L. – had been a founder member in 1903.]
1914 – January – appointed Head of School.
    – Whit Monday – 1st June – Open Athletics Champion.
    – passed Entrance Examination for the Royal Military College at Sandhurst.
    – Colour-Sergeant in the O.T.C.
    – July – left the School.
Entered Sandhurst direct from School, and was commissioned in the Army Service Corps.
First World War –   Mentioned in despatches.
1914 – M.C.   Mentioned in despatches.
    – Contracted lung trouble.   **DIED, 1914.**
[There were four Carter brothers; three died in the First World War. The fourth brother fathered a son who attended the School between the wars. *His* son in turn became a Physics teacher at the School, and served for 24 years (1982-2006). He in *his* turn had four sons, all of whom attended the School, all of whom went on to Peterhouse, Cambridge, like their father. There were also two or three cousins – Wakefields – in the School. See the Carter fee saga in the Governors' Minutes for 18th November.]

F. HOOPER   Entered January, 1907.
Courtenay dormitory.
20th May – Athletic Sports – 1st in Under 13 220 yds.
1908 – promoted to Form III during the year.
July – left the School.

Walter Wills OWBRIDGE, Teignmouth. b. Feb., 1895.
[His leaving 'CV' says he entered in June, 1907. But he is listed as being a member of Form II in the *Register* of February, 1907. So it seems likely that the above 'June, 1907' is a misprint for 'June, 1906'.]
Listed as 'Junior Fortescue and day boy'. Later recorded as in the Courtenay dormitory. [So he probably switched to boarding, and so became fit to be included in a dormitory.]
The Spring Runs – 25th March, 11th in the Short Run.
23rd July – House Swimming Competition – second in Junior Long Race.
The Autumn Runs – 19th October – 20th in the North-West Run.
30th November – 11th in the Bray Run. [Now listed under 'Courtenay'. See above.]
1908 – awarded Running Colours.
1909 – 25th May – confirmed by the Bishop of Exeter at South Molton Church.
    – presented two books to the Library – "The Secrets of the Sargasso" and "When Terror Ruled".
    – Open Swimming Champion. Also in 1912.
    – won the Under-15 *Exmoor* Medal. [He was also second in the Senior *Exmoor* four times – which must be some kind of record.]
1910 – Easter – donated nine more books to the School Library, including two by 'Capt. F.S. Brereton' [any relation?].
    – December – donated yet more books to the Library [by authors like Rider Haggard, Dumas, Kingsley, Baroness Orczy – reckoned to be pretty 'good stuff' at the time].
1911 – April – more books to the Library [only four this

time] – "The Hollow Needle", "Stranleigh's Millions", "The Wife He Never Saw", and "The Black Spider".

– awarded Second XI Cricket Colours.

– December – more and more books – seven actually, including the "Boys' Own Annual" for 1911. [So he hadn't kept it long – didn't he like books?]

1912 – Spring – books for the Library [and still they came, including one by Dumas I bet you hadn't heard of – 'Memoirs of a Physician'].

– appointed Prefect.

– appointed Captain of Running.

– Certificate 'A'.   Colour-Sergeant in the O.T.C.

– awarded First XI Football Colours.

– awarded First XI Cricket Colours.

1913 – a book for the Library [just one, it seems – perhaps he was running out].

– Rifleman's Certificate.

– Open Athletic Champion.

– September – appointed Head of School.

– November – passed entrance exam for R.M.C., Sandhurst.

– December – left the School.

– [As a sort of parting gift, he] presented one final book to the Library – "Morning Star", by Rider Haggard. [Then, in 1914, his *brother* began donating books to the Library.]

1914 – 24th – 27th July – attended the Old Boys' Gathering.

First World War –

Young Walter, Form II, from the 1907 School photograph.

1914 – 2nd Lt., East Yorkshire Regiment.

– 'at the front'.

– 'both his shoulder and leg damaged'.

1916 – promoted 2nd Lt. East Yorkshire Regiment.

– 7th Nov. – wrote from the BEF, so say that he was feeling 'an awful slacker to be dodging about at the base when everybody else whom I knew at School seems to be "up in the line" '.

1929 – joined his battalion in India.

1966 – 12th June – died. [Recorded as 'Major'.]

Ernest PEARCEY,   Silverton.

Listed as 'Junior Fortescue and day boy'.

The Runs – 25th March, 18th in the Short Run.

Easter – left the School.

Served in First World War.

Bertie WEBBER,   South Molton.

Entered January, 1907.

A day boy.

End of Summer Term – left the School.

First World War –

1914 – serving in the Royal North Devon Hussars.

[The following entered the School in May:-]

R.B. BOATFIELD,   Torrington.

Brereton dormitory.

20th May – Athletic Sports – 2nd in Under 11 100 yds.

1910 – Easter – left the School.

C.E. BROOKS,   East Buckland.

Day boy.

20th May – Athletic Sports – 2nd in Under 13 100 yds.

1909 – July – left the School.

Walter Wills Owbridge. He went on to become Head of School, and a prodigious contributor of books to the School Library.

[The following entered in September:-]

George Bryan ANSTEY, Filleigh. b. Aug., 1895.
[The brother of 'G.W. Anstey, Filleigh' (Form III)?– see 7th January.
Yet both have the same first Christian name. Perhaps cousins then?]
Day boy.
[So he probably walked every day from Filleigh. Nothing
remarkable in those days; another pupil used to walk from
Chittlehampton – six miles.]
December – on the results of the December exams,
promoted to Form III.
1909 – awarded Form III Science and Form prizes.
    – member of the Officers' Training Corps.
    – April – left the School.
    – May – recorded as a "new" Old Boy, who had
        'gone into engineering works at
        Taunton'.
First World War –
1916 – promoted Petty Officer, R.N.S.
1922 – 27th December – married Alma Mary Squire, at
South Molton. [His brother/cousin, 'G.W.' (see above), had also
married a Miss Squire, also at South Molton, only 17 months before.]

Gordon Lyne BLIGHT, Port Isaac, Cornwall.
b. May, 1895.
Son of an Old Boy.
Courtenay dormitory.
December – on the results of the December exams,
promoted to Form III.
    – 25th May – confirmed by the Bishop of Exeter at
South Molton church.
December – Junior Cambridge Local Examinations – also
in 1910.
1910 – won the *Exmoor* Under-15 medal.
    – awarded Form V. Prize.
    – awarded Running Colours.
    – December – Senior Cambridge Local
        Examinations.
1912 – January – elected President of the Reading and
        Debating Society.
    – made a Prefect.
    – awarded Football 2nd XI Colours.
    – Rifleman's Certificate.
    – Certificate 'A' in O.T.C. Promoted Sergeant.
1913 – April – left the School.
1914 – Friday, 16th January – attended the Old Boys'
        Dinner at the Restaurant Frascati in London.
First World War –
1916 – promoted 1st Lt. [References from his friends reveal
        that his nickname was 'Dolly'.]
    – wrote to Harries … 'We are producing a trench
        magazine for Christmas. As Editor I have some
        doubts as to its success.'
1917 – obtained a Regular Commission in the Berk-
        shires, and became Adjutant to the cyclists of a
        Division. [In other words, he had decided to become a
        professional soldier; he was no longer content to be a
        volunteer for the duration. To fall in love with soldiering in
        the middle of a war. . . .]
1919 – joined his regiment in Mesopotamia [Iraq now.]

1956 – presented a chair to the Memorial Hall.   [This was
        a regular tradition. Hundreds of these chairs must have been
        presented over the years, and hundreds survive, with the
        donor's name and dates of attendance carved on the back. It
        says a lot for the craftsmanship that they have withstood the
        treatment of generations of pupils for so long.]
1976 – 27th March – died. [He is recorded as 'Brigadier', so he
        had clearly made a success of his professional soldiering.
        Like 'Mickey' Roberts of Form III.]

A.E. BROOKS   East Buckland.
Day boy.
1911 – Cambridge Local Preliminary Examination.
1912 – Junior Cambridge Local Examinations.
    – awarded 2nd XI Cricket Colours.
1913 – July – left the School.

J.E. PIDSLEY, Sidmouth.
Brereton dormitory.
The Autumn Runs – 19th October – 19th in the
North-West Run.
1908 – Form II prize.
– Easter – left the School.

John WELLS, Winchester.
Brereton dormitory. Son of an Old Boy.
The Autumn Runs – 30th November – 13th in the
    Bray Run.
December – won a prize for his performance in the
    December exams – *Robinson Crusoe*. Promoted to
    Form III.
1909 – won Under-13 Swimming Medal.
    – awarded Form III Mathematics Prize.
1910 – Junior Cambridge Local Examinations.   1911 –
        ditto.
    – won Under-15 Swimming Medal.
1912 – awarded Second XI Football Colours.
    – Open Swimming Champion.
    – Certificate 'A'.   Sergeant in the O.T.C.
    – Senior Cambridge 'Locals'.   1913 – ditto
1913 – awarded First XI Football Colours.
    – appointed Prefect.
    – awarded Running Colours.
    – December – left the School.
First World War.
1914 – serving with the Honourable Artillery Company.
1915 – Feb. – wrote to Headmaster Harries, 'We did not
        have a very jolly Christmas, as the Regiment went
        into the trenches on Christmas Eve. [Artillery in
        trenches? Or a gap in the evidence?] I did not go with
        them as I was laid up with bad feet, slightly
        frostbitten. Since New Year's Eve I have been in
        a Convalescent Hospital. . . I was very pleased to
        see the list of Old Buckland men serving, and I
        am proud to think that I was one of the first out.'
1916 – 23rd May – wrote from northern France – out of
        service for six weeks with influenza. 'I was
        awfully sorry to hear what a time you must have
        had last term [a scarlet fever outbreak]. You must have
        found it very difficult to carry on.' [This from a

John Wells. There is no individual picture of him that I can locate, but we know that he attended this Old Boys' Dinner at the Talbot Restaurant, on 10th January, 1947. This was at the height of the 'austerity' regime after the War. Note the lounge suits, even military uniforms; the meat and two veg; and the beer mugs instead of the battery of wine glasses. Light years away from the Lucullan opulence of the Old Boys' Dinner in 1907 – see 11th January. Ex-Headmaster Harries, long retired now, is standing on the left, third from the right-hand end. Current HM, Howells, is standing fifth from the left-hand end.

soldier on the Western Front!]
  – visited the School during the summer.
1917 – 22nd May – [He wrote to tell Harries of a rather eventful day he had just survived]: in one day on the Western Front, he was saved when shrapnel hit his spade instead of him; he was buried by shellfire from his own side – twice; he was knocked down and 'slightly' gassed; and he was reported 'missing'. He went on to say that he had discovered he was in the same Corps as 'Dolly' Blight (Form II), went to visit him, and found he was digging not a trench but an allotment. [At the end of the letter, he apologised for wasting Harries' time !]
1918 – now serving in the Devonshire Regiment – awarded the Military Cross 'for conspicuous gallantry and devotion to duty in command of a Support Company. When the two front companies had lost all their officers, he led up his Company, organized the remains of the two companies, and, though wounded, dug in on a line which he held until relieved two nights later'. (From the *Gazette* of 23rd April.) [He was later awarded a bar to his M.C.]
1919 – returned to the Paris branch of his old bank, and 'expects shortly to sail to Brazil'.
1924 – 20th January – his wife gave birth to a daughter.
1925 – visited the School.
1947 – 10th January – attended the Old Boys' Dinner at the Talbot Restaurant .

1949 – 14th January – attended the Old Boys' Dinner at the Dorchester.
1954 – won the morning round of the East Berks spring golf meeting [!]. [He is referred to in this *Register* entry as 'Wing. Cdr.' Was this a simple error? Or had he joined the R.A.F. in the Second World War?]
1956, 1957, 1958 – attended the Whitsuntide Gathering.
1961 – 10th February – attended the Old Boys' Dinner at the House of Commons, as guest of Jeremy Thorpe, M.P. for North Devon.
  – 15th March – died. *The Times* printed an obituary, in which it said: 'He entered the book trade comparatively late in his life, but because of his great experience in other fields, had contributed in a short while a great deal to the counsels of bookselling, culminating last year in his election as president of the Booksellers' Association of Great Britain and Ireland.'

William James Bryan WOOD, Bristol.
Brereton dormitory.
1910 – December – left the School. [He is listed among the leavers as belonging to Form III. So, between September, 1907 and December, 1910, he was promoted just once. And that is the only thing we know about his school career. What had be been doing for three whole years?]
First World War – he joined the Forces. [Even the anonymous ones joined up.]

End of Form II biographies.

To mark the School's fiftieth anniversary, members of the Fourth and Fifth Forms were dragooned into performing scenes from As You Like It, *in the open air in the School grounds. The* Register *thoughtfully supplied their names, which has been a great help with identification in other team pictures and so on. The photograph was from 1908, and so, strictly, beyond bounds, but it was too good a picture to be left out.*

Of the 90 boys who were in or who entered the School in 1907, 40 were recorded as having joined the Old Boys' Association. 30 of those were recorded as being still alive nearly sixty years later. There could, of course, have been many more, whose fate we don't know. So – bearing in mind that the male expectation of life at the time was about 65, to say nothing of two world wars – not bad going. Or of course the statisticians could argue that 30 per cent living beyond the average age was about right.

The End.